ISBN 978 0 904491 92 0

Front cover
Northeast corner of Bedford Square
(photo 'Russ, London', 2007)

THIS BOOK is one of a series of fourteen that survey the history of all parts of the London Borough of Camden. The present volume is a complete revision and reworking of part of *Streets of Bloomsbury and Fitzrovia*, which appeared in 1997. In the years since it was published so much new information has become available that we have decided to produce two new books, each focusing on one of the two areas.

In this volume we cover the part of Bloomsbury west of Woburn Place and Southampton Row. It includes the historic manor of Blemundsbury, which became the Duke of Bedford's estate, as well as some non-Bedford land northward to the Euston Road. (For the rest of Bloomsbury, extending eastward to Gray's Inn Road, see *Streets East of Bloomsbury.*)

We explore our survey area in seven walks, starting with the first part to be developed in the late 17th century, Bloomsbury Square. We then work our way gradually northwards in a broadly chronological fashion. Much of Bloomsbury's Georgian architectural grandeur survives, most notably in Bedford Square but in other squares too, although as it has expanded the University of London has added Modernist and more recent blocks. This area developed from a preserve of the fashionable, through residences for lawyers and merchants in the 18th and 19th centuries to a home of academia. Many writers and scholars chose to reside in an area close to the British Museum with its famous Reading Room (the forerunner of today's British Library). Bloomsbury's reputation as a haunt of intellectuals also derives from the so-called Bloomsbury set, the early-20th-century group of authors and artists who, rebelling against their solid Victorian upbringing, notoriously 'lived in squares … but loved in triangles'. Virginia Woolf and her friends crop up time and again.

Other notable former residents of Bloomsbury have been so numerous that in some streets we have had to be selective, but the roll call is impressive. Authors range from Thomas Gray to Graham Greene alongside Carlyle, Dickens, Trollope, Edgar Allan Poe and Arthur Conan Doyle, poets such as Christina Rossetti, Wilfred Owen and W B Yeats, and the noted thespians Sarah Siddons, Charles Kean and Ellen Terry. Other performers have included music-hall artistes Vesta Tilley, Little Tich and Hylda Baker. Painters who have lived here include Godfrey Kneller, John Millais and Burne-Jones, as well as architects George Dance, Pugin and Lutyens. Thomas Cook was one of several travel pioneers who made Bloomsbury their home. Those connected with science or medicine have included Henry Cavendish, pioneer of vaccination Edward Jenner and Charles Darwin. Several Bloomsbury residents have been champions of women's rights: Mary Wollstonecraft, Emmeline Pankhurst and Millicent Fawcett.

We gratefully acknowledge the assistance of all the staff of the Camden Local Studies & Archives Centre (CLSAC), and in particular its Archivist Tudor Allen. We also thank Ricci de Freitas of the Marchmont Association for enlightening us on some of the residents of Russell Square.

The Bloomsbury research team
Sheila Ayres
David Hayes
Ruth Hayes
Steve Denford (team leader)

A survey of streets,
buildings & former residents
in a part of Camden

Streets of Bloomsbury

Compiled by
Camden History Society

Edited by
Steven Denford and David Hayes

Designed by
Ivor Kamlish

General Editor of Camden History Society Publications
F Peter Woodford

Diagram of the walks

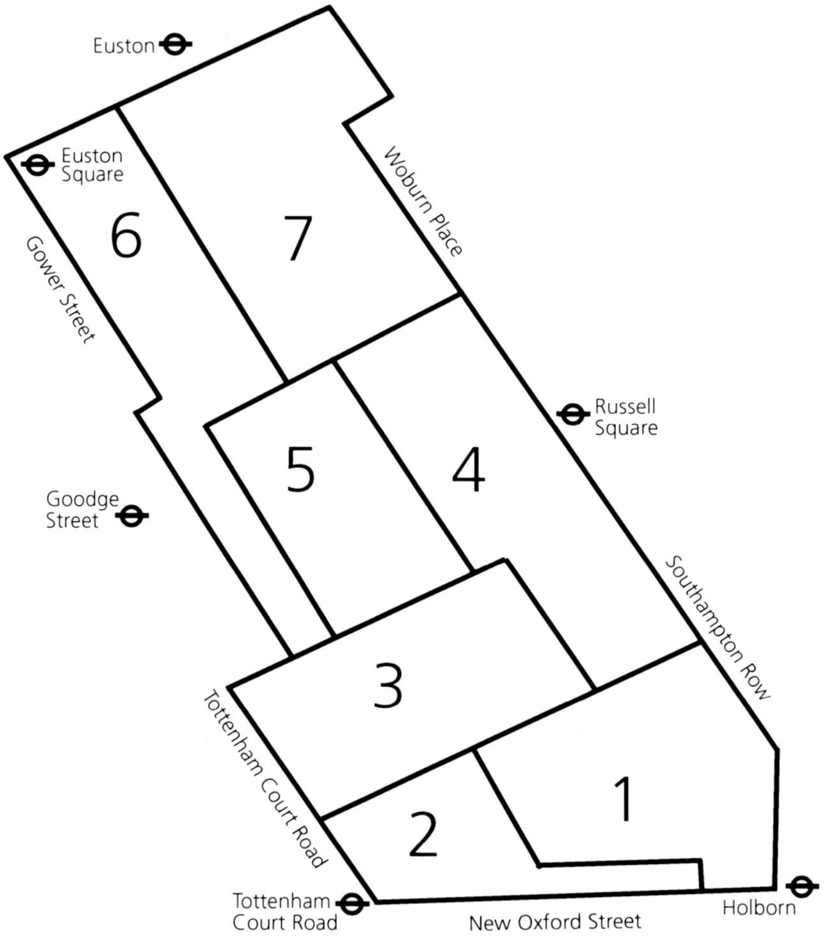

Contents

List of illustrations

Illustrations numbered

2, 4, 6, 9, 10, 11, 14, 20, 24, 26, 27, 31, 32 and 34 are reproduced by courtesy of Camden Local Studies & Archives Centre.
7, World Monuments Fund/Richard Holttum
17, Wellcome Images
18, geograph.org.uk
28, © UCL, Department of Geography
33, Tate (Creative Commons)
other images, Wikimedia Commons

Historical overview

By the late 17th century, London had broken out of the confines of its ancient wall: from the street connecting the City with Westminster, a continuous built-up area stretched northwards to Holborn, reaching as far as the ancient church of St Giles-in-the-Fields. However, the northern half of its parish, with which much of this book is concerned, was still rural. There was a large Liquorice Field growing medicinal plants between what are now Bury Place and Coptic Street, and a cherry orchard covered what is now Bloomsbury Square. Most of the fields served as pasture for dairy cattle.

Much of our area **[1]** lay in the manor of Bloomsbury, earlier known as Blemundsbury, after William de Blemund, who in 1201 bought land here previously granted to the Abbey of Westminster by Edward the Confessor. To drain the then marshy ground he made a ditch, known as Blemund's Dyke, along the present line of Bloomsbury Way. Blemund, or Blémont, was a gallicised version of Cornhill; William was the brother of an Anglo-Norman merchant either with a mansion near Cornhill in the City, or married to an heiress called Cornhill (accounts differ).

1 Underlying fields and parish boundaries c.1760

The estate subsequently passed through many hands until its owner in 1375, a wealthy fishmonger called Nicholas Exton, made a deal with the London Charterhouse, bequeathing the manor to them in return for a life annuity for himself and his family.

At the Dissolution, Henry VIII annexed all the estates of the Charterhouse and in 1545 gave the 'messuage called Blumsbery and the fields northwards' to his Lord Chancellor, Thomas Wriothesley, later created Earl of Southampton. Between 1201 and 1545 someone had built a twin-gabled manor house at the south-east corner of the property, which its new owners renamed Southampton House.

The Earls of Southampton farmed the estate throughout the rest of the Tudor period and through the reigns of three Stuarts. The 3rd Earl was allowed by James I to extend his estate southwards from Blemund's Dyke to High Holborn over what had previously been Crown property known as the 'king's gore'. The Southampton title was extinguished when in 1667 the 4th Earl died without male issue. Rachel, his widowed daughter and co-heiress, married William Russell, eldest son of the 5th Earl (later 1st Duke) of Bedford. Lord William was executed for alleged treason in 1683, but the manor passed to his son, and much of what we shall be describing is still part of the Bedford Estate.

The northern fringe of our area lay in the manor of Tottenhall, part of the large Middlesex parish of St Pancras. The manor house, known as Tottenham Court, once stood just north-west of our area, near the site of Tolmers Square. Since 1672 the copyholders of the land had been the FitzRoy family, descendants of Henry FitzRoy, an illegitimate son of Charles II, who became Earl of Euston and Duke of Grafton. Charles Fitzroy, a grandson of the 2nd Duke, who inherited the family's Tottenhall property in 1757, became the 1st Baron Southampton in 1780 – a new creation quite independent of the earlier extinct earldom. Thus, by historical accident, we have within our area two adjoining properties, both known at different times as the Southampton Estate, but belonging to two unrelated families.

During the Civil War, fortifications were constructed against a possible attack on the capital by Royalist forces based in Oxford. Earthen bulwarks lined what was then the northern edge of London, passing a little to the north of Southampton House, where a fort was constructed in its fields. The earthworks, never tested in battle, were not dismantled until long after the War; those in Bloomsbury were incorporated into the gardens of the great houses soon to be erected there.

The Earl of Southampton had wanted to build himself a modern house since before the Civil War, but royal policy forbade the erection of important London houses beyond the City walls, and he obtained permission to do so only at the Restoration. Emulating the Russells' development 30 years earlier in Covent Garden, the 4th Earl laid out Southampton (now Bloomsbury) Square, with his new house (later Bedford House) on its north side and a 'little town' to the south to service it, complete with shops and a market. A neighbouring plot was offered to an in-law, the Duke of Montagu, on which to build Montagu House, the second version of which, after the first burned down, later became the first home of the British Museum.

Plague and fire (1665-66) prompted further migration west from the City. Houses were built in the 1680s on the Pitaunce Croft immediately north of St Giles church. These would eventually degenerate into the notorious slums of the Rookery, which were finally swept away in the mid-1840s by the building of New Oxford Street, our southern boundary. By 1720 the whole area north to Great Russell Street was built up. 1731 saw the creation of a new parish, St George's Bloomsbury, carved out of that of St Giles and corresponding, very roughly, to Bloomsbury manor. The fields to the north remained as farmland. Agricultural needs often conflicted with those of the townsfolk, who would come here to walk, gather watercress, shoot ducks, fight duels, or indulge in rough games.

The northward march of the built-up area resumed in the second half of the 18th century, encouraged by the building of the world's first urban by-pass, the New Road from Paddington to Islington. Authorised by Act of Parliament in 1756, it was meant to ease the movement of troops and to enable cattle to be driven to the markets while avoiding the congested streets of Holborn and St Giles. Renamed Euston Road in 1857, its Camden section, since widened, forms the northern boundary of our area. In the controversy surrounding the road's construction, the Russell and FitzRoy families were in opposing camps. The 4th Duke of Bedford opposed the by-pass, fearing the loss of his fine views northward to Hampstead and Highgate. The 2nd Duke of Grafton, a promoter of the road, saw it as an opportunity. Later, in 1768, his grandson Charles Fitzroy (the future Lord Southampton) shrewdly purchased the freehold of the Tottenhall demesne lands at a bargain price, securing development rights over some 255 acres, including a field called Murrells, the eventual site of Euston Square. The New Road was built, and the inevitable urbanisation of the fields to its south was soon under way.

Although development on the ducal estates was fitful, it was entrusted to architects or speculative builders of stature. Wide streets and grand squares fit for the gentry were the order of the day – though in fact the cream of society had by then migrated further west to Mayfair, Hyde Park or Belgravia. On the Bedford Estate, the 4th Duke apparently repented of his opposition to the New Road; to improve access to it, he upgraded an old track along his eastern boundary (on the line of Woburn Place) into a private road.

Bedford Square materialised after his death in 1771, and his widow was the driving force behind the onward development of the estate. She began at the lower end of Gower Street, and bought land in Cantelowes Close from the Duke of Newcastle to lay out what is now Torrington Place. In the same spirit the 5th Duke, her grandson **[2]**, gave up his 1660 town house (Bedford House) in 1800, and commissioned James Burton, John Nash's favourite builder, to demolish it and develop the land northwards. Burton built Bedford Place, much of Russell Square and the east side of Tavistock Square.

Around 1811, Euston Square was laid out, astride the New Road on the (Fitzroy) Southampton Estate. After a hiatus during the Napoleonic Wars, Tavistock Square was completed in 1820 by Thomas Cubitt, the first builder to employ a permanent skilled workforce. He started work on Gordon Square in the 1820s, but financial problems delayed its completion, by his executors, until 40 years later. Torrington and Woburn Squares were built by James Sim and his family in 1821-28. On nearby (non-Bedford) land, a projected Carmarthen Square was pre-empted by the building of University College (UCL).

2 Francis Russell, 5th Duke of Bedford (1765-1802), after Hoppner

When Victoria ascended the throne in 1837, the development of our area was all but complete, and a street pattern substantially unchanged to this day was in place. The next decade saw the construction on our southern boundary of New Oxford Street, sweeping away the slums of the notorious St Giles Rookery.

Despite the aristocratic origins of the Bedford Estate, its Victorian householders were decidedly middle-class, (mostly!) highly respectable and employing an army of low-paid servants. Well-to-do businessmen rubbed shoulders with doctors, lawyers and architects, academics employed at UCL or attracted to the area by the British Museum and its Reading Room and an assortment of artists and writers. On Charles Booth's late-19th-century colour-coded 'poverty' maps, the area is a sea of middle-class red and upper-middle-class gold. The few streaks of blue denote the poverty of the human inhabitants of the various mews, where private stables and coach-houses met residents' transport needs, and livery stables those of visitors. To protect residents from the intrusion of undesirable traffic from outside, the Dukes of Bedford maintained six bar-gates, with uniformed gatekeepers, at entrances to the estate.

The area's character changed rather little until towards the end of the Victorian era, when fashionable residents had moved away westwards. Most of their grand houses were preserved, some becoming lodging- or boarding-houses, or small private hotels, conveniently sited near the three mainline railway termini along the Euston Road. Others were divided into flats, or converted into offices, typically with a flat above. Some were to become the national headquarters of charities or trades unions.

Edwardian Bloomsbury was still regarded as a pleasant place to live, or simply walk about in, as celebrated in a 'Spring Song' by John Davidson printed in 1906 in the *Pall Mall Magazine*:

Laburnum and Lilac

What? Russell Square!
There's lilac there!
And Torrington
And Woburn Square
Intrepid don the season's wear.
In Gordon Square and Euston Square –
There's lilac, there's laburnum there!
In green and gold and lavender
Queen Square and Bedford Square,
All Bloomsbury and all Soho
With every sunbeam gayer grow,
Greener grow and gayer.

From the closing years of the 19th century to the outbreak of WWI, there was a flurry of rebuilding. Some blocks of mansion flats were built, along with large (in some cases grandiose) purpose-built hotels. Institutions expanded, with extensions to University College and a new 'Cruciform' building for University College Hospital (UCH).

Properties in and around Keppel Street were declared to be of substandard construction and pulled down, together with neighbouring insanitary mews, and a new road called Malet Street was laid out on part of the site. Nearby, a wide British Museum Avenue (p 80) was constructed, intended as a grand northern approach to a newly extended British Museum. The Avenue proved a white elephant, and during its short, 30-year lifespan was never more than a roadway lined by vacant land. The hole thus left in Bloomsbury's Georgian fabric was only gradually filled and, indeed, was enlarged in the 1930s, when further land was controversially cleared to make way for a new University of London precinct of which only the University's Senate House materialised.

Over the years, Bloomsbury has been home to numerous notable men and women. The *Oxford Dictionary of National Biography* has articles for some 600 past residents of the area covered by this book. Alongside such household names as Charles Dickens and Charles Darwin is a host of lesser-known, but important figures in the fields of art or literature, science or medicine, and social or political reform.

The name Bloomsbury has become indissolubly linked with the Bloomsbury Group, a coterie of writers and artists active locally in the early decades of the 20th century, noted for their rejection of Victorian moral and religious norms, and for their own contrastingly unorthodox lifestyles – mocked by those excluded from the Group, or admitted but failing to stay the course. Cropping up repeatedly on our walks will be the names of such leading 'Bloomsberries' as novelist Virginia Woolf and husband Leonard; artists Vanessa Bell and Duncan Grant; art critics Clive Bell and Roger Fry; biographer Lytton Strachey; publisher David Garnett; and economist John Maynard Keynes. 'Bloomsbury Group' was not a term ever used by its 'members', and is arguably a misnomer, as its centre of gravity was at different times as much in Fitzrovia as in Bloomsbury. Although undoubtedly the most important intellectual grouping of its day, the Bloomsbury Set **[3]** epitomised just one phase in the story of the district's long and rich cultural past.

There was considerable bomb damage during WWII, after which wrecked buildings were replaced by new, often nondescript, blocks of offices or flats. The University and other institutions made further encroachments into the Squares. Plans in the 1980s for an extension of the British Library, involving the clearance of the whole area south of the British Museum (where the Library was then based), met with strong opposition. Planning blight occurred until an alternative site for it was secured on the Euston Road. Thereafter, the story was one of preservation and restoration. Almost the whole of our area lies within the Bloomsbury Conservation Area, and all of its pre-1850 buildings are Listed. Environmental change in recent years has been largely confined to the refurbishment of existing buildings.

Present-day Bloomsbury is dominated by the disparate worlds of tourism and academe. Its more northerly streets and squares have seen further, seemingly relentless incursions by academic institutions, most notably by an ever-expanding UCL. Further south, tourists throng the pavements, whether as guests of the area's still numerous hotels, or as visitors to its many attractions, not least the British Museum, the nation's busiest tourist destination. Bloomsbury remains a pleasant place to visit, and away from the fumy traffic on its congested main roads, pleasingly tranquil backwaters are there to be explored; and in the gardens of Bloomsbury's famous Squares, lilac and laburnum still bloom.

3 Left to right: Lady Ottoline Morell and some (sometime) Bloomsbury Set adherents: Maria Nys (the future Mrs Aldous Huxley), Lytton Strachey, Duncan Grant and Vanessa Bell; photographed at Garsington in 1915

Present street names and their origins

Adeline	Adeline Marie Somers Cocks, wife of 10th Duke of Bedford
Bainbridge	Henry, C17 builder of street's first houses
Barter	Allusion to C17-C19 Bloomsbury Market
Bayley	Sir John, judge and Bedford Square resident
Bedford	Dukes of Bedford, ground landlords
Bloomsbury	Corruption of Blemundsbury
Bury	William Van Keppel, Viscount Bury, father-in-law of 4th Duke of Bedford
Byng	Georgiana, 1st wife of 6th Duke of Bedford, daughter of George Byng, 4th Viscount Torrington
Coptic	Important Coptic manuscript collection acquired by British Museum
Dyott	Married name of daughter of Henry Bainbridge
Endsleigh	Endsleigh Cottage, Devonshire holiday home built by 6th Duke of Bedford
Euston	Estate in Suffolk; principal seat of Dukes of Grafton
Galen	Ancient Greek physician; Pharmaceutical Society HQ once adjoined
Gilbert	Gilbert Holles, 3rd Earl of Clare, friend of William, Lord Russell
Gordon	Georgiana, daughter of 4th Duke of Gordon, 2nd wife of 6th Duke of Bedford
Gower	Lady Gertrude Leveson-Gower, daughter of 1st Earl Gower, wife of 4th Duke of Bedford
Grafton	Duke of, head of the FitzRoy family, local landowners
Keppel	Lady Elizabeth, daughter of 2nd Earl of Albemarle, mother of 5th & 6th Dukes of Bedford
Malet	Sir Edward Baldwin, son-in-law of 9th Duke of Bedford
Montague	Ralph, 1st Duke of Montagu (*sic*), father-in-law of 4th Earl of Southampton
Morwell	Estate in Devon owned by Dukes of Bedford
Museum	British Museum, which the street approaches
(New) Oxford	Mid-C19 continuation of Oxford Street
Pied Bull	C18-C19 public house
Ridgmont	Ridgmont (*sic*), village on Duke of Bedford's Woburn estate
Russell	Family name of Dukes of Bedford
Southampton	Thomas Wriothesley, 4th Earl of Southampton, first developer of land
Store	*Unknown*
Streatham	Baron Howland of, another title of Duke of Bedford
Tavistock	Marquess of, courtesy title of Duke of Bedford's heir
Taviton	Estate in Devon owned by Dukes of Bedford
Thornhaugh	Property of Duke of Bedford near Peterborough
Torrington	Viscount, father-in-law of 6th Duke of Bedford
Vernon	Elizabeth, mother of 4th Earl of Southampton
Willoughby	George Philip, Mayor of Holborn 1903-04
Woburn	Bedfordshire, principal seat of Dukes of Bedford

Route 1

Around Bloomsbury Square

A sinuous circular walk from Holborn Station

'Bloomsbury started with the creation of Southampton Square'. So opined Sir John Summerson, the eminent historian of London's Georgian architecture, at a Camden History Society event in 1976. We will visit and discover the history of this earliest named square in the capital, now Bloomsbury Square, and then continue with a tour of the small but interesting streets built to service its upper-class households.

Leave Holborn Underground Station by its smaller exit, into High Holborn. Cross the busy intersection diagonally to the Metro Bank and turn right to walk briefly up **SOUTHAMPTON ROW**, the Bedford Estate's eastern boundary. The left-hand carriageway follows the line of old King Street, which became part of Southampton Row in 1864.

The early buildings shown here on the 1682 Morgan map included 'small inns for stabling and coach houses'. Michael Mattaire (1668–1747), classical scholar and typographer, was living in King Street at the time of his death. The poet Thomas Gray lodged there in 1759, and in the 1820s it was home to caricaturist Robert Cruikshank, brother to the more famous George. Later in the century there were many small businesses here. The 1878 directory, for example, lists a servants' registration office and an *accoucheuse* at No.9 Southampton Row, while next door at No.11 were a chronometer maker, a solicitor and a watchmaker. No.19 was the workroom of Misses Eleanor and Jane Faulkes, *modistes.*

The road was greatly widened in 1904 as part of the LCC's Kingsway development to the south. None of the existing properties pre-date the widening, and several have had recent makeovers. The new office block named One has this number chiselled in bold letters in stone on either side of its doorway (actually Nos.3-9). It was designed by Sheppard Robson. Nos.17-23, with a gated driveway, and interesting dark brown doors with brass handles and decoration, form the southern wing of the much admired Edwardian **Sicilian Avenue**.

This pedestrian shopping street was built by R J Worley for the Bedford Estate in 1905-10 (at the same time as Kingsway). Its name is grandly announced on the colonnaded entrances at either end, while the upper storeys sport exuberant *tourelles* in brick, terracotta and marble. On the left (west) side is Sicilian House, followed by Vernon House, while opposite are the former Arcade Chambers. The ground-floor shops and eateries all have elegant, good-quality fittings. Fores Gallery Ltd, 'specialists in sporting engravings', was based at **No.15** from 1980 to 2000. Note the cherubs' faces on the lamp posts where they are not surrounded by tables. Like the Avenue itself, the lamp posts, with blue faience pedestals, are Grade-II-Listed.

Emerging at the west end of Vernon Place (p 20), turn left along the south side of **BLOOMSBURY SQUARE**. Across the road, in the square's south-east corner, stands a K6 red telephone box designed by Giles Gilbert Scott in 1935. Past the square the road continues westward as Bloomsbury Way (p 23), following the line of the medieval Blemund's ditch (p 7), the original boundary between Bloomsbury and St Giles manors.

In 1640 Thomas Wriothesley, 4th Earl of Southampton, obtained a licence from the Privy Council to build a mansion on his Bloomsbury estate, but the Civil War intervened and it was not completed until 1660. At first it was often called Southampton House in the Fields, both to distinguish it from the Earl's previous house near Holborn Bars and because of its isolated position.

This isolation did not last long, however, for in 1661 the Earl was given a licence to build between his new mansion and the

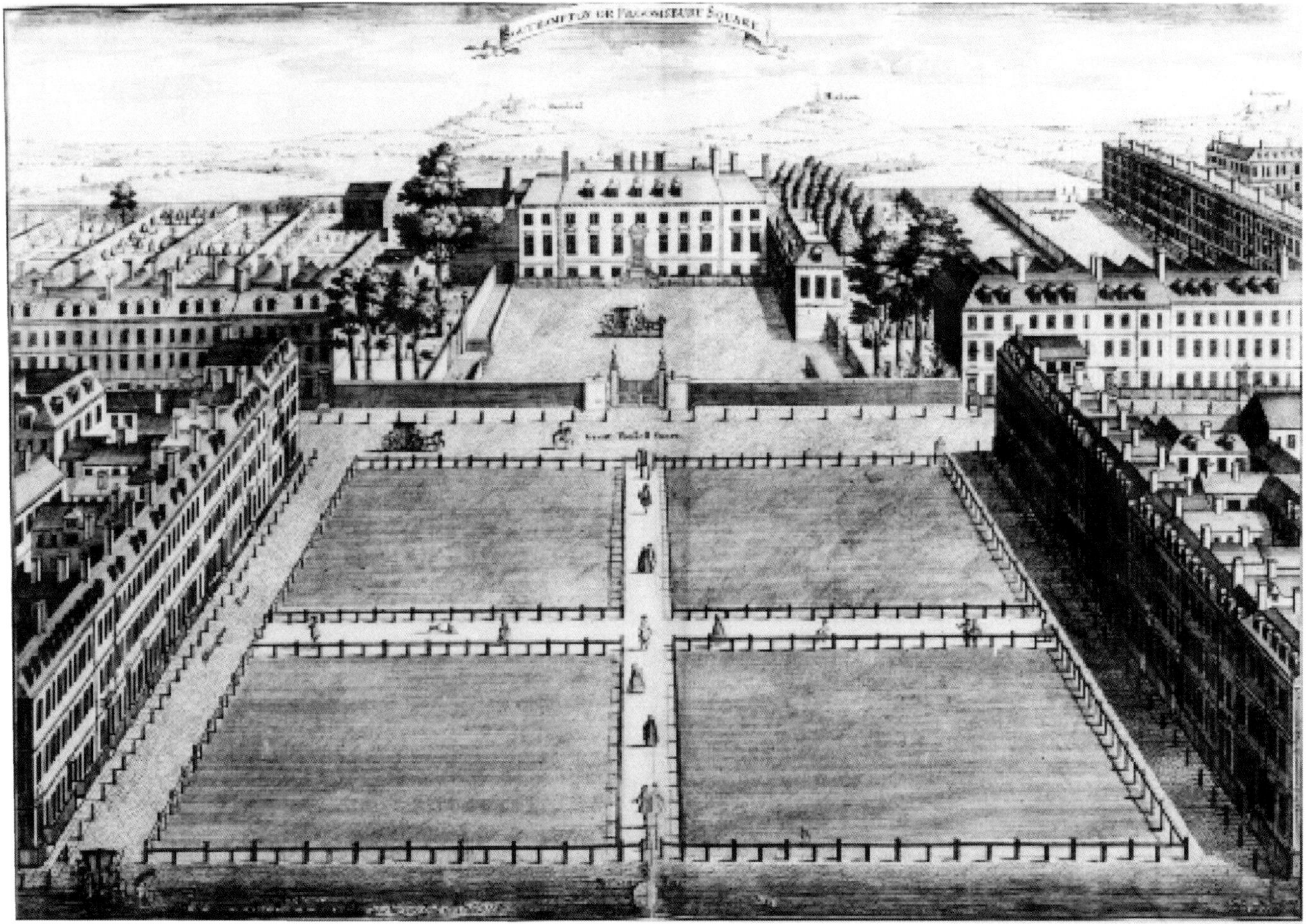

4 Southampton House and its Square in the early 18th century. Note the uniformity of the houses at this stage.

Holborn highway (High Holborn). He had no architect but is thought to have been influenced by the new Covent Garden Piazza built by Inigo Jones in the 1630s for the Earl of Bedford. Southampton's surveyors laid out a square garden immediately to the south of his mansion, over a former cherry orchard. A row of houses was erected on either side **[4]**. According to Boyle's Court Guide of 1799, Seymour Row (Nos.1-11) was on the east side, and Allington Row (Nos. 13-24) on the west, while the mansion was listed as No.12. This numbering was reversed in the 18th century, to run clockwise from the middle of the south side, which had by then been built on.

The early leases, for just 31 years (and later for 42 years), were sold piecemeal by the Earl's agent to small-scale builders, who sub-leased the new buildings to developers and usually it was they who then rented them to tenants. At the end of the main lease the property reverted to the Earl. A similar system was used over the next couple of centuries to develop the west end of London.

Southampton's new estate was a great success. Residents were attracted by the clean air and proximity to one of the great families of England. The Earl continued to develop and expand his 'little towne' by building a market beyond the south-west corner of the square (see p 21).

The Earl died in 1667 and two years later his daughter Rachel married William Russell, son of the 4th Earl of Bedford, whose family thus acquired the estate. William was executed in 1683 on a trumped-up charge of treason (he was unashamedly opposed to the succession of a Catholic monarch) and his widow continued the development. The mansion became known as Bedford House and the square as Bloomsbury Square. The 5th Earl of Bedford was created 1st Duke of Bedford in 1694.

The 5th Duke of Bedford (succeeded 1771) was ruled by a passion for farming at his ancestral home at Woburn and had little interest in Bedford House. An Act of Parliament of 1800 allowed him to pull it down, and Bedford Place, with houses on either side (and with an adjacent road, Montague Place, to the west) was built northward from the Square, bisecting the site of the mansion. It led to the Russell family's new attraction, Russell Square (p 59), a much larger and grander development.

We will walk clockwise round three sides of Bloomsbury Square, beginning with the south side. In the initial layout of the estate this was called Vernon Row (or Vernon Street). Here, in a building called the Golden Head, the engraver and painter John Faber was based from the mid-1730s. Nos.43-45 were built originally c.1760 but re-developed in 1830-40. James Orrock (1829–1913), the painter and art collector, lived at **No.43**. The architect Ewan Christian, who designed the National Portrait Gallery, lived and worked here from 1842 to 1847. On the corner, **No.45** has a bronze plaque recording the fact that three Earls of Chesterfield lived in an earlier house on this site, including the 4th Earl (1694-1773), famous for his letters to his son on how a gentleman should behave. They were written as private advice but his impecunious daughter-in-law published them for cash.

Nos.46&47, across Southampton Place (p 20) were built c.1840-50, as was **No.1**, the terraced house next door. The biblical scholar and bibliographer Thomas Horne died at his home at No.47 in 1862.

'Bloomsbury House' at **Nos.2&3** was built originally to house the College of Preceptors, the first professional body for teachers. It was put up in 1887, designed in a sort of Flemish Renaissance style by one Frederick Pinches. Note the sculpted heads in the roundels. The College of Preceptors became the College of Teachers in 1998 and moved in 2003 to the University of London's Institute of Education (p 69). The building was sympathetically restored in 2007 and now houses the International Institute for Strategic Studies, which also hosts conferences and weddings. An earlier No.2 was home to Edmund Lodge, a senior herald at the College of Arms, who died there in 1839. Red-brick and terracotta **No.4** is home to the Froebel Society and National Froebel Union, which in 1904 spearheaded the kindergarten movement.

Across the road, the south-west corner of the square saw the first houses built. An early resident of the corner house was Dr John Radcliffe (1650-1714), Royal physician and a benefactor of Bart's Hospital, Oxford University and Oxford's Radcliffe Infirmary. The building was much altered by Flitcroft in 1744. By 1853 it was the office of the Greek Revival architect, James Brooks. In 1880 the house was divided into **No.5**, facing Bloomsbury Way, and **No.5A** in the square itself. It has an impressive Georgian frontispiece with a thermal window surmounting a Palladian one. The writer Jack Lindsay was based here at the time of the General Strike. No.5A was purchased by the Pushkin House Trust, which moved here from Kensington in 2005. After restoration it is now 'a thriving centre devoted to the provision and support of Russian culture in Britain and beyond'. Its public events offer opportunities to admire some of the original internal fittings.

Now walk north beside the new, low hornbeam hedge of the square's central garden. Pass **No.6**, a house built by Isaac Ware in a style similar to nearby Chesterfield House (former No.45). A plaque erected by Herbrand Russell, 11th Duke of Bedford and the Liberal Unionist first Mayor of Holborn, records the residence of the Tory Disraeli family, including, from 1817-29, the young future Prime Minister Benjamin. The house was from 1852-1901 the family home of Edward Prior, an architect active in the Art Workers' Guild. The surgeon and smallpox vaccinator Charles Aikin and his scientist brother Arthur, both members of a prominent Unitarian family, died at **No.7** in 1847 and 1854, respectively.

A gate in the garden hedge leads to the underground car park and ahead is its unobtrusive entrance ramp, the exit being on the other side of the garden. Excavated for Camden Council in the 1960s, this is London's deepest car park, going down seven storeys, or 60ft. Taking inspiration from the double-helix structure of DNA, the ramp has been called 'a corkscrew in a drum'.

Cross to the pavement opposite. In former No.8 Thomas Leverton Donaldson was born in 1795. He was later the architect of University Hall (p 108). Nos.7&8 were rebuilt in 1881 and playwright Francis Marshall and his actress wife Ada Cavendish lived in the new **No.8** until he died in 1889.

In 1909 Nos.9-11, first built in 1662-65 but much altered, became the White Hall Hotel, as still announced on the pediment and the large entrance step. The building is now apartments. **No.10** has a blue LCC plaque for the dermatologist Dr Robert Willan, who died here in 1812. He was the first person to classify diseases of the skin. He was also an advocate of the curative effect of mineral waters, and in 1803 published the luridly-titled *Account of the Dreadful Effects of Dram-Drinking*. Nos.10, 11 and 13 were re-fronted c.1770-72 and stuccoed in 1862. At Listed **No.12**, the ground-floor front room served towards the end of his life as the office of the architectural historian Nikolaus Pevsner (1902-83), compiler of *The Buildings of England*. The house is now occupied by the Chartered Institute of Arbitrators.

No.14 dates from 1662-65 and has also been stuccoed. It was home to Richard Bright (1789-1858), the discoverer of Bright's Disease. Next door, the good-looking bull's head above the covered entrance indicates that it leads to Pied Bull Yard, which we shall visit later (p 26). **Nos.15&16** was remodelled by John Nash but its interior is recent. The British branch of the famous Parisian Cordon Bleu cookery school has been based here since the early 1980s.

On the corner with Great Russell Street (p 41) stands **No.17**. Its first known owner was Sir William Jones, Charles II's first Attorney General, to whom the house was given by the Earl of Southampton. George Compton, the 4th Earl of Northampton, refurbished it in 1687-88 and used it as his town house until his death in 1727. Fifty years later Sir John Rushout, 1st Baron Northwick, negotiated a contract with the then unknown architect John Nash, to reconstruct the building and erect houses on the hitherto undeveloped land running along Great Russell Street (Nos.66-71). Nash converted the corner building into two separate houses, one with an entrance in Great Russell Street, and the other in Bloomsbury Square. The interiors were refurbished and the frontage was remodelled in neo-Classical style, with Corinthian columns and a moulded cornice, all covered in plaster; Nash employed the firm of Robert and James Adam to apply the render.

The two houses failed to sell and one was unoccupied until 1800. In 1841 No.17 was leased to the Pharmaceutical Society of Great Britain, founded that year to improve pharmacists' professional standing through better training. It expanded into Nos.72&73 Great Russell Street in 1857 and three years later added another storey to provide laboratories. Initially it shared its new premises with the Royal Literary Fund which had offices at Nos.72&73 from 1842-62. The Royal Pharmaceutical Society (RPS) acquired the freehold in 1958. In 1976, under plans to expand the British Museum, the government placed a compulsory purchase order on the buildings and the RPS left for Lambeth. The government's plans were, however, opposed by the Bloomsbury Society, and the buildings were resold at auction. They are now occupied by the German Historical Institute London, which moved here in 1982.

Move on round the square to face Bedford Place (p 64). The Earl of Southampton's development was described by John Evelyn in his diary entry of 9 February 1666: 'dined at my Lord Treasurer's, the earle of Southampton, in Blomesbury, where he was building a noble square or piazza, a little towne; his own house stands too low, some noble roomes, a pretty cedar chappell, a naked garden to the north but good aire'. The 'naked garden' had an unusual feature, as it included the site of the line of fortifications built in 1643 by the City Corporation to resist possible royalist attacks during the Civil War. The earthen bulwarks ran behind the Bedford House, crossing the line of Bedford Place about halfway along.

Along the north side of Bloomsbury Square are the houses built on the site of the *front* garden of Bedford House after it was demolished in 1800. Two rows of five houses stand on either side of Bedford Place, which was driven through the site of the mansion. The original leases were for 61 years. Designed and erected by James Burton (1761-1837), Nash's favourite builder, who was to be responsible for much of the subsequent development of Bloomsbury, all the houses have attractive iron balconies, and those at No.19 and No.21 come with hoods.

No.18 was the home of Dr George Pinckard, first physician of the Bloomsbury Dispensary (p 48). He died here in 1835. **No.19** was the HQ of the Institute of Public Health and Institute of Sanitary Engineers in 1902. In the same year Gertrude Stein rented an apartment at **No.20** with her brother Leo before moving to Paris. It also formerly housed the Paul Mellon Centre for Studies in British Art before this moved to Bedford Square (p 51). The painted inscription 'PS 304' suggests that there was access here to a public air-raid shelter during WWII. Beyond Bedford Place, **No.23** became the first headquarters in 1875 of the Metropolitan and National Nursing Association, founded in 1874 to raise the standard of district nursing.

Protected by railings at the north end of the square's garden is the bronze statue by Sir Richard Westmacott of Charles James Fox, the radical Whig politician (1749-1806). Its site was suggested by the 6th Duke of Bedford and the statue was erected here in 1816 by Whig supporters. Dressed in consular robes and sandals, and holding Magna Carta in his right hand, Fox is seated, probably because he was too portly to appear dignified if standing. In Louis MacNeice's poem *October in Bloomsbury*, 'Charles James Fox unconcerned in a bath towel sits on his arse in Bloomsbury Square, while plane tree leaves flop gently down and lodge in his sculptured hair'. Fox gazes north up Bedford Place at the statue of his patron, the 5th Duke of Bedford, in Russell Square.

Now enter **Bloomsbury Square Gardens**. The present planting scheme differs from the original formal layout shown in **[4]**. In 1806 Humphrey Repton, a prominent exponent of the Picturesque landscape movement, was commissioned to redesign the garden, which he laid out with new promenades, including a lime walk. This arrangement was changed in the 1820s to include a large lawn, which by the early 20th century featured scattered trees. By the end of the century the garden had became neglected and a refurbishment project by a newly formed Friends group was set up to work with Camden Council. In 2003 the 15th Duke of Bedford reopened the garden which, now reflecting Repton's original plan, has become a valuable community resource with a children's play area. Near the west gate is a 'physic garden' planted by schoolchildren in 2011-12 as part of a Heritage Lottery-funded 'Healing Histories' project involving several Camden schools as an *homage* to the Chelsea Physic Garden of the most famous local resident, physician Sir Hans Sloane (p 20). Only two of the attractive interpretation boards placed around the perimeter of the garden at the time now remain.

Look across to **Victoria House**, the colossal building with imposing Ionic pilasters occupying all of the east side of the square and the whole block eastward to Southampton Row. It was designed by Charles William Long for the Liverpool Victoria Friendly Society, with a brief to 'add to the dignity and beauty of the metropolis'. The company had bought the land in 1920, but as some existing leaseholders were reluctant to vacate their properties, building work started at the north and south ends, meeting in the middle of the Southampton Row side in 1926. Some staff who had already moved in had had to reach their offices by ladder.

The building was finally completed at the centre of the west side, allowing a (second) opening ceremony to take place in August 1932. Once completed, Victoria House was the nation's largest office block other than in Whitehall. Pevsner described it as 'a very large Beaux Arts Grecian composition'. The sculptures in the pediment, by Herbert William Palliser, represent the bounty of nature. There were three halls, two equipped with superbly sprung floors for dancing. During WWII the basement housed air-raid shelters, first-aid and gas-contamination stations and police and fire brigade sub-stations – all on hand for any emergency within the property.

In 1998, on the departure of Liverpool Victoria for Bournemouth, the building was unsuccessfully shortlisted as a possible City Hall to house the new Mayor of London and Greater London Authority. The next year it was bought by Garbe (UK) and refurbished over the next four years. The preserved Grade-II-Listed areas, said to look 'virtually unaltered', include the south hall, now known as the Ballroom. William Alsop, the architect of the refurbishment provided a surprise for visitors: 'two egg-shaped pods bracketed from the cantilevered floors and suspended in the new atria'. These are meeting rooms reached via narrow walkways.

Buried under Victoria House at the north end are the foundations of the original Nos.28-29, the house of the judge and politician William Murray, 1st Earl of Mansfield. This was sacked and set alight during the Gordon Riots of 1780, and Mansfield and his wife had a narrow escape by the back door. His magnificent library was only one of the family's possessions that were lost in the fire.

Dickens in *Barnaby Rudge* mentions that Barnaby was to be hanged in Bloomsbury Square for his part in the Gordon Riots (though he was later reprieved). There were other instances of disorder in the area. In the 18th century, rioting Spitalfields weavers invaded the square and attacked Bedford House several times, incensed that the 4th Duke had opposed their petition to Parliament to bar the import of French silks. Close to the slums of the St Giles Rookery (p 38), the square was also a haunt of footpads and thieves, who looked for easy pickings here.

Later buildings on the site of Mansfield's house included a new No.29, which from 1862-64 was home to the social philosopher, 'survival of the fittest' Herbert Spencer. It became the office of the architect Richard Norman Shaw in 1876. Later, from 1897-1914, it was the marital home and office of the young architect Edwin

Lutyens **[5]**. Born here were his daughters, the writer Mary Lutyens (b.1908) and her elder sister Elisabeth (b.1906), the composer. Incidentally, composed eight years later was Vaughan Williams' *A London Symphony*, the second movement of which is meant to evoke Bloomsbury Square on a November afternoon.

Other residents of the east side of the square included the architect Thomas Edward Collcutt, who built No.36 to his own design, and in No.38 John Wheeley Gough Gutch, the surgeon, botanist and editor of the *Literary and Scientific Register*, who died in 1862. No.39 became the home of the Hahnemann Hospital in 1850s and is named after the founder of homeopathy Samuel Hahnemann (see also p 55). The landscape architect Sir Geoffrey Jellicoe (1900–1996) started his own practice at No.40.

5 Free Church, Hampstead Garden Suburb, designed by Lutyens when resident in Bloomsbury Square

By Victorian times Bloomsbury Square had lost its appeal to the aristocracy but was favoured by the professional middle classes. On his retirement in 1865, the librarian Sir Edward Panizzi moved from his quarters in the British Museum to a house at No.31, also on this east side of the square. Today, there are several Colleges for learning English established in the vicinity, which attract many foreign students.

Before leaving the square, we should list some of its more notable residents not already mentioned. Among its early inhabitants were painters Isaac Fuller and Henry Cook who died here in 1672 and 1700 respectively; the religious writer Richard Baxter who moved to the square in 1673; the politician Sir Samuel Barnardiston, who died here in 1707; and the writer and politician Sir Richard Steele, a resident in 1711-14.

Residents in Georgian times included several prominent judges such as Lord Ellenborough, who lived here from 1789 to 1808; poets such as Mark Akenside, who lived in the square until 1759 at the same time as fellow poet Anne Penny and Anna, Lady Miller, the salon hostess and gossip. Painters included Isaac Whood (d.1752) and Stephen Slaughter (d.1765), who set up a successful portrait practice in the square, which attracted many patrons. From 1785

Britain's leading 'animal magnetizer', John Boniot de Mainauduc, was based here, as were the Meux family of brewers.

Move on now from the garden to **BLOOMSBURY PLACE**, a short street that was initially part of Great Russell Street and skirts the north side of Victoria House. Facing this are some well preserved early-19th-century houses, all stuccoed. The actress and singer Evelyn Laye (p 58) was born in 1900 at **No.8**.

In 1695 Sir Hans Sloane moved to a house on the site of **No.3** when he returned home from Jamaica. He rose to become the President of the Royal Society and physician to Queen Anne, but also treated the local poor for free. He popularised the drinking of chocolate, which he had brought back from Jamaica. He acquired an enormous collection of books, MSS and natural history specimens and bought a property on the site of **No. 4** to house them (see plaque). When he died he left them to the nation and this later became the nucleus of the British Museum collection. He retired in 1742 and bought the manor of Chelsea, where he was a patron of the Chelsea Physic Garden and where he is remembered in such street names as Sloane Square and Hans Place. In 1871 **No.2** was the office of the Registrar of the Corporation of the Sons of the Clergy, although it bears the plaque to Sloane.

At the junction ahead we regain **SOUTHAMPTON ROW**, and turn right along its middle section, which was known as Upper King Street until 1864. All of the present buildings postdate the widening of the road in 1915. On the right stands Victoria House. The pediment sculptures on this side, not easily viewable even from opposite, represent trade and navigation. Supplanted here was an eclectic mix of 19th-century small businesses and a pub called the Red Lion, with a Red Lion Yard behind. Next door to the pub, at No.28 Upper King Street, was until 1852 the bookshop of Charles Mudie, founder of the well-known circulating library (p 32). Walk past the shops on the ground floor of Victoria House, collectively known as **Victoria Colonnade**. Each shop has a frontage of plate glass and stainless steel fittings. Note particularly the fittings and staircase of **No.74**, presently occupied by Amway.

On the opposite side of the street, note the elaborate carving over the door of **No.80A** (Bristol House). The green plaque on Faraday House at **No.70** recalls that the Electrical Engineering College was based here from 1903 to 1967.

At the next intersection cross over and turn right. We are back at **VERNON PLACE**, an eastward continuation of Bloomsbury Way named after Elizabeth Vernon, the mother of the 4th Earl of Southampton. Charles Combe, physician and numismatist, died at his house here in 1817. Erstwhile No.1 was lived in by George Ansell (1826-1880), the investigative chemist who researched the dangers of fire-damp in mines and also wrote a standard book on the Royal Mint. His daughter Gertrude, the reformer and suffragette, was born here in 1861. By the end of the century the longstanding Albion public house at No.7 on the Southampton Row corner had become the Albion Hotel, while next door at No.5 stood the Hôtel de France et de Belgique. Notice on the building opposite the inscription 'Avenue Chambers', the original name of the triangular northern block of Sicilian Avenue (p 13).

Vernon Place merges into the south side of the Bloomsbury Square. Turn left into **SOUTHAMPTON PLACE**. We are now walking over the land that the 3rd Earl of Southampton was able to acquire from the Manor of St Giles that gave him the important and easy access from his previous southern boundary, present day Bloomsbury Way, to the main road (High Holborn) ahead of us.

The street was known as Southampton Street until 1939. Colley Cibber, actor, dramatist, theatre proprietor and poet laureate, was born here in 1671. In 1720 John Strype described the street as 'very spacious with good houses...well inhabited and resorted unto by gentry for lodgings'. Charles Combe (see left) was born here in 1743. From 1757-63 the street was rebuilt on either side with two fine rows of Palladian style houses by Henry Flitcroft, celebrated for his previous work at nearby St Giles church. Pevsner noted the

Doric or Ionic columns and pediments attached to some of the door cases.

The physician and chemist William Prout practised as a specialist in stomach and urinary diseases from his home in the street from 1821, and the Home and Colonial School Society was founded here in 1836 by John Reynolds and John Bridges to train teachers in Pestalozzian principles. **No.8** was home to the lithographer, and later photographer, Francis Bedford, probably born here in 1816. In 1862 he was the first photographer to be asked to join a royal tour – with the future Edward VII. On his return, Bedford's photographs of the Middle East were exhibited to great acclaim. J M Barrie was said to have lived here with his friend Thomas Gilmour in the 1880s. In 1920 it housed the office of the (private) National Detective Agency. At that time a cluster of architects was based in neighbouring houses, mostly now forgotten but including Charles Fitzroy Doll, who was appointed the Duke of Bedford's surveyor in 1885 and designed the Hotel Russell. His studio was at **No.5**. At the former No.9 was the HQ in the 1920s of the Polish Community in Great Britain and subsequently until 1949 the radical bookshop 'Left on the Shelf'.

At the end of the street cross over very carefully to **No.13**, a house occupied in 1910 by the National Froebel Union, now removed to No.4 Bloomsbury Square. To the north a plaque records that **No.17** was the childhood home of Cardinal John Henry Newman (1801-90), a Protestant at the time, but after his conversion in later life to become one of the pillars of the Catholic church.

Stuccoed **No.19**, from 1884, housed an unusual not-for-profit enterprise called the Universal Knowledge & Information Office. Launched and personally supervised by Lord Truro, it was intended to provide both a public service and employment opportunities for women. For a minimum fee of one shilling (5p) people worldwide could enquire by post 'upon every thing' and receive an answer in their own language. A staff of 30, including subject specialists and linguists, worked at No.19, while 200 others were employed to undertake research in the British Museum or the London Library. The service seems to have ceased after Lord Truro's death in 1891.

Pass through the covered entrance into **BARTER STREET**, here known as Silver Street until 1937. This entrance was originally wider and open to the sky, but was subsequently arched over by an extension to No.19 and narrowed, perhaps to prevent market traffic from using residential Southampton Street. We are entering the area once known as Bloomsbury Market **[6]** developed to house the community of shopkeepers and artisans who were to service the residents of the nearby upper-class houses.

Being close to a pretty smelly and dirty market, the original housing was on cheaper leases. But while not grand – Strype in 1720 described it as 'indifferent well built and inhabited' – it never degenerated into a slum, as did much of nearby St Giles. A key factor was the strict control exercised by the Bedford Estate. Here was the childhood home of the physician and poet, Sir Edward Hannes (1664-1710). The draughtsman Robert White (1645–1703) published his often very large engravings at his home in the Market; and John Collins, the mathematician and scientific administrator, was living in 1671 in a house next to the sign of the Three Crowns.

The present, early-19th-century buildings on both sides of the street are Listed Grade II. Now converted into private apartments, the handsome warehouses lining the north side were occupied from the 1850s and for well over a century by the wine and spirit merchants W J Hollebone and Son, who had offices at No.19 Southampton Street.

On the left, **Nos.16-20** have attractive preserved shop fronts. The locked driveway past No.20 corresponds to an ancient path, first known as Fountain Alley. It later led to King's Arms Yard and from the 1920s was called Monarch Yard. Just beyond, on a site that was once stables and later a confectionery warehouse, the flats of **Lytton Court** were built after WWII on a more human scale than the buildings ahead.

At the next intersection, the footway

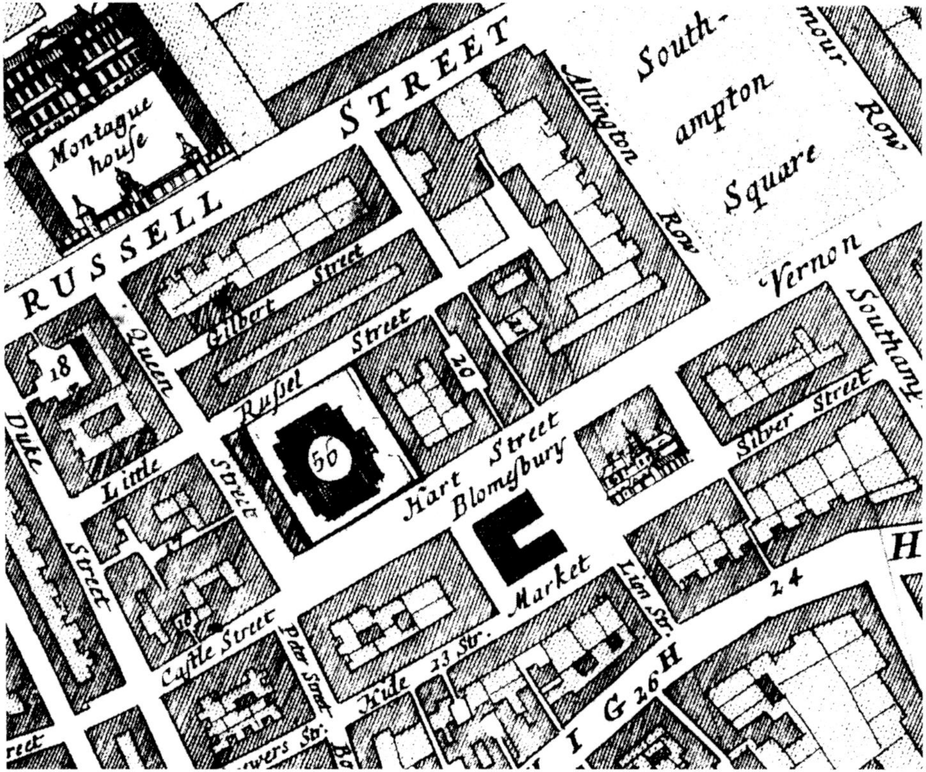

6 Bloomsbury Market on a map of 1720. Southampton Square is now Bloomsbury Square, Hart Street is Bloomsbury Way, and Silver Street part of Barter Street

known now as **Bloomsbury Court** and leading south to High Holborn, was called Fountain Court in 1720. The short street leading north, and formerly known as Market Street, was the earliest part of present-day T-shaped Barter Street to be so renamed, in 1884.

Continue straight ahead, with Bupa House (p 23) on your right. Here, in a 7-roomed corner house at Nos.1-3 Silver Street, the Pedic Clinic was opened in 1913, a dedicatory service being conducted by the Bishop of Willesden. It was the first clinic of its kind in the country; treating poor people for disabling foot disorders. Clinics were held in the evenings, as the staff gave their chiropody service here for free and needed to earn a living during the day. In 1920 the Pedic Clinic moved to Fitzroy Square, where four years later it was renamed the London Foot Hospital.

We are now approaching the heart of the old market area. In 1662, the Earl of Southampton, keen that his development should be self-contained, was granted a licence to hold a market here on three days of the week (and later also a cattle market on Fridays). Southampton's market was tucked away out of sight and smell of the wealthy, with small houses and shops facing either towards the market place or in short roads nearby. They were built much smaller and closer together, the earliest dating from 1666. A further licence granted that year allowed the Earl to provide a fish market and a Market House, and to open on four days a week.

The Market House stood on the Bupa House site. Pictured in **[6]** with a belfry, it had seemingly been rebuilt on a cruciform plan by the time of Roque's map of 1745.

The roadway in front of it was known as Bloomsbury Market until it was absorbed into Silver Street in 1877. The leases for the market buildings were issued in 1668, but those for the 28 indoor shops in the Market House were kept by the Earl. In its early days the market was a popular place to visit. Samuel Pepys records a trip to 'the new market of my Lord Treasurer's' in August 1666 and another in December 1668 to a nearby apartment 'a bye [out-of-the-way] place but with a good prospect of the fields'.

Situated beyond an open market place, and on a site *west* of Bury Place (ahead), were the 'fish shambles', selling fish from the Thames, and the 'flesh shambles', where animals were both slaughtered and sold. These occupied a long building facing east with wings on either side. A public house, the Dolphin, slaked the thirsts of market workers.

Later accounts vary as to the success or otherwise of Bloomsbury Market but, writing in 1720, John Strype already thought it 'of small account by reason [it] is of little use and so ill served with provisions in so much that the inhabitants are served elsewhere'. By the end of the century, as Horwood's map reveals, both market buildings had disappeared to be replaced by more housing. Trading seems to have continued outdoors for about another 60 years, with stalls in neighbouring streets and in the 'Market Square', now **BURY PLACE**.

Originally part of a track linking High Holborn with the fields to the north, this was later continued at its southernmost end by a narrow Lion (or Lyon) Street, now buried under New Oxford Street on your left.

On the left-hand corner today, at the rear of the Holborn Tower, an inscription in stone records that between 1914 and 1957 the Women's Freedom League had its headquarters 'on this site' (actually, at No.144 High Holborn). Moderate suffragists Edith How, Teresa Billington and Charlotte Despard had founded it in 1907 as an alternative to the Women's Social and Political Union (WSPU) run by the Pankhurst family after the latter's change of policy from peaceful protest to a campaign of vandalism.

Now turn right into Bury Place. At its widest point, the east side was used as a cab stand in the late 19th century. No taxis now wait for the staff of **Bupa House**. Built in 1928, this began as a U-shaped building at Nos.15-19 Bloomsbury Way (still its postal address) and was long known as New Oxford House. It housed the Co-operative Permanent Building Society until this moved in the early 1960s to the newly built Holborn Tower. Extended through to Barter Street, the building was renamed Chesterfield House, possibly recalling the nearby earlier Bloomsbury Square residence of the Earls of Chesterfield. After remodelling by Frederick Gibberd Partnership, with an impressive new reception area, it was occupied by Bupa in 1996. The wall of the white Portland stone ramp leading to the main entrance is inlaid with an abstract pattern in African black granite called *Chain of Events*, the work of sculptor Peter Randall-Page. On the pavement beside it sits his earlier (1991) work in Kilkenny marble, entitled *Beneath the Skin* and resembling the enormous grub of a giant insect. The slippery surface on the top of the creature is said to have been caused by many tired tourists resting on it after a visit to the British Museum.

Bury Place continues across the main road ahead and we shall meet it again later. For now, turn left into **BLOOMSBURY WAY**, which was formerly known as Hart Street and, originally residential, home to some notable people (see p 27). Today it carries heavy eastbound traffic, with (beware!) a contraflow bus and cycle lane. Cross at the traffic lights to the north side and turn left to walk the few metres to **St George's Bloomsbury**.

This church was built after the passing of the Fifty New Churches Act of 1711 in the newly formed parish of St George's, separated from St Giles. It was the sixth and last of the 12 churches that were designed by Nicholas Hawksmoor and was consecrated in January 1730. Hawksmoor's highly original steeple was meant to resemble the ancient (long-vanished) Mausoleum of Halicarnassus, with the lion and unicorn (supporters of the Royal Arms) at the base of the pyramid **[7]**. The new church allowed the fashionable

7 Steeple of St George's Bloomsbury

residents to the east and north-east to attend worship without having to pass through the slums by the parish church of St Giles. It was constructed on a cramped site purchased from Lady Rachel Russell and already hemmed in by houses. It was a triumph for Hawksmoor that he was able to create a magnificent interior orientated to the east despite the land's north-south axis. However, this design meant that only 447 worshippers could be seated, and an extra 337 seats were added in 1781 only by adopting a north-south orientation and inserting galleries. During restorations begun in 2002 by Molyneux Kerr and completed by Inskip & Jenkins, the reredos and the north gallery were returned to respect the original intentions of Hawksmoor and the east-west orientation was restored.

The Church is open most afternoons, but if it is shut there is an information board to the left of the steps. There is an excellent handout in the church that covers all aspects of its history. One notable event held here, on 14 June 1913, was the funeral service, organised by the WSPU, of the suffragette Emily Davison, who died after flinging herself at the king's horse in the 1913 Derby. Thousands of suffragettes accompanied the coffin and many thousand people lined the streets as it made its way to King's Cross station for burial in Northumberland.

A flight of stairs to the left of the church leads down to the free exhibition *Hawksmoor and Bloomsbury*, and also in the Undercroft the Museum of Comedy (closed Mondays), which boasts artefacts ranging from Charlie Chaplin's cane to the Steptoes' stuffed bear.

From the pavement outside gaze up to the figure of George I, standing on a stepped spire modelled on Pliny's description of the ancient Mausoleum at Halicarnassus. This had at one time been considered by Wren for the spire for the new St Paul's. The lions and unicorns (union of England and Scotland) around the base of the tower which had been removed as unsafe in the 19th century were remodelled by Tim Crawley and returned to their original positions in 2006.

The footpath to the left of the church is usually open but if it is shut, walk on to Museum Street and make two right turns to reach the same spot. If the path is open, the traverse of the narrow passage, squeezed between the west front of the church and neighbouring buildings is unforgettable. The architectural critic Ian Nairn waxed lyrical about this in his *Nairn's London* (1966): 'Seven steps down, seven steps up. It sounds simple but in fact has a drama of a full symphony movement, charged up by the stupendous classical detail that bores a hole in your right flank'. Admire the north elevation of the church, which Nairn considered its best part, and cross the small churchyard. The sculpted stone remains give it the appearance of some ruined ancient site, reflecting the 18th-century enthusiasm for ruins. They lie beneath two towering plane trees, which obscure the cleaned and repaired north front of the church. The architectural critic Gavin Stamp recently fulminated against Camden Council's refusal to remove the trees.

We have now reached **LITTLE RUSSELL STREET**. On our left, within the church grounds and with a semi-circular apse lit by large windows, is the present **No.6**, the vestry hall, with steps up to the door. It was the base for the First Editions club run by A J A Symons from 1922-31 as a dining club and a centre for biographical information.

Through the gate, and across the road at **Nos.25-27**, is a yellow-brick building with dark red banding and a niche containing a statuette. Close to the ground is the foundation stone of the St Giles and St George's Parochial School laid by the Bishop of Rochester in 1879-80. A plaque at first-floor level explains that it was 'for the children of the two parishes in lieu of the original building in Museum Street'. The new school was the work of the local parish architect Joseph Peacock. With 40 girl boarders and 80 day boys, it was essentially an industrial school, training the girls for domestic service. For their general education the pupils attended the nearby National School (see right). By 1923, and until the end of WWII, Nos.25-27 were occupied by an antique furniture dealer. To the left, at **Nos.28-30**, is New Ruskin House, Adam-style with medallions of pretty ladies' heads on the door. Grade-II-Listed in 2010, this is occupied by various firms mostly connected with the arts, including the London Review of Books and the old-established American firm of Library Fine Arts.

Walk east along the north side of the street past several small houses that date from the early 1700s but were refaced and stuccoed in Victorian times. Across the street is the side entrance, complete with ferocious lions' heads, to Museum Chambers, early mansion flats of 1884, which date is prominently displayed.

At the end of the street we join the north end of **BURY PLACE**. This began life as one arm of a then L-shaped Little Russell Street. To your right, in the earlier 18th century a narrow alleyway known as Hole in the Wall ran south to join Hart Street. Off its east side was a tavern of the same name, 'known for the Cheese Cakes, Pyes, Tarts, &c. there made at the house so called'. By the end of the century this had been swept away and a new street built on the line of the alley. Combined with the earlier arm of Little Russell Street, this was at first known as Compton Street, and then, by 1819, as Bury Street. Viscount Bury was one of the titles of the Keppel family (cf. Keppel Street, p 77). In 1937 the street became part of the Bury Place we have already traversed. On your right today are **Museum Chambers** on the west side and **Russell Chambers** opposite, both with prominent bay windows. The main entrance doors have elaborately carved pediments. A blue plaque on the latter block notes that Bertrand Russell, philosopher and campaigner for peace, lived here in 1911-16 in Flat No.34.

On the corner of Little Russell Street at **No.15** (then No.17 Bury Street), a latter-day incarnation of the ancient Pied Bull Tavern was still standing in 1871. Across the road is gated **GALEN PLACE**. Formerly known as Pied Bull Yard, this was so renamed in 1888 after the examination halls of the Royal Pharmaceutical Society (p 17) were built in its north-east corner. Galen (c.130-201) was a Greek physician and it is said that no-one before or since has exercised so great an influence on medical practice. One source suggests that the old T-shaped Pied Bull Yard contained a slaughterhouse before it was given over to stabling. George Shillibeer, whose pioneering 3-horse Omnibus famously plied along the New (Euston) Road in 1829, was at one time based here as a cabriolet proprietor. An 1870s map shows it furnished with a pump and a urinal. It was not exactly salubrious and in updating his poverty map in 1898 Booth marks it purple, or containing some poor, although only three buildings were then occupied.

Left of the entrance was the (Anglican) National School for girls, boys and infants. Later on the same site, at No.9, and exempt from paying rates to Holborn Council, was the Central Library for Students, founded in 1916 and subsequently to become the National Central Library (p 92). From the late 19th century Bloomsbury Hall (p 27) abutted the south side of Galen Place, where a florist's now occupies modern **Nos.30-32**. Established here for some years was the Bloomsbury Workshop, a gallery which sold books and artworks, and held small exhibitions devoted to the Bloomsbury Group.

The Bedford Estate chose Chapman Taylor Partners as their architects for their 1980s development here. The northern section preserves the historic name of **PIED BULL YARD** and can be reached via a gate further along that is open Monday to Saturday. Outdoor restaurant seating fills much of the courtyard, where the ambiance is decidedly upmarket. Looking up on the north side, note the well preserved 18th-century windows of the tidy backs of properties in Great Russell Street, a reminder of the beneficial effects an efficiently run estate can have on the local environment (no rubbish here).

Leaving by the **BURY PLACE** exit, look up again to observe the novelty clock installed in 1988. It no longer functions but when it did the two hard-hatted workmen on top struck the bell to mark the quarter hours, while chasing each other round and round below were the now static five figures, a businessman, a punk, a policeman, a scantily-clad female jogger... and a bull.

Since 2003 the window display at adjacent **No.14** has encouraged the reader inside to browse in the independent London Review Bookshop. High-profile author readings and other events are held in the evenings and there is a coffee shop next door.

Crossing the road and briefly walking north, turn left into quiet, car-free **GILBERT PLACE**. Known as Gilbert Street until 1939, this was named after Gilbert Holles, 3rd Earl of Clare, a friend of the ground landlord, William Lord Russell, who had the first houses here built c.1670. None of them remain, but the later **Nos.8-14** and **Nos.17&18** are Listed. The former block, halfway down on the left, has a pattern of iron window-guards, retaining plants which add some cheer to the street. **No.29**, further along on the north side, was rebuilt in the 1880s and from 1899-1902 was the bindery of the Arts and Craft bookbinder, Douglas Bennett Cockerell. This may explain the once splendid *trompe l'oeil* 'Renaissance' panels that flank the front door. The painting, alas, is now barely visible.

Reach **MUSEUM STREET**. Before the 1820s, and the building of the British Museum, this was known as Queen Street. By 1713 the engraver and art dealer Gerard Vandergucht, was based at the Golden Head in Queen Street, where he trained his sons Gerard and John.

Enjoy the exuberantly pastel-coloured terraces on both sides at this north end of the street. Dating from the 18th century, they were given a makeover in the 1850s, by William Finch Hill in a 'modified French Renaissance style'. Enjoy the pattern of oval roundels. Booth's researcher in 1898 noted that the street was full of shops with their owners 'of a good class' living above.

To your right, **Nos.37-39** retain their 19th-century shop fronts. On your left, note the splendid 'old fogey' clothes in the windows of the corner shop at **No.40**, now called 'Thomas Farthing' and displaying a penny-farthing bicycle outside. Until his death in 2007 the shop was owned by Peter Jolliffe, the poet and antiquarian bookseller, who specialised in modern first editions and ran the Ulysses Bookshop here. Occupying No.40 in Edwardian times had been Men's League for Women's Suffrage. Hanging above is an intricate metal sign made (possibly by Walter Crane) for the publishing firm Allen and Unwin, which moved here from Rathbone Place, Fitzrovia in 1914, after (Sir) Stanley Unwin took over the bankrupt business of George Allen. In 1936, J R R Tolkien submitted for publication a tale called *The Hobbit*. Unwin paid his 10-year-old son Rayner sixpence (2½p) to write a report on the manuscript. The boy liked it and the book was soon published by Allen & Unwin, as nearly two decades later was *The Lord of the Rings*.

No.40 was long known as Ruskin House. George Allen (d.1907) had not only been a publisher of the later works of John Ruskin, but had also married Ruskin's mother's maid. **No.41**, next door, is now named Ruskin's Tea Rooms in honour of the Victorian art critic, who sold not cups of tea but packets of pure leaf tea to the poor in the shop he opened in Marylebone.

Cross the road to the **Plough** public house, remodelled in 1855, where a sign on the corner summarises the history of the area, noting *inter alia* the foundation locally, by the 4th Duke of Bedford, of the 'Bedford Gang' (of Whigs) in 1765. The pub was frequented by artists and writers in the interwar period, when it was nicknamed the 'Baby's Bottom', presumably as it was painted pink.

Continue across Little Russell Street towards Bloomsbury Way. On the left hand side, at the former No.6, the bookseller and publisher John Major was based in 1839. William Carey, the art critic and dealer, lived nearby before moving to Birmingham in 1835. At **No.47** was previously the Museum Street Galleries. In 1962 the artist Robert Colquhoun was preparing for an exhibition here when, aged just 47, he suffered a fatal heart attack in rooms above. The following year the gallery displayed paintings by Dr Stephen Ward, shortly after he committed suicide, having been made the scapegoat during the Profumo scandal.

Cross over to Tavistock Chambers (1888) on the east corner ahead. On its ground floor is **No.49A**, the Atlantis bookshop, the oldest established occult bookshop in London, opened in 1922 by Michael Houghton. It stands on part of the site of the Parochial School for Boys and Girls, which stood here beside the parish church until its move to Little Russell Street (p 25) in 1879-80.

Turn left into **BLOOMSBURY WAY**, known as Hart Street until 1938. Strype in 1720 remarked that it was 'large and open, with well built houses'. On Booth's poverty map of 1899 it was coloured a middle-class red (as were most main roads in the area). Enjoy another look at the spire of St George's. Beyond the church is the striking Edwardian **Kingsley (Thistle) Hotel**, at first and for many years a temperance hotel.

Opposite at **No.10** is an immense, newly refurbished former Ministry of Defence office block, which has another long frontage in New Oxford Street (see p 31). Once standing here was a terrace of houses, Nos.1-14 Hart Street. The physician John Haslam, who specialised in the treatment of insanity, was living at No.1 in the 1820s. No.3 was the home of Charles Farley (1771-1859), the actor, dramatist and theatre manager, who supervised Covent Garden pantomimes for three decades, and served as mentor of the clown Grimaldi, before spending most of his last 25 years in quiet retirement here. No.12 was home to the physician and actor Sir John Hill (d.1775). The architect, designer and antiquary John Woody Papworth, elder son of J B Papworth, died at No.13 in 1870.

When his cartographic business prematurely collapsed, Christopher Greenwood (1786–1855) turned, unsuccessfully, to publishing county historical guides from an office in Hart Street. After their marriage in 1832 Sir Charles Lyell and his wife moved into No.15 Hart Street. He was the author of *The Principles of Geology*, and a friend and supporter of Charles Darwin.

Several public houses have disappeared from the north side of the street. A small turning led to the Bugle Bull Inn, described by Strype in 1720 as being 'of good account'. Pubs once stood on either corner of the junction with Bury Place – the Bull and Mouth (which closed only in 2005 to become a Chinese restaurant) and a Victorian Yorkshire Grey in a building now occupied by a branch of Richer Sounds.

Beyond, **Nos.24-28**, fronted by Georgian-style railings as if to resemble a short terrace of 19th-century houses, actually form a 1980s office building extending north to Galen Place (p 25). It covers the site of the late-Victorian Bloomsbury Mansions (actually offices) and the entrance to Bloomsbury Hall, which extended back to Galen Place. In the 1880s, when known as the Neumeyer Hall, it shared the premises with the London 'depot' of the Berlin-based piano makers of that name, the American organ builders Bell & Co and the office of the Royal College of Organists. The hall was much used by various socialist bodies, including the Social Democratic Federation and the Fabian Society. William Morris spoke here more than once. In November 1884 he and George Bernard Shaw put on an 'Art Evening', a fundraiser for the Socialist League. It included a performance by Eleanor Marx and her cad of a partner Edward Aveling (p 48) of a play based on their own lives. The entrance to Bloomsbury Hall was at No.25A Hart Street and the Hall was described in 1906 as 'a long, oblong room, with a level floor. At one end of it is a kind of dais of two different levels, winged with tapestry curtains'. Surviving **Nos.20&21** and **No.23** are Listed, together with their railings.

Living at No.17 (on the south side of the street, now under Bupa House) in the 1870s was the controversial Miss Sarah Stride, the Lady Superintendent of her Home for destitute girls and fallen women at No.12 Great Coram Street. It was said she kept a similar home here at No.17 and she was taken to court for alleged non-payment of bills, and exposed by the Charity Organisation Society as an unsuitable person to run such establishments. Next door at Nos.19-21, and with a portico facing Barter Street, is a former 18th-century town house, now **Swedenborg House**, home of the Swedenborg Society since 1925 when they moved from Bloomsbury Street (p 36). The society publicises the works of Emanuel Swedenborg (1688-1712), the Swedish mystic, theologian and scientist. Internally one of the main attractions is the ground-floor Swedenborg Hall, described by *The Guardian* as 'one of London's most atmospheric venues'.

We have come almost full circle. Before finally taking leave of Bloomsbury Square, look at figure **[8]**, which shows an assemblage of overpowering office blocks. These were designed by Ernö Goldfinger in 1962 for the developer Hammerson, whose plans to erect them onthe south side of the square mercifully never materialised.

To return to Holborn Station, retrace your steps through Sicilian Avenue and turn right along Southampton Row.

8 What might have been: Ernö Goldfinger's scheme for the south side of Bloomsbury Square

Route 2
Along and off New Oxford Street to the north

A linear walk from Holborn Station to Tottenham Court Road Station. For more information on streets and buildings south of New Oxford Street, see *Streets of St Giles*.

The walk begins at the east end of New Oxford Street, which is reached from Holborn Underground Station. From its Kingsway exit cross the road to Sainsbury's and walk beyond the store along High Holborn. Cross over at the second traffic lights, and pause on the small island where **NEW OXFORD STREET** forks off to the right.

A relatively new thoroughfare, this dates only from the mid-19th century **[9]**. By then the ancient, slightly curved east-west route for horse-drawn traffic, via St Giles High Street, had become seriously congested. In 1839 an Act was

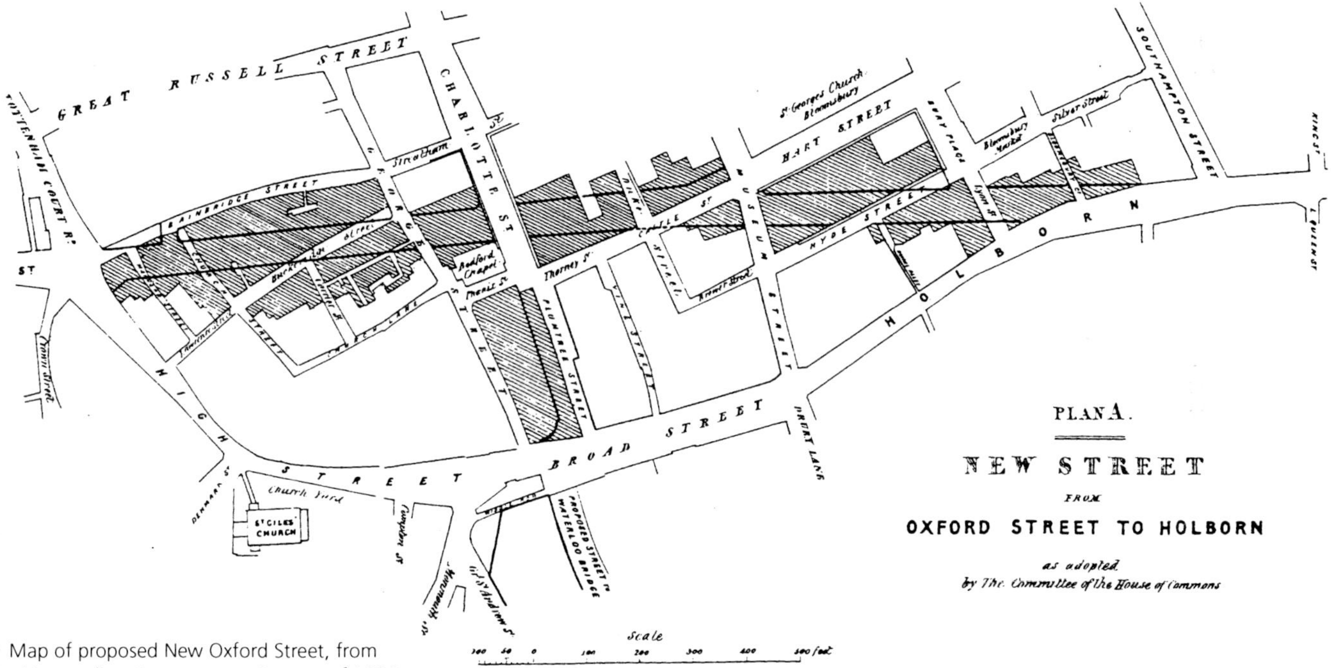

9 Map of proposed New Oxford Street, from the Metropolitan Improvement Reports of 1836

passed to permit the construction of a bypass road running directly from Oxford Street to High Holborn; the necessary powers to buy up the land were authorised two years later. Overseen by (Sir) James Pennethorne, Surveyor of Works to the Crown, construction began in 1844 and was completed by 1847. The new, much admired buildings were described as exhibiting 'a great advance in taste'. Leases were soon taken up, and the new street became a popular shopping destination. It was initially named and numbered as part of Oxford Street, with Nos.441-494 running sequentially eastward on the south side and Nos.495-552 opposite returning west. In 1881, it was renamed New Oxford Street and renumbered, with even numbers running westward on the north side and odd numbers opposite. No.494 thus became No.1.

Stretching from the corner is the large 9-storey **Commonwealth House** (Nos.1-19), dating from 1939 and designed by the architect H P Cart de Lafontaine in a *moderne* style. Its current (2016) redevelopment will see the building's rounded 'prow' clad in the hexagonal glazed green tiles originally proposed by Lafontaine, but vetoed by Sir Giles Gilbert Scott (as advisor to the Crown estate), who considered them too much of an 'innovation'. The numberless clock high above, characteristic of the period, is to be preserved.

Offices here were occupied for many years by the Remington Typewriter Co. and in the 1980s by the publishers IPC and the editorial office of *New Scientist*, and from 1998 by the Cavendish publishing group. Long occupying No.1 on the corner was the National Bank (of Ireland), founded in 1835 by a group of MPs, including the Irish statesman Daniel O'Connell. The branch here closed in 1970 when the bank's English operations became part of Williams & Glyn's.

Coincidentally, next-door No.493 Oxford Street (later No.3) served briefly, in 1846, as the base of the National Land Bank newly formed by the leading Chartist and MP, Feargus O'Connor. His National Land Company was based almost opposite, at No.144 High Holborn on the site of the modern Holborn Tower (on your right).

By a further coincidence, old No.145 High Holborn, destroyed in the construction of New Oxford Street, had been the birthplace in 1813 of the radical Henry Vincent, who became another prominent Chartist. The Vincent family moved to Hull in 1821; soon after, the engineer Augustus Siebe, later famous for his diving suit, set himself up at No.145 as a watchmaker and silversmith.

Walk along the south side of New Oxford Street, where as part of the Commonwealth House refurbishment new shopfronts 'informed by the Art Moderne period' are to be installed. Here until very recently at **No.5** was the Wellspring bookshop, belonging to and promoting the Rudolf Steiner Society. On this site in 1853-57, No.492 Oxford Street was the business address of William Horsell, an advocate of vegetarianism.

Beyond No.19 is a closed gateway to **Dunn's Passage**, long known as Dumb's Alley. Now a desolate sunken service road open to the sky, but once a narrow pedestrian tunnel, this was a hive of activity in the 19th century, housing a ragged school for 500 children (until 1857) and a factory that successively made gun-cases, sports equipment and (later) photographic apparatus. On the right-hand wall you can still see the old Borough of Holborn street sign.

Apart from buses, there is only a trickle of traffic in this part of New Oxford Street. Renewed traffic problems arising after WWII led to the introduction of a one-way scheme, with City-bound vehicles routed along Bloomsbury Way, and westbound traffic following the historic route via High Holborn and St Giles High Street.

Opposite is the huge, 9-storey, red-brick building at **Nos.2-28**, until recently known as St George's Court. It occupies a triangular site, with its other long side facing Bloomsbury Way (p 27). Designed by the architects Lewis Solomon & Son, it was originally intended as offices for J A Phillips, a major estate agent. Only the foundations were completed in 1939, and during WWII the site was requisitioned and its basement used for a large air-raid shelter (and a coal dump). Completed in 1948, the block subsequently housed a succession of government departments, including the Ministries of Supply, Aviation and Technology, and latterly of Defence. Newly refurbished by Buckley Gray Yeoman, its 150,000m² of office space is now being marketed as '10 Bloomsbury Way'. At the building's east end, a re-housed Victorian pub, the Oxford & Cambridge Stores at No.2, was still trading in the 1980s.

Before St George's Court was built much of this site housed the huge West End branch of tailors and outfitters E Moses and Son, which opened in October 1850. Once famous for their cheap, ready-made clothes their new branch outshone (literally because of its many gas-lights) their large building in Aldgate, which in the 1840s had been the largest shop in London. The German visitor Max Schlesinger referred to the New Oxford Street establishment in 1853 as a 'dazzling blaze'. Among its many departments, it advertised bespoke tailoring for the gentry, with a carriage halt and private entrance in Hart Street (now Bloomsbury Way). The firm ceased trading in 1883 soon after the death of its founder Isaac Moses Marsden.

On the south side, at **Nos. 21-31** and extending through to High Holborn, is a neglected, oppressive Modernist block, with long bands of Portland stone and glass. This was built for the General Post Office by E T Serjent in 1961-69 as its West Central district sorting office, replacing its earlier premises. These had opened on Hyde Street to the south in 1894 and gradually expanded before and after WWI with the purchase of properties on neighbouring streets. In 1927 the Post Office opened its own underground railway which required ventilation shafts and lifts that took up a lot of space and necessitated further expansion, culminating in 1960 in the purchase of the site and erection of the block we see today. On its closure the block was acquired by the British Museum and used for storage, but plans to turn it into a study centre fell through. In recent years the empty building, black-faced at street level, has lain empty, its dark voluminous interior playing host to various 'pop-up' events, ranging from fashion shoots, design shows and a Christie's art exhibition, to an illicit all-night internet-fuelled 'rave' in 2010. Camden Council's 'draft planning framework' (2014) proposes a major mixed-use redevelopment of the site.

At the next junction, glance along the south end of Museum Street, here a combination of earlier Peter Street and Bow Street. Lost in the construction of New Oxford Street was much of Hyde (earlier Hide) Street, which began as a continuation of Barter Street (p 21), then ran across the sorting-office site to cross Museum Street a few metres to your left. Intersecting there from the right is the old street's surviving rump, originally named Brewer Street, later absorbed into Hyde Street, and finally renamed West Central Street in 1938 after the adjacent sorting office.

Where New Oxford Street is joined obliquely by Bloomsbury Way, the acute-angled corner was once occupied by the popular Café Vienna (or Wiener Café) **[10]**. It was a favourite haunt of the Vorticist

10 Interior of the Café Vienna, 1897

poets, and at lunchtime of staff and users of the British Museum, among them Arthur Waley (p 66), the poet Laurence Binyon and the artist Lucien Pissarro. The mirrored ceiling of a triangular room on the café's first floor witnessed Wyndham Lewis's first meeting with Ezra Pound in 1910. Entirely staffed by 'enemy alien' Germans and Austrians, the establishment was forced to close on the outbreak of WWI. Later occupied by the National Trade Union Club and a Barclays bank, the building was demolished in 1939 to make way for the (eventual) St George's Court.

Over the road at **No.34** (now a Prezzo restaurant) is the site of the famous Mudie's Select Library, probably the best remembered of all the buildings in New Oxford Street. In 1852 Charles Mudie moved his business from Upper King Street (p 20) to a large, handsome building here at Nos.30-34 (then Nos.509-511). The library had as many as 120,000 books in circulation and a further 100,000 in reserve. Subscribers **[11]** paid a guinea (£1.05) a year but could borrow only one book at a time. Mudie carefully selected his stock, excluding works he deemed unsuitable. Publishers were afraid of him, for if he did not take a book, sales were doomed. As a popular rhyme had it:

As children must have Punch and Judy
I can't do without my Mudie.

By 1884 Charles Mudie had retired and his son Arthur took over the business, which continued until 1937.

Born in 1862 at No.509, the son of a Mudie's cashier, was Charles Abel, later to become a prominent Christian missionary in Papua New Guinea. No.30 was home to the mathematician and astronomer Arthur Downing, who died here in 1917.

Crossing Museum Street, continue ahead beside a row of original 1840s buildings at Nos.33-45, which were erected on the site of an earlier Castle Brewery. Pass the **Old Crown** public house at No.33 on the corner, with its three large hanging lamps. **No.35** next door once housed the late-Victorian 'magical warehouse' of James Bland, one of several magic shops in the street at the time. In 1902 it was taken over by Hamley's, serving as one of their several toy shops until 1915. **No.39** was re-fronted in 1927 in art deco style for the Hackney Furniture Co.

Nos.43&45 have been described as 'the most prominent intact survival of Pennethorne's most important Metropolitan Improvement'. Handsome stuccoed and balustraded **No.45**, now a betting shop, initially housed Stocker's Prize Beer Engine Manufactory and later the wine and spirit merchants Marshall & Elvy. The building continues around the corner along West Central Street, which debouches here, having made a 90° turn along what was originally the southern part of Duke Street (now Coptic Street).

Soon intersecting from the left, by the Listed Bloomsbury pub (of 1904, by Charles Fitzroy Doll) is Shaftesbury Avenue, opened in 1886 and the

11 Exchanging books at Mudie's subscription library, 1901

last of the street improvements of the Metropolitan Board of Works. Here at its north end the Avenue splits into two branches, forming two sides of a triangular island. The north side of the open space (directly ahead) corresponds to earlier Thorney Street, a short continuation of erstwhile Castle Street. Born in 1792 at its west end, on the corner with Plumtree Street (now Shaftesbury Avenue's other carriageway) was the painter John Linnell, whom we shall meet again later (p 37).

Standing until 2002 against the blank wall facing you, was a red-granite drinking fountain erected in 1887 to celebrate Queen Victoria's Golden Jubilee, and now relocated to nearby Princes Circus, down on your left.

Crossing over this branch of Shaftesbury Avenue at the lights, continue west past a further row of 19th-century survivals. **No.49** was once a café run by Stavros Georgiou, the father of the pop singer Cat Stevens (aka Yusuf Islam), who was born here in 1947 and spent much of his childhood waiting on tables and working in the kitchen. The building has another entrance (No.245 Shaftesbury Avenue), as does the adjoining **Crown** public house, which is signalled by a large old lamp topped by a crown.

Beyond, at **No.53** (*alias* Hazelwood House), is the renowned shop of James Smith & Son, makers, sellers and repairers of umbrellas, walking-sticks and whips. Established in 1830, the shop arrived here in 1865, originally as a branch of the Smiths' main store in Savile Row. Listed Grade-II*, it is the only survivor of the splendid emporia that graced New Oxford Street in Victorian and Edwardian times. It has an elegant shop front in mahogany and brass. The business still thrives, and tourists can be seen queuing in the morning before opening time.

Cross to the north side of New Oxford Street and walk back east to peer through the wrought-iron gate that guards **Stedham Place**, an open courtyard ablaze with greenery and flowers during spring and summer. This was once a stabling area called Charlotte Mews. The old warehouse on the right-hand side is late Victorian, and the iron balconies on the far side belong to Stedham Chambers (p 34).

Further along, turn left along **COPTIC STREET**. Earlier known as Duke Street, it was renamed in 1894, when the British Museum acquired an important collection of manuscripts from the early Christian (Coptic) churches in Egypt. The consecutive numbering was retained. It begins with a run of brick-built late Georgian houses, Nos.5-10, originally all with shops below. Fluted Ionic pilasters adorn the old shop front at **No.5**, which since 1985 has housed the Greek restaurant Konaki, with a courtyard at the rear. In the mid-1930s food and social historian Dorothy Hartley rented a room here while working for the *Daily Sketch* and researching in the British Museum Reading Room. Across the street are two stuccoed houses at **Nos.24&26**, the former a Korean restaurant (note the delightful lion-shaped corbels supporting the architrave). The 1990s housing development by Avanti Architects, with a corner tower feature, covers the site of No.27 Duke Street, the home from 1792 of the painter Isaac Cruikshank, where his two sons Robert and George, later famous as caricaturists, spent their childhood. The house was the late-19th-century base of the Charity Organisation Society.

To the right of the raised paved area (to prevent through traffic), and on the corner of Little Russell Street, is St George's House at **Nos.30-31**; inscribed in brick high up on both frontages is the legend 'Dairy Supply Co. Ltd'. The company was part of the Express Dairies empire founded by George Barham and one of the earliest wholesale suppliers of milk to the capital. By 1899 it occupied nine properties here and in neighbouring streets; Charles Booth's researcher had noted the year before that chambers above the shops were let out to the company's carters and employees. A wall plaque facing Coptic Street lists four directors. The corner building was designed by R P Whellock in 1888, and adorned with the sunflower motif popular at that time. Its round-arched windows were a hallmark of Express Dairies premises. Later used by United Dairies, the building was converted in 1967 into a Pizza Express restaurant, in a trend-setting scheme by Enzo Apicella, creating one of London's earliest 'theme restaurants'. Still preserved within are some of the original fittings and tiling, and various dairy memorabilia.

Deviate briefly into the west end of **LITTLE RUSSELL STREET** (p 25), where beyond an arched entry, the beautifully incised stone fascia at **No.35** repeats the dairy company's name. Now occupying the building is the Cartoon Museum, which moved here from the Brunswick Centre in 2006. The building formerly housed the Matrix Studios where Adam & The Ants recorded their first hit album in 1980.

Returning to **COPTIC STREET**, look beyond the Pizza Express building to two interesting early-19th-century houses. **No.32** incorporates a covered entrance to a yard. A German spy of WWI, Lizzie Wertheim, lodged here in 1915 before she was imprisoned in Aylesbury Gaol. She died in 1920 of TB in Broadmoor Hospital for the criminally insane. The tall **No.33**, with its central door, is now a hostel providing student accommodation for Oxford House College.

Turn left into **STREATHAM STREET**, rounding a corner once occupied by a pub called the Fox. Now standing on either side of the junction are the two red-brick blocks of **Stedham Chambers**, privately built in 1886 as 'artisans' dwellings' and initially known as Duke Street Chambers. The 30 flats were later renamed after the Sussex village where the blocks' owner, Major Caleb Collins, was born. This east end of Streatham Street was originally much narrower and named Woburn Court. Woburn Abbey is the Duke of Bedford's seat in Bedfordshire.

On the right pass featureless **WILLOUGHBY STREET**, known as Woburn Street until renamed after George Philip Willoughby, Mayor of Holborn, in 1903-04.

Continue west to where a locked gate on the left guards a modern alleyway running through to New Oxford Street. Never a right of way, it was recently closed. Beyond this, Streatham Street crosses **BLOOMSBURY STREET**. Facing onto the former but numbered in the latter, the left-hand corner house has a Doric portico surmounted by a head of Menelaus, king of Sparta and husband of Helen of Troy. In 1820 an art school for aspiring painters, opened two years earlier at No.50 Great Russell Street (p 47) by Henry Sass, moved here to what was then No.6 Charlotte Street, Bloomsbury. The property was renumbered No.21 Bloomsbury Street in 1845 and survives as present-day **No.10**.

Henry Sass was not a successful painter but his Drawing Academy became very much part of the early Victorian art world. Its pupils included Edward Lear, Augustus Egg and D G Rossetti. William Powell Frith lodged here aged 16, whilst Millais enrolled in 1838 as a 9-year-old child prodigy. Sass's establishment has been called the preparatory school for the Royal Academy and the fees were high. It was also known from 1832 for admitting females; Henrietta Ward, who studied here, was later to found an art school for women.

In 1840 Sass became ill and passed his academy on to Francis Cary **[12]**, whose father Henry, a translator, died in the house in 1844. In that same year Sass also died, and the establishment became known as Cary's Painting School. Cary continued to live and work at No.21 Bloomsbury

12 Francis Cary, drawing by James Hayllar

Street until the 1870s before retiring to Surrey. Today, the building houses Oneworld Publications, an independent publishing firm founded in 1986.

Bloomsbury Street began life as a cul-de-sac, the northern end of the variously spelt Plumtree Street, which ran north from what is now Princes Circus to a point just south of present-day Great Russell Street. It was developed c.1686 by Henry Plumbtree who came from a well-to-do Nottinghamshire family. The narrow street was widened in the 1760s, extended to meet Great Russell Street and named Charlotte Street, probably after George III's consort. It became known as Charlotte Street, Bloomsbury (occasionally Lower Charlotte Street) to distinguish it from its northward continuation known as Charlotte Street, Bedford Square. The two Charlotte Streets were numbered separately. All very confusing for postmen, no doubt, especially as there was yet another Charlotte Street a few minutes away in Fitzrovia.

This Route concentrates on the former Charlotte Street, Bloomsbury, i.e. from New Oxford Street up to Great Russell Street. The west side was renumbered slightly in 1824, with the addition of two houses. Several of the buildings at its southern end were demolished when New Oxford Street was pushed through in 1845. Charlotte Street was then renamed Bloomsbury Street, subsuming a widened Plumtree Street, whose remaining houses were numbered as part of the newly-named thoroughfare. To the north of New Oxford Street numbering began at No.17, running consecutively up the east side and down the west to No.36. The numbering was changed yet again in 1894 when Charlotte Street, Bedford Square also became part of Bloomsbury Street, with even numbers on the east side and odds on the west (south to north, so No.36 for example became present No.1). By then the street had lost its southernmost section in the mid-1880s construction of Shaftesbury Avenue.

Early residents of Charlotte Street included the auctioneer John Sotheby, before he moved to Chigwell in 1778, and the painter George Keate (1729-97), who had his friend Robert Adam decorate his house. It was also the birthplace in about 1780 of the philosopher and writer Thomas Morgan, known by his pseudonym μ.

Among the houses in Charlotte Street Bloomsbury that were demolished for the construction of New Oxford Street was No.14. Before her marriage in 1806 to Charles Kemble, this was the home of the noted actress and singer Maria Theresa du Camp. Also broken up was the Charlotte Street School of Medicine at No.15 in the home of its principal George Dermott, which had offered students 'unlimited dissection'. It moved briefly to No.28 Bedford Square before closure.

On the **east side** of Bloomsbury Street, the block **Nos.12-18**, stretching north from where you are standing to Great Russell Street, is a 1980s development called Bloomsbury Plaza, a development of shops with flats above that unusually each bear a letter rather than a number. This replaced Oakley House at Nos.14-18, an early-20th-century block, which during WWII housed amongst others the British Industrial Design Group. The shop at **No.12** is Oxfam's flagship second-hand bookstore in London, opened by the author Ian McEwan in 2007. Previously on this site were the purpose-built premises of the Bloomsbury Dispensary, which opened here in 1880 having moved from Great Russell Street (p 48). It was bombed out in 1941, when it transferred temporarily to No.5 across the street. Its successor body, the St Giles-in-the-Fields and Bloomsbury United Charity, has an office further north at No.15A Gower Street.

Bloomsbury Plaza also covers the site of (pre-1980) No.16, which as No.24 was occupied from 1848 by the Natural History Agency. This was run by Samuel Stevens, who was the agent for and sold the collections of Alfred Russel Wallace and Henry Bates. He was a member of the Stevens family of natural history auctioneers and sold the business in 1867 to follow his entomological interests.

The late-1980s block **Nos.2-8**, running south to New Oxford Street respects the height of the remaining house at No.10. In the former house at No.6 (then No.9) a pioneer of photography, German-born John Henry Dallmeyer, founded his eponymous company, which stayed there until 1888 (and only went out of business in 1993). He developed lenses which were good enough for astronomical observations and taking photographs of the sun. On his departure the premises became the London shop of the French numismatists and antiquities dealers Rollin and Feuardent, where they often organised exhibitions of coins and medals.

No.4 was the home in the early 20th century of the Pelman Institute, offering popular classes in memory training or pelmanism, a system of 'scientifically training the mind'. During WWI the efficient brains produced by Pelmanism were claimed to be as effective a means of defeating the enemy as tanks. During WWII the Institute moved to Albion House (p 38) in New Oxford Street. In the house in 1836, when it was No.9 Charlotte Street, a Rev. Dr Willis opened a house for lunatics, for which he ended up in court. He was allowed to continue under his real name of William Willis Moseley for several decades, advertising that he could cure mental illness in just a few hours.

No.2 (when No.17) housed the Benefit Penny Bank, which catered for small investors, many of whom ransacked the building when the bank folded in 1883. The HQ of the National Institute for the Deaf (later at No.105 Gower Street, p 89) was based at former No.2 in the late 1920s.

Walk briefly south to the New Oxford Street junction and cross over to the **west side** of Bloomsbury Street. **Nos.1-5** are three Grade-II-Listed houses built c.1766-67. The once longer terrace was truncated when New Oxford Street was created. At **No.1** is *Bookmarks*, the Socialist Bookshop founded in the 1960s and stocking publications of Socialist and Marxist interest; it is also the official bookshop of its near neighbour, the TUC (p 43). As No.22 Charlotte Street this was the home in his last years of the chemist David Booth (1766-1846), the author of a seminal book on brewing which advocated the use of thermometers in the brewing process. In 1854, as No.36 Bloomsbury Street, the building was purchased on a 72-year lease by Augustus Clissold for the Swedenborg Society, to serve as its library, reading room and first permanent home. The Society left for its present headquarters in Bloomsbury Way (p 28) in 1925. Its early years here were unhappy: it became entangled in a legal dispute with its manager, a Mr White, who ran the bookshop on the ground floor. He decided to stock spiritualist works rather than the Society's own New Church literature and the Committee members ejected him; he took repossession forcibly with the aid of prizefighters. Law suits ended in his leaving, to be replaced by the much-respected Charles P Alvey.

At the corner with Streatham Street is **No.5** (at present a café). When first built in 1766 this was the home of Paul Saunders, tapestry maker, whose commercial premises (now demolished) lay behind. In the 1930s No.5 was the office of the architectural firm of James, Bywaters & Rowland Pierce, who designed Norwich City Hall and Hertford County Hall. During the Regency there was a 'Lock Dispensary' on the site, with a patients' entrance in Streatham Street. By 1821 it boasted it had cured over 2,000 people of syphilis. (The first 'Lock Hospital' for the treatment of venereal disease had opened in Southwark in 1747, the name deriving from the rags or 'locks' that covered the patients' sores.)

The block between Streatham Street and Great Russell Street, built in 1907 as the Ivanhoe Hotel (for its twin the Kenilworth see p 43), it is now the **Radisson Blu Edwardian**. Old No.33, now covered by the tower at the corner of Great Russell Street, housed in the mid-19th century a dairy run by Jane Newman until she died. The next occupant was the architect and surveyor Wyatt Papworth (1822-94), younger son of J B Papworth and remembered for his *Dictionary of Architecture*. In the early 1820s at No.26 Charlotte Street the dancing master Mr Levien taught quadrilles. Several of the old houses had become lodging houses before they were replaced by the hotel.

Turn left into the western end of **STREATHAM STREET**, here at first named Nottingham Street, after the home town of

Henry Plumbtree, the late-17th-century developer of what is now Bloomsbury Street.

No.2 Streatham Street (precise location unclear, but probably here on the left) was the childhood home of the landscape painter John Linnell, whose birthplace in 1792 we noted earlier (p 33). By 1800 the Linnell family had moved via Soho to near-slum conditions at No.2 at a time when it lay on the edge of the St Giles Rookery (p 38). Linnell later wrote in his autobiography a vivid description of his life here: 'At first we lived in the kitchen and parlour and the first floor. The second floor was let. Later, however, the whole floor was occupied by my father's business as a picture framer and gilder, for he prospered here for some years through the bad times when bread was half a crown a loaf and press gangs roamed the streets.' Linnell's father James also sold pictures and published prints. By the age of ten his precocious son was drawing portraits in pencil and chalk, and copying paintings of George Morland. In 1843, above a cowshed in Streatham Street, London City missionaries founded the St Giles and St George's Ragged School & Refuge, later to occupy more salubrious accommodation near today's Princes Circus.

On the corner of Dyott Street stands Listed **Parnell House**. A bold inscription at first-floor level explains why its flats were built – as 'Model Houses for Families'. The Duke of Bedford provided the site, previously Streatham Mews, at a nominal ground rent of '1½d (0.6p) per foot'. Intended to house 'the deserving poor in regular employment', the 48 flats were built in 1849-50, shortly after the development of New Oxford Street, by the Society for Improving the Condition of the Labouring Classes. The block was at first variously known as Streatham Street Buildings or as Ashley Buildings, after Lord Ashley (soon to be Earl of Shaftesbury), the Society's chairman. The builders were the major local firm of Winsland and Holland based in Duke Street, just to the south of New Oxford Street.

All the flats were entered and chiefly lit from balconies overlooking an internal courtyard, by which device the architect, Henry Roberts hoped to avoid window tax. He argued that each gallery was an elevated street so each flat was an independent dwelling house. The authorities did not agree, but the Society successfully appealed and their much publicised case led to the repeal of window tax in 1851.

Each flat contained a living room, scullery, two bedrooms and a water closet off the scullery – a tremendous improvement in sanitation over previous arrangements in the poorest housing – and was let for 4s (20p) a week. The rent of basement flats was half this, though still beyond the reach of the poorest. The internal arrangements were altered in 1956 to a design by Frederick Gibberd. In 1965 the block was taken over by the Peabody Trust, which, needing money to renovate its older properties, later put the flats up for sale to private buyers, to the dismay of many locals. The flats were fully modernised in 1987.

DYOTT STREET was known before 1877 as George Street. Once standing on the north-west corner was a pub, the Two Brewers, and to the north of it the Irish Free School mentioned by local surgeon William Blair in evidence to a House of Commons enquiry in 1816. In this he stated that the local boys were now more orderly and that 80-85% of the local population was Irish Catholic. The school stood on the south side of diminutive New Street, always so named (its marking as 'Kent Street' on Stanford's map of 1862 being apparently a cartographical error). Once L-shaped, the street had been reduced to a short cul-de-sac when the Horseshoe Brewery (see p 38) was extended in the early 1800s.

On visiting Dyott Street in 1898, Charles Booth's researcher described two of the 4-storey houses at its north-east end, and those in adjacent New Court, as 'very poor' and its residents as 'casual coster class'. 'Some windows broken', he wrote, 'bird cages at side windows, blinds drawn across windows instead of curtains, noisy especially when pay day comes round for "reserve men", children very dirty and carelessly dressed, one very mangy cat prowling about'.

Ahead of us, but unworthy of exploration, is **BAINBRIDGE STREET** (once sometimes spelt 'Bembridge Street'), now a gloomy canyon between the backs of buildings in adjacent streets. Towards the far end is the stage door of the Dominion Theatre in Tottenham Court Road. Henry Bainbridge built the street's first houses in the 1670s. His daughter, Jane Dyott, was possibly the wife of Simon Dyott, a St Giles vestryman listed in 1676. The street later lay on the northern edge of the Rookery. Trading here in the early 19th century were several pubs, including the Ship and the Cart & Horses, and another called the Admiral Nagle after Sir Edmund Nagle, a hero of the French wars, whose name was quickly corrupted by locals to 'Admiral & Eagle'. In the 1850s Mayhew called Jones Court in Bainbridge Street 'a haunt of coiners and thieves', while a contemporary, Flora Tristan, wrote of it as a 'veritable cesspool' and being 'almost suffocated by its poisonous smell' .

The north side of Bainbridge Street was long occupied by the Horseshoe Brewery, whose origins are obscure, its first known owner (c.1785) being one Thomas Fassett. Specialising in the brewing of porter, it was acquired in 1809 by Henry Meux (pronounced 'Mewks') and greatly enlarged. To mature the porter Meux installed several enormous vats. At 5.30 pm on 17 October 1814 one of these, not the largest, burst one of its iron hoops, releasing 3,555 barrels (127,980 gallons) of maturing porter into the neighbouring streets. Flooded properties in nearby Great Russell Street included the Tavistock Arms at No.22. A wave of hot liquor at least 15ft high swept along New Street (see p 37), washing people out of first-floor windows and ruining three houses. Eight people, all women or children, lost their lives. Poignantly, five of them had been mourners at a wake in a New Street cellar for a 2-year-old boy who had died the previous day. The Horseshoe Brewery closed in 1921, when production moved to another Meux brewery at Nine Elms. Pulled down in 1922, it was eventually replaced by the TUC and (now former) YWCA buildings facing Great Russell Street (p 42).

Turn left along Dyott Street to re-emerge into **NEW OXFORD STREET** at its bustling, congested western end. When constructed in the 1840s, this cut through the infamous St Giles Rookery. Dyott Street, which continues south ahead of you, was usually regarded as its hub. Originally developed in the later 17th century as a respectable suburb close to the old parish church, the area declined into a slum notorious for its poverty, prostitution and crime.

Though viewed as a slum-clearance venture, the construction of New Oxford Street actually caused further deprivation: the Royal Statistical Society found that 5,000 people had lost their homes and that streets just outside in the affected area had seen a 76% increase in population. While the newly homeless received no assistance, the Duke of Bedford, as owner of over 100 of the freeholds, received £114,000 in compensation.

We have re-entered New Oxford Street beside recently refurbished Isis House at **No.74** on the left. Replacing bombed property after WWII, it was originally advertised as having 'a revolutionary, thermally efficient, full height glazed curtain wall'.

Across the road to the left, at **No.55**, is former Albion House, a modern successor to an earlier building of the same name, numbered 59A. This in turn had been built on the site of the Bedford Episcopal Chapel, a proprietary Anglican establishment dating from 1771, which had eventually become Unitarian.

On 23 November 1910 Dr Hawley Harvey Crippen was hanged for the murder of his wife.

The first Albion House had been mentioned repeatedly at his trial. Here were the London offices of the (American) Munyon's Homeopathic Remedy Co., where he had lately been manager. And here too was the Yale Tooth Specialists Co., the dental practice in which Crippen had become a partner and where, working as typist and bookkeeper, was his lover Ethel Le Neve (with whom he was to flee on a transatlantic liner, only to be arrested in the first use of radio to catch a criminal). Also in Albion House was the office and weekly meeting-place of the Music Hall Ladies Guild, including its treasurer, the singer Mrs Cora Crippen (stage name, 'Belle Elmore'), whose body would soon be discovered, preserved in slaked lime, beneath the Crippens' Holloway home. Recent DNA tests on preserved scar tissue have suggested that the victim was actually male, and the evidence against Crippen therefore faulty, but this has in turn been disputed.

On your right is modern Fairgate House at **No.78**. At this address, from 1867, were the glamorous offices of Thomas Holloway, a purveyor of pills and ointments. The fortune he made by selling these remedies allowed him to found the Holloway Sanatorium at Virginia Water (Surrey) for the care of the 'insane of the middle class'; and in 1879, at the suggestion of his wife, the palatial (Royal) Holloway College for well-heeled young ladies at nearby Egham. This became part of London University in 1900, admitted male undergraduates from 1965, and merged with Bedford College (p 55) in 1985.

Turn right into New Oxford Street. At Nos.80-112 is the Listed, white-stone former Prospect House, recently refurbished for Hermes Real Estate, with an entrance at **No.100**. Based at No.80 from 1880 were the popular linen drapers, costumiers and milliners Henry Glave, founded in Islington in 1848. Next door was the entrance to the short-lived Royal Arcade, described as a 'miniature imitation of Burlington Arcade'. This was gradually taken over by Glave's, whose shop soon occupied Nos.82-88 as well. In 1929 the architects Gunton & Gunton built them a splendid new building in a neo-classical style, also subsuming Nos.90-112. Glave's planned a further expansion, buying up land behind as far north as Great Russell Street, but they had overreached themselves. Their store closed in 1933, to be fondly remembered, particularly for its large stock of gloves and its club allowing customers to buy their purchases by weekly instalments. Swan and Edgar then occupied the property for a time. Taken over as government offices on the outbreak of WWII, the building survived the conflict, unlike many nearby, and its handsome Corinthian pilasters can still be admired above the modern shop fronts.

In 1908 the former No.102 housed the Aural Clinic Co., another of the several dubious medical practices in which Dr Crippen (see above) was involved; while three doors away, a shop at No.108 was occupied by the chemists Lewis and Burrows. Here, on 19 January 1910, Crippen infamously signed the poison register to buy 5 grams of hyoscine hydrobromide intended for his wife. On the site today is a branch of All Bar One.

On the south side opposite No.82 is another survivor of WWII, the triple-bayed building at Listed **Nos.71-75**, designed by W B Catherwood in 1887 for soap manufacturers A & F Pears. The interior was remarkable 'for the decoration in the Italian-style of mosaics, marble statuary, fountains and pools'. The upper floor, reached by a marble staircase, was hung with very costly paintings, including the famous *Bubbles* by John Millais, showing a too-good-to-be-true, golden-haired little boy sitting on the floor blowing bubbles. It became very well known when it was used to advertise Pears' soap. From the 1920s and for several decades, a Midland Bank was on the ground floor here. Above, in the 1960s, was the HQ of the multi-millionaire music publisher Dick James, who co-founded Northern Songs and at one time owned a controlling stake in The Beatles' songs. His recording studio here was made available to a young pianist named Reggie Dwight, later to gain fame as Elton John. From the early 1980s the building was home to Forbidden Planet, purveyors of comics and sci-fi merchandise. It now houses the Toni and Guy Hairdressing Academy.

The buildings on either side were lost to WWII bombing. Now at Nos.77-91 is the vast **Castlewood House**, designed by Lewis Solomon & Son and built after the war as government offices, but now privately occupied. The block extends to Earnshaw (earlier Arthur) Street, on opposite corners of which once stood the original No.91, from c.1860 to WWII home to the curriers and leather factors John S Deed & Sons; and at No.93 the Hand & Crown public house.

Continuing along the north side of New Oxford Street, **Nos.114-116** is former Imhof House. Installed by 1862 on this site, at No.547 Oxford Street, was Imhof & Mukle, a partnership of Daniel Imhof, a Bavarian organ builder, and Leopold Mukle, a clockmaker from the Black Forest listed here as a 'professor of music'. The partners made musical clocks, and also the Orchestrion, a clockwork 'self-acting' organ **[13]**, said to have been installed in every royal house in Europe. Imhof & Mukle seem to have been the first firm to sell a gramophone, and in 1903 gave the first public record recital in nearby Endell Street Baths. In 1929 they rebuilt their headquarters as Imhof House, with the same roofline and white stone as their neighbours, Glave's. Likewise fondly remembered for their good service, they later sold radios, records and television sets before closing in 1981. A branch of a ubiquitous coffee house now occupies the ground floor.

Across Bainbridge Street, the last building on the north side, at **Nos.118-132**, replaced an earlier shop of the men's outfitters Horne Bros. Of six storeys and in 'neo-Grec' style, it was built by Harry Wilson in 1929-30 as a shop and HQ for Montague Burton's clothing empire, founded in 1903 and by that time with 400 shops nationwide. After WWII, men discharged from the forces were issued with a complete outfit, including a three-piece suit with waistcoat, shirt and underwear. Montague Burton won the government contract to supply these suits, which if topped off with a hat and tie were known as 'The Full Monty'. The store here now combines branches of Burton for men and Dorothy Perkins for women.

13 An Imhof & Mukle Orchestrion, now in Blackpool Tower

Impossible to miss on the left is **Centre Point** tower (Nos.101-103). Of 33 storeys and 398-ft high, Richard Seifert's skyscraper built in 1961-67 has ever been controversial. Long left empty by property tycoon Harry Hyams, it was eventually used by the Centrepoint charity for the homeless, to which it lent its name, and later occupied by the Confederation of British Industries. Although disliked by Pevsner, it was Grade-II Listed by English Heritage in 1995. Under wraps in 2016, the block was undergoing an internal transformation by designers Conran & Partners to provide 82 luxury apartments.

We have reached St Giles Circus, where this walk ends. The huge construction site on the left is (in 2016) part of a major redevelopment of Tottenham Court Road Station, to include new platforms for Crossrail and a new public plaza on the west side of Centre Point. The tremendous change taking place here will doubtless impact on a wide area, including New Oxford Street. New Oxford Street was a 19th-century 'improvement' and here is one for the 21st-century – opinions will doubtless vary on the end-product.

Route 3
Great Russell Street and Bedford Square via the British Museum

A circular walk from Tottenham Court Road Station

Leaving the station by Exit 1, cross St Giles Circus to the Dominion Theatre diagonally opposite; then walk northwards and take the first turn right into **GREAT RUSSELL STREET**.

The street was originally built from 1670 along the line of an old field path, marked as Green Lane on Tudor maps. At first it ran past Southampton (now Bloomsbury) Square into Southampton Row. By the time John Strype surveyed the street in 1720 it was lined with handsome private residences, particularly on its north side, with gardens offering open views to Hampstead and Highgate. Strype wrote that 'this Place by Physicians is esteemed the most healthful of any in London'.

Among early residents were the antiquary John le Neve, born here in 1679; the playwright John Crowne (d.1712); the painter Godfrey Kneller, newly arrived from Germany, and later one much influenced by him, Gerhard Bockman. 18th-century residents included the physician William Battie (c.1703-76) who made a fortune treating the insane; Dr James Hawley (d.1777), who in 1761 acquired land in what became Camden Town; Robert Knight, the financier who ruined many in the South Sea Bubble; the engraver and pantomime artist Edward Rooker (1724-74); and Arthur Onslow (1691–1768), Speaker of the House of Commons. As the grander houses either disappeared or were divided up, there was a gradual decline in the status of the street. The south side became steadily more commercial in the 19th century.

On the Tottenham Court Road corner at **Nos.1-3** is the Barbados High Commission, whose ground floor houses the Barbadian Tourist Authority. The present block also encompasses the offices of **No.4**, the first home of the British Film Institute when it was set up in 1933.

14 The first Central YMCA building (1912) in Great Russell Street

Opposite is towering **No.112**, the London Central YMCA building by Elsworth Sykes Partnership, completed in 1976. Its predecessor, an Edwardian Baroque building by Richard Plumbe **[14]**, was opened by royalty in 1912 as the YMCA flagship. It catered to members of HM Forces during WWI and served the same function in WWII. Hit by a bomb in September 1940, it was quickly repaired with Government help. From 1971-76 the building was completely rebuilt to provide further facilities, including the St Giles Hotel, first run as part of the YMCA but now independent. The hotel is on the upper floors, which are set obliquely to the main structure.

In the 18th century the south side of the street here consisted primarily of modest terrace houses, which backed on to the Horseshoe Brewery. In 1764 the Bedford Estate erected a terrace of 4-storey houses that include No.5 and Nos.8-12. All these buildings were stuccoed in the mid-19th century. From the 1870s **No.5** was part of the Horseshoe Hotel on Tottenham Court Road which had been extended over part of the Brewery site. The area to the rear was redeveloped in 2007.

The terrace is interrupted by **No.7**, Nederlander House, which has an attractive art deco frontage. Its ground floor provides an exit from the Dominion Theatre. Some writers have placed James Boswell's first meeting with Samuel Johnson 'in the back room of Tom Davies' bookshop' at **No.8**, but the meeting in fact took place in Russell Street, Covent Garden, which until 1859 was also known as Great Russell Street (a source of no small confusion to historians). In the 1840s two painters of miniatures, Daniel Byrne and William Wallace Scott, were living at **No.9** and **No.10** respectively.

No.12 was in 1787 the last recorded home of the cabinet maker Christopher Furhlong, an accomplished inlayer whose clients included the Prince of Wales. In 1916 the 'Tramp Poet', W H Davies, after a lifetime of living rough and losing a leg in the process, settled at a flat here with his pet toad, Jim. He had self-published his *Autobiography of a Super Tramp* in 1908, which brought him to the attention of London's literary and artistic circles (he was painted by Augustus John). Davies is best known for the couplet

What is this life, if full of care,
We have no time to stand and stare...

Nos.13&14, the building before the car park, is also 18th-century. At No.13 the mezzotint engraver Henry Hudson was based in 1782-86. No.14 bears a blue plaque inscribed 'Here lived Charles Kitterbell as related by Charles Dickens in *Sketches by Boz* "The Bloomsbury Christening".'

Past the car park entrance is a large neo-Classical building by Lutyens, dated 1931. It was built to house the YWCA headquarters, but in recent years has become **The Bloomsbury Hotel**. Among the houses demolished in its construction was No.16, where the aged actor and playwright Henry Grattan was living in 1927. He had been a star of musical comedies around 1900 and wrote many revues during WWI including the recruiting song *We don't want to lose you, but we think you ought to go*. The writer and traveller George Borrow lived briefly at the former No.17 in 1829-30, while No.18 was the home 1856-77 of Richard Berridge, partner with Sir Henry Meux in the Horseshoe Brewery; he left large sums to educational charities.

On the **north side**, the politician and political economist Francis Horner (1778-1817) once lived at **No.107**; it provided the HQ of the English Folk Dance Society before its move in 1930 to Cecil Sharp House, Regent's Park. **No.106** bears a bronze plaque designed in 1908 by Charles Fitzroy Doll, commemorating the architects Augustus Charles Pugin (p 78) and his more famous son Augustus Welby Northmore Pugin, who both lived here. Pugin senior died at the house in 1832, having taken in pupils since the early 1820s. One such was the architect Benjamin Ferrey, who from 1834-36 went into partnership with fellow pupil Thomas Larkins Walker next door at **No.105**.

No.105, with a lovely 200-year-old wooden shopfront, now houses the artists' colourmen L Cornelissen & Son. It was once home to the pioneering photographer Frederick Scott Archer, who invented but failed to patent a collodion process that became the dominant form of photography worldwide from the 1850s to the 1880s. He died in poverty in 1857. With the two houses further on, No.105 dates back to the late 17th century, but was refronted in the 19th century. **No.103** housed piano makers George Luff & Co., who displayed their wares at the Great Exhibition in 1851 and had a factory in Caroline Mews to the rear, while **No.104** was the business address of engraver Samuel Cousins in the 1820s. It was later home to architect Elijah Hoole (1837-1912), who designed Toynbee Hall and similar settlements.

Beyond The Bloomsbury Hotel is **Congress House** at Nos.23-28, the headquarters of the Trades Union Congress (TUC). Terrace houses on this spot were demolished in the early 1930s for the projected expansion of Glave's department store in New Oxford Street (p 39). However, the firm was closed in 1933 and the whole site was sold, though Congress House (designed by David du Roi Aberdeen in 1948) was not opened until 1958. Above the portico is a striking sculpture by Bernard Meadows, symbolising *The Spirit of Trades Unionism*. In the courtyard behind, Epstein's sculpture of a mother carrying her dead son commemorates the sacrifices of trades unionists in two world wars.

Former houses here included No.24, where the American writer Nathaniel Hawthorne and his family lodged for several months before leaving for the Continent in January 1858. The ground floor was the shop of the noted apothecary and chemist William Jones, who moved in in 1756; the business he founded was based here until 1908. In the 1920s the building housed the Challenge Gallery, and the studio of the designer, calligrapher and painter Margaret Calkin James. From 1785 David Williams had special teaching facilities at No.28, where in 1790 he set up the (Royal) Literary Fund to support indigent authors and their families; early beneficiaries included the widow and children of Robert Burns. The portrait painter John Hayes lived at No.28 in 1849-51.

Across from the TUC the three houses Nos.102-100, refaced by Thomas Cubitt in 1821, have pilasters carrying an entablature with a bracketed cornice. They are on the site of, and may incorporate the shell of, Thanet House, built in 1686. Aristocratic occupants of Thanet House included the 6th Earl of Thanet; his son-in-law Sir Thomas Coke of Holkham; and in 1771-78 Henry, Earl Bathurst, a lacklustre Lord Chancellor. In the last year of his life Topham Beauclerk (1739-80) was the occupant, witness the bronze plaque on **No.100**. A great friend of Dr Johnson, Beauclerk was said to have such a large book collection here that 'the British Museum's nose was quite out of joint'. His wife was the amateur artist Lady Diana Beauclerk, née Spencer (1734-1808). When his house in Bloomsbury Square was destroyed by the Gordon Rioters (p 18), the Earl of Mansfield moved into Thanet House and stayed until 1785, when he left for Lincoln's Inn Fields. The last tenant was the anatomist John Sheldon (1752–1808), who embalmed the body of a female patient to whom he had become deeply attached, displaying it in a glass-topped cabinet at his house.

The house was divided into two after 1787, when the brewer Harvey Christian Combe lived there and held legendary suppers for royalty and his aristocratic friends. **No.101** was home in the late 1780s to the painter and engraver John Sanders and later to the comedian Charles Mathews (1776-1835), who wrote most of his autobiography here. The British Institute of Preventive Medicine (now the Lister Institute) was based at No.101 in 1894-98. In the 1920s the publishers Heinemann had offices here, as did the architect Beresford Pite. The publishing firm Robert Hale & Co. was set up in 1936 at **No.102**, which had become a separate house in 1820 following a further division of the structure.

Nos.99&98, slightly recessed, have their house numbers prominently displayed on hanging signs, and there is a parish boundary mark (St George's Bloomsbury, 1823) on No.99. The first physician of the Bloomsbury Dispensary (p 48) in 1801-35 was George Pinckard, who lived at **No.99** from 1801 before moving to No.18 Bloomsbury Square. James Bell started his stained-glass business from **No.98** in 1865. The house was home in the 1890s to the writer Arthur Machen, when he translated Casanova's *Memoirs* and wrote several macabre novels, including *The Great God Pan*.

Beyond Dyott Street, two hotels face each other across the street. They were built as part of a temperance hotel empire founded by Robert Cranston (1815-92) of Edinburgh, clearly a Walter Scott enthusiast judging by the names. Now both owned by Radisson, **the Kenilworth** on the north side came first, designed in 1903 by G Waymouth; and the Ivanhoe, later the Marlborough and now the **Radisson Blu Edwardian**, followed by 1906, designed by Sir Thomas Rhind. The façade of the Kenilworth features a Scottish shield above the entrance and there are two Scottish heraldic lions holding the lamp standards above the tall porch. Helene Hanff, author of *84 Charing Cross Road*, was staying here when the British edition was published in 1971. She gave so many interviews that the hotel staff dubbed her 'the Duchess of Bloomsbury Street': this became the title of her next book. During WWII the Ivanhoe was used to house Irish labourers repairing bomb-damaged buildings. It was then squatted for a time.

Houses supplanted by the hotels included on the south side No.32, where the writer Sir Archibald Edmonstone, who was to travel across Egypt, was born in 1795, the son of the Scottish politician Sir Charles, second Baronet. In 1824 the Medical, Clerical and General Life Assurance Society was founded here by George Pinckard (p 43). At No.33 the chemist John Thistlewood Davenport went into business in 1856 with the former British Army officer Dr John Collis Browne, who had invented the medicine chlorodyne, used in India to treat soldiers suffering from cholera. It was to be produced and marketed by J T Davenport and Sons until the 1960s for all manner of illnesses with the exhortation 'Do Not Untimely Die'. Davenport himself did not die until 1902 and served as President of the Pharmaceutical Society. Incidentally, he was the nephew of Arthur Thistlewood, the Cato Street Conspirator, executed in 1820.

The Kenilworth Hotel lies on the site of Nos.94-97. At No.94 Samuel Greig, the Russian Consul General, whose father had served with honours in Catherine the Great's navy, died aged only 29 in 1807. Two years earlier his wife – later famous as Mary Somerville, science writer and mathematics expositor – had given birth here to their son Woronzow Greig. He became a noted barrister who helped publish and promote his mother's scientific research. Throughout the Victorian period No.95 housed the offices of the General Cemetery Company, which ran Kensal Green Cemetery; its General Secretary lived above the shop. Buried at Kensal Green in 1852 was the civil engineer, John Sylvester, who specialised in heating systems. He had lived at No.96, which was later home to the British Society for the Propagation of the Gospel among the Jews, a nonconformist organisation founded in 1842.

Along the north side of Great Russell Street beyond Bloomsbury Street is a run of three Georgian houses dating from c.1760. **No.91**, with an elegant frieze above the door, bears a blue plaque marking the home (1863-68) of George du Maurier, best known for his novel *Trilby*. The shop below was run at the time by A & F Pears, the soap merchants (p 39). Later, in the 1930s, the house provided a London base for the detective writer Margery Allingham. Timothy Williamson, master clockmaker, operated at No.90 from 1788. King George III asked him to create two mechanical musical clocks as gifts for the Emperor of China, which are now in the Palace Museum, Beijing. From 1800 the building was used as a lodging house, where Percy Bysshe Shelley stayed in 1817. In 1876-81, the gemologist Bryce M Wright had his shop here, which he claimed had the largest stock of minerals in Europe. During the 1920s until her retirement the photographer Lizzie Caswall Smith, who specialized in society and celebrity portraits, had her studio in this building. The publishers Hamish Hamilton were at **No.90** from the 1940s until 1978. At **No.89** was the home and practice of Dr John Epps (1805-1869), an early convert to the teachings of Hahnemann and the leading practitioner of homeopathy in London by the 1850s (see also p 19). A radical dissenter, he was a friend of Robert Owen, John Bright, Richard Cobden and several Italian revolutionaries. He saw medicine as a tool of liberation for the poor and lower classes. The numismatist Sir Stanley Gotch Robinson, an authority on ancient Greek coins, died in his home at No.89 in 1976.

On the south side, Nos.35-38 form a taller, stuccoed and rusticated terrace. The carver and gilder Thomas Allwood worked at **No.35** from 1772-93; George Romney used him to frame his paintings. The National Unemployed Workers Union was based here during the Depression, when its leaders were often charged with sedition. At **No.36** lived William Davidson, a landscape gardener who specialised in cemeteries. While here in the 1850s he landscaped the new City of London Cemetery. The house was later home to the architect and archaeologist E F Loftus Brock (1833-95). The Egypt Exploration Society, founded in 1888, was based at **No.37**; it funded Petrie's expeditions for nine years until it ran out of money. The British National Association of Spiritualists was set up in 1877, moving to **No.38** soon after. In 1926-35 this housed Harold Edward Monro's Poetry Bookshop.

Nos.39-42 form a uniform terrace of four townhouses, swathed in stucco. Note the lions' heads on the entablature. We are now in the centre of an area long devoted to bookshops and publishers. **No.39**, on the corner of Willoughby Street, was long occupied by the bookselling firm of Stevens, Son & Styles. When they moved out in 1961, the publisher Ben Weinreb took over the building. 'Gosh! Comics' were here 1980-2011.

After Coptic Street (p 33), Nos.43-48 form another highly decorative block. Dating from about 1735 the buildings were given a facelift by the Bedford Estate in the 1850s, to designs by William Finch Hill; the Georgian interiors were untouched. The block has a symmetrical frontage to the street stepping up in height at each corner. Notice the ironwork gates at the entrance to **No.43**. Here the art metal workers Jones & Willis produced items of Victorian church furniture. By 1891 it was home to the actress Kittie Carson. That year she founded the Theatrical Ladies Guild, whose members joined weekly sewing bees at her home to raise money for theatre folk who had fallen on hard times. The organisation grew and moved out in 1896; it has since become the Theatrical Guild. Mrs Carson also founded The Actors' Charitable Trust (TACT), which still provides education grants for actors' children. Next door, **No.44** was from the close of the 19th century the shop of O E Janson, natural history agent; his son continued the business until the 1970s. Above it was the HQ of the Simplified Spelling Society founded in 1908, now TESS (The English Spelling Society), which aims to improve literacy through spelling reform. In the 1880s the novelist and social activist Margaret Harkness lived at **No.45**. It was here that her cousin Beatrice first met Sidney Webb. **No.46** has a blue plaque to Randolph Caldecott, the artist and book illustrator, who lived and worked here in 1872-79. Since 1890 it has been a bookshop, first run by the oriental booksellers Luzec & Co., and then from 1986 by the antiquarian booksellers Jarndyce. Earlier, Peter Mark Roget of Thesaurus fame moved into rooms here in 1800. The upper floors housed the office and home of the architect and town planner Stanley Davenport Adshead, where his only child, the mural painter and designer Mary, was born in 1904.

The **Museum Tavern** on the east corner of Museum Street (p 26) is on the site of the Dog and Duck hostelry, which may have begun serving alcoholic refreshment informally as early as 1705: duck hunting with dogs was then still common around the numerous ponds in northern Bloomsbury. The pub was renamed the British Museum Tavern in 1762. Rebuilt in 1798, it was extended and refaced in 1855 by William Finch Hill to match the distinctive block we have just passed. For example, spot the oval niches above first floor level both here and on No.48 opposite. *British* was dropped from the name in 1873 and the pub was remodelled in 1889 by Wylson & Long, to include a magnificent mahogany backfitting and two stained-glass windows, rare survivals today.

The **British Museum** dominates the north side of the street. The land here was originally leased by Lady Rachel Russell to Ralph Montagu, later 1st Duke of Montagu, husband of her stepsister; he had Montagu House built here in 1678. It was designed by the brilliant scientist and architect Robert Hooke, and decorated by Verrio. It burned down only eight years later and was rebuilt even more lavishly in a fashionable French style, attributed to a little-known French architect Pierre Puget, and similar to the Montagu family's Boughton House. The cost to Montagu was enormous but he had the means. After the death of his first wife he married the extremely rich but mad Duchess of Albemarle. She had declared that she would marry none but a crowned head, so Montagu persuaded her he was the Emperor of China, and as Empress she was served at Montagu House on bended knee.

When an Act of Parliament in 1753 brought together Sir Hans Sloane's antiquities with the manuscript collections of the Cotton family and of Robert Harley, Earl of Oxford, they were assembled in Montagu House, purchased for the purpose by the Crown after the death of the 2nd Duke. The antiquities were at first grudgingly shown, by appointment only, to groups of not more than five people at a rate of ten per hour **[15]**. In 1757 King George II gave to the museum the Royal Library of 12,000 volumes, and with it the privilege of copyright deposit. Over the next 60 years the collection grew rapidly, with the arrival of Sir William Hamilton's first collection of Greek vases (1773), the Rosetta Stone (1802), the Townley collection of Greek sculpture including the Discobolus (1805), the head of Ramses II (1815) and George III's Library, presented by George IV in 1823.

Sir Robert Smirke was commissioned to expand the space available and from 1823 designed a great quadrangle in a style modelled on several Ionian Greek temples. Montagu House was gradually replaced, the last element being demolished in 1845. Smirke's mighty portico rests on a 6-ft concrete base, an early use of the material for such a purpose. The sculpture in the central pediment is by Sir Richard Westmacott and by his own account represents the Progress of Civilisation.

15 Visitors to the British Museum mounting the Grand Staircase of Montagu House shortly before its demolition

Construction of the Museum lasted until well into the 1850s. After Smirke's retirement in 1846 the work passed to his brother Sydney (who also designed the fine railings in front) and then to the latter's son, Sydney Smirke Jr. Foot-high bronze lions used to mark the museum boundary, some of which now surround the Duke of Wellington's monument in St Paul's Cathedral. The plane trees lining the street in front of the museum soften the effect.

The famous round Reading Room was not part of the original design but was constructed within the quadrangle at the instigation of the Principal Librarian, Sir Anthony Panizzi. In 1852, desperate at the congestion resulting from the ever-expanding collection of books and manuscripts, Panizzi took up the idea (already several times put forward) of constructing a circular building within the square courtyard, but this time coupled it with the newly popular use of cast iron to create tall and airy buildings. By 1854, after one rejected design, Sydney Smirke produced an acceptable solution incorporating the giant dome whose diameter (140 ft) exceeds that of St Peter's in Rome. The Library was first opened to the public in May 1857. Panizzi later welcomed the Italian hero Garibaldi on a visit to the Museum in 1864, amidst ecstatic crowds.

In 1881 the natural history collections were removed to South Kensington and in 1905 the newspaper archive was relocated to Colindale. At this time the Edward VII Galleries (p 50) were built to the north. A West Gallery was completed in 1938 to house the Parthenon marbles.

After WWII, with the book collection once again exceeding all bounds, there were plans to demolish the little streets between Great Russell Street and New Oxford Street and to build a new, separate British Library. Vehement opposition delayed implementation and the whole area suffered planning blight until in the late 1960s Camden Council found a site for a new Library next to St Pancras Station. It was another 30 years before the building there opened its doors in 1998. The book stacks surrounding the Reading Room were removed and the space was transformed into a public area – the Great Court – covered by a stunning glazed roof by Norman Foster and Buro Happold, and paid for by a large injection of Lottery funding.

This book is not the place for a catalogue of the extensive collections of one of the world's greatest museums. Before we leave, let us instead consider the houses along Great Russell Street (Nos.78-88) that were demolished in the 1840s when the present forecourt was created. No.78 was leased by the Medical, Clerical and General Life Assurance Society, who were based here from 1837-46. A grand house at No.79 was the home of the actor John Philip Kemble until his death in 1823. His brother Charles then took over the lease using profits he had made from the Covent Garden performances of his daughter Fanny, who was living here in 1831. Christopher Haedy, steward to the 7th Duke of Bedford, lived at No.80 in the 1840s. No.85 was home to the architect Benjamin Ferrey (p 42) from 1838. The antiquary and engraver Henry Shaw lived at No.88; in 1834 he published his influential work *Details of Elizabethan Architecture*. On the western edge of what are now the British Museum's grounds, there once stood a house that was rented by the poet and politician Andrew Marvell, and where he died in 1678.

Beyond the Museum Tavern, at former No.50 the artist Henry Sass set up his School for Drawing and Painting, with room for a live-in pupil, in 1818, before moving to larger premises (p 34) in what is now Bloomsbury Street in 1820. Next door, No.51 was in the 19th century home to the manufacturing ironworkers, Messrs C Jeakes & Co. At **Nos.52-57** is a grand, French-inspired 5-storey block, replete with gables, erected in 1888-95. It was built as a family hotel called the Thackeray, as the writer was said to have lived here when a boy. It is now a hostel for women called **Helen Graham House**, named after a President of the YWCA, which ran it until recently; it is currently managed by Viridian.

Former No.52 was home in 1800 to the President of the Society of Engravers, John Samuel Agar; and then housed Thomas Harris & Sons, opticians to the Royal Family, who also made microscopes and telescopes. At former No.55 the American ornithologist and bird artist Audubon took lodgings in 1827, while looking for an engraver and wealthy subscribers. Dr Edward Aveling lodged here in 1884-86, courting scandal by living openly with his lover, Karl Marx's daughter Eleanor, despite being married **[16]**. On her 31st birthday in January 1886 the first English performance of Ibsen's *A Doll's House* was given in their living room, with Eleanor, May Morris and George Bernard Shaw all taking part. The couple founded the Bloomsbury branch of the Socialist League, which unlike other branches was in favour of seeking change through parliament; they decided to leave the League in 1888. Aveling then left Eleanor, who ten years later killed herself with prussic acid, which Aveling had procured for her.

Benjamin Wilson, the portrait painter whose talented pupil was John Zoffany, died in his home at former No.56 in 1788; his son, the colonial governor Sir Robert Wilson, was born there in 1777. The historical engraver Philip Audinet also died in the house, in 1837. The home and office of the lawyer William Bray was at No.57; he allowed his friend Thomas Robert Malthus to use it as his official address around 1800, when the political economist was living in a succession of London garrets.

Helen Graham House is followed by two blocks of mansion flats. The first is **Great Russell Mansions**, completed in 1893 in a similar style, with oriel windows and decorated balconies, one with a head of Nebuchadnezzar. At the former No.59 the travel pioneer Thomas Cook opened his first London office in 1863; he lived above the shop. At No.60 the watercolour painter George Bryce lodged in 1854, where he was visited by his friend John Ruskin.

16 Eleanor Marx, socialist activist and her lover Edward Aveling

The second block is **Museum Mansions** (Nos.62-65), with shops below, in stock brick with classically-influenced stucco detailing in horizontal bands. At Flat No.17 the brothers Sewell and Leslie Stokes lived for many years and co-wrote a series of plays, including *Oscar Wilde* in 1936, which launched actor Robert Morley's career.

At the former No.62 the Bloomsbury Dispensary was founded in 1801. This served the health needs of the poor inhabitants of the slums of St Giles to the south and those of Little Coram Street (now part of Herbrand Street) and its neighbours to the north. Dr Edward Jenner **[17]** (see also p 64) delivered free smallpox vaccinations here, and served on the Dispensary's medical committee from its inception until his death in 1823. The Dispensary also had the distinction of appointing London's first Medical Officer of Health, in 1846. When its lease ran out in 1881, it moved to Bloomsbury Street (see p 35).

Above the Dispensary at No.62 were rooms into which Edward Burne-Jones and his new wife Georgiana moved in 1861 after the painter Henry Wallis left. Burne-Jones' son Phillip was born here soon after. Upon the couple's move to Kensington in 1865, the painter Edward Poynter, who had recently married Georgiana's sister, took over the rooms. He was followed by Frederick Jameson (1839-1916), architect and musician, who translated the libretti of Richard Wagner. During 1868-69 the artist James Whistler used the apartment as his studio when his friend Jameson was away, but it was not a fruitful period for him.

East of Bury Place at Nos.66-71 is a 4-storey terrace built in 1777 to the designs of the young John Nash, to whose memory not one but two plaques have been placed on the façade (the official one only recently). The houses retain their clean Georgian lines and are covered in stucco; an early use of the material for which Nash became renowned. He lived at the corner house **No.66** for three years until his bankruptcy, after which he retreated to Wales to rebuild his reputation. No.66 was later the shop and home of James Tregaskis, seller of rare books, who died here in 1926.

The Danish painter Vilhelm Hammershøi lodged at **No.67** on a trip to London in 1905-06 and painted a rather spare view of Montague Street opposite. The stained-glass artist Horace Wilkinson was living at **No.68** shortly before WWI. The Theosophical Society had its publishing house here in the 1940s and 1950s. **No.69** housed the offices of the Inter-Aid Committee for Children from Germany and Austria, one of the charitable groups that helped organise the Kindertransport in the 1930s, bringing Jewish and non-Arian Christian children to the UK. **No.71** was the home of Norman MacDermott when he founded the Everyman Theatre in Hampstead in 1920 and made it a centre of experimental drama.

Nash's terrace abuts **Nos.72&73**, a larger building coterminous with No.17 Bloomsbury Square (see p 16). On the north side of Great Russell Street opposite stand Nos.77-74, also stuccoed, the final group of houses in the street. The fabric is 17th-century, the remnant of a terrace built between Southampton House and Montagu House in the 1670s. The houses now form the HQ of the publishers Faber & Faber (p 67), but for many years from the end of WWI they were the offices of the Zionist Foundation, established in 1899 to campaign for a permanent homeland for the Jewish people. The Jewish Agency set up its main political office here and conducted government negotiations; its Chairman was David Ben-Gurion, who became the first Prime Minister of Israel. **No.77** bears a blue plaque to the architect Thomas Henry Wyatt (1807-80), who became President of RIBA and lived and died in the house.

17 Edward Jenner injecting adults and children with cowpox (note cow looking in at the window)

It has a pretty iron balcony on its side elevation along **MONTAGUE STREET**, put up when that street was formed.

This street lies along the former boundary between the grounds of Montagu House and Southampton House, and was constructed in 1803-06 by the builder W E Allen to designs by James Burton. On the right, towering plane trees shelter a brick wall with an entrance to **No.29A,** the former Bedford Estate office; a detached villa, this was built in 1842-43 after the expansion of the British Museum had destroyed the earlier office opposite. The terrace beyond, beginning at **No.29**, is typical of Burton's plain but well proportioned houses, stuccoed on the ground floor. Each townhouse is three-bays wide with a recessed, semi-circular arched doorway and iron balconies to first-floor windows. No.29 itself was home in the late 1830s to the art patron Lewis Pocock (see also p 87), who founded the Art Union of London with his friend the architect George Godwin, and the writer Edward Edwards.

Most of the houses in the street are now used as hotels. **No.20** on the right was home to the architect Charles Foster Hayward (1831-1905). To its side are some decorative iron gates, dating from 1899, which bar a roadway that once led to Montague Mews. This was built to service the houses both here and in Bedford Place but by the 1890s, when few residents kept carriages and as the leases fell in, the Bedford Estate demolished the stables and other buildings, including a pub called the Montague Arms. These were replaced by landscaped gardens. After WWII local people successfully petitioned the Council to let their children play in the gardens, but the hotel owners eventually managed to make them private once more. Just past the gates is **No.21**, once home to the Victorian watercolour painter Edwin Thomas Dolby; and later to the folklorist Alice, Lady Gomme, who had a vast knowledge of traditional children's games. She had helped found the Folklore Society in 1878 with her husband Laurence, and she moved here in 1916 after his death.

Opposite, the terrace houses begin past the side wall of the British Museum, which uses **No.1A**. This was built in the 1830s as No.30 to house the Montague Street Savings Bank, which lasted as an independent organisation until 1914. The building served as an RAF recruiting office just after WWII. At the front steps of **No.1** next door, according to later reminiscence, a stag was cornered in the 1820s – George Grantley Berkeley's Middlesex staghounds then frequently trespassed into the burgeoning outskirts of London. Two butcher boys are said to have captured it after the owner (unsurprisingly) refused to let it in to be slaughtered. The tinplate and sheet metal manufacturer William Blizard Williamson, who developed the lever lid tin, died here in 1895; his family business was to merge with Metal Box in 1930. John Henderson (1797-1878) of **No.3** amassed an important collection of art and antiquities which he bequeathed to the National Gallery and the British Museum; and the architect and surveyor Daniel Cubitt Nichols died in the house in 1895.

The houses on the east side are now part of the **Montague On The Gardens** hotel, and unnumbered. Thomas Cockayne, the leading philologist of his day, lived at **No.17** from 1837, taking in student boarders to supplement his meagre income. At **No.12** the sculptor Edward Roscoe Mullins was living in 1876-87.

On the west side, the terrace merges almost imperceptibly into that fronting Russell Square (p 65). Shortly afterwards there is a left turn into **MONTAGUE PLACE**. This was first laid out in 1802 to the north of the gardens of Montagu House. Three decades later the British Museum began to encroach on the gardens, with the construction of Smirke's North Wing (1833-38); the tenants here petitioned against the development, but to no avail. In the early 20th century the houses themselves were demolished, and replaced by the **Edward VII Galleries**, built by Sir John Burnet. They were opened in 1914 by King George V after his father's death. Walk ahead to the imperious stone lions that guard the entrance.

Opposite, the north side of Montague Place is mainly occupied by 1930s buildings, outposts of Senate House (p 78). Indeed, none of the street's original houses survive, though they once had some notable residents. The archaeologist Sir Charles Fellows (1799–1860), who found the ruins of Xanthus, the ancient capital of Lycia, died at his London home, No.4. No.10 became the home in 1878 of author and Positivist James Cotter Morison, who moved here to be close to the British Museum. No.22 was home in the 1830s to the barrister and legal writer Samuel Richard Bosanquet, who held the then unusual view that poverty was not the fault of the poor. Arthur Conan Doyle lodged at former No.23 when first in London in 1891 and his *The Sign of Four* has Sherlock Holmes living in Montague Street. The medical botanist Albert Isaiah Coffin, who promoted the use of cayenne pepper for warmth, died at No.24 in 1866. No.30 was home in 1834 to Dr Alexander Tweedie, physician to the London Fever Hospital. The Gothic Revival architect G E Street (p 65) rented No.33 from 1856-62.

Booth's researcher in updating the poverty map in 1898 wrote that Montague Place and the surrounding area were for part of each year an American colony, with the visitors using lodging-houses, all run, as he blithely put it, by 'Jewess she-dragon' landladies.

Beyond the Edward VII Galleries, a new 9-storey wing, designed by Rogers Stirk Harbour and Partners, opened in 2014. It is on the site of Nos.1 and 2, the latter rented from 1905 by Sir John Burnet from the British Museum, for whom he was then working on a master plan for the eventually abortive British Museum Avenue (p 80). Early in 1912 he moved into No.1, which was both his office and home until 1948.

Opposite is a sunken, leafy green space – Malet Street Gardens (p 78) – at the back of the corner house, which is **No.11 Bedford Square**, standing in isolation from the rest of the square. This was the London home of the scientist Henry Cavendish, brother of the 3rd Duke of Devonshire and the outstanding natural philosopher of the late 18th century. He is recorded as living here from 1783. He set up a laboratory, museum, and library in the house and discovered that water consisted of hydrogen and oxygen. No.11 was later the childhood home of Charles Shaw-Lefevre, politician and Speaker of the House of Commons, and the birthplace in 1797 of his civil servant brother John, one of the three Poor Law Amendment Act Commissioners. Today, the house is the London home of the Surrey-based Royal Holloway College, part of the University of London.

Ahead is **BEDFORD SQUARE**. Built between 1775 and 1783, it was the first example in London of a square with houses of uniform proportions and design and has survived virtually unscathed, the architectural highlight of this Route. Four sides of palace-fronted terrace houses, each treated as an entire block with a central pedimented feature and wings, surround a central garden open only to residents.

After the Peace of Paris in 1763, which marked Britain's triumph over France in the Seven Years' War, great riches flowed into the country, which according to the 4th Duke of Bedford 'excited a rage for building and houses rose like exhalations'. The Duke was a great admirer of the Circus at Bath, and envisaged a Bedford Circus on his land in Bloomsbury. After his death in 1771 the idea metamorphosed into a square, to be developed by his widow, Gertrude Leveson-Gower.

Thomas Leverton is generally considered the designer of Bedford Square, although the Coade stone decorations that frame the doors can be seen in many catalogues of the time. The north and south sides each have a central pair of stuccoed houses surmounted by a pediment; the east and west sides have a similar pediment, but over a single large house. The quality requirements imposed on the builders were stringent: facings, balustrades and window sills had to be of Portland stone, roofs of slate, gutters and rainwater pipes of lead, floors of best Memel or Riga wood, the pavements wide and of York stone. Coach houses and stables were provided on three sides of the square, in what are now Gower Mews (p 94), Morwell Street (p 54) and Bedford Avenue (p 57).

The first leases had to be signed by two

duchesses (Bedford and Marlborough) and by Robert Palmer (the 4th Duke's man of business). Each lessee was precluded from doing anything in or upon the premises which 'may be or grow to the annoyance, grievance, damage or disturbance of the said duchesses and Robert Palmer or their heirs'. To this day, the last condition governs the behaviour of lessees (including the University of London) throughout the Bedford Estate.

From the start Bedford Square attracted residents who were solidly upper middle-class rather than aristocratic; it was the 'aristocracy' of the Inns of Court and to some extent the City who flocked to Bedford Square. For long the official residence of Lord Chancellors, the square was consequently inhabited over many years by distinguished lawyers and judges, too numerous to mention in full. During the 19th century there were many medical men and architects as well. It remained a safe residential haven until the early 1890s, when the gates across the roads which had protected the Bedford Estate from the lower orders (p 100) were removed. In 1898 Booth's researcher said it was 'less good than formerly', although no boarders were allowed. Over the next 50 years the private houses gradually gave way to offices.

On the northern side, balustraded **No.12** on the eastern corner has a fine roofed iron balcony at first-floor level. It was home to the organist Sir George Smart, who conducted the music at the coronations of George IV, William IV and Victoria, and taught many singers, including Jenny Lind. He was a close friend of the composer Weber, who died of TB in Smart's earlier London house. **No.13** carries a blue plaque to the famous internal-combustion engine designer Sir Harry Ricardo, who was born here in 1885, the only son of the architect Halsey Ricardo, and was still living here during WWI. The building is known as Leverton House, as from 1795 until his death it was home to the architect Thomas Leverton.

No.16 houses the Paul Mellon Centre for Studies in British Art. Founded in 1970, the Centre has been based here since 1996 and has an outstanding library. A J A Symons (1900-41), the dandy and biographer of Baron Corvo, lived at **No.17**. Stuccoed **Nos.18&19** form the centrepiece of the north side. In the former lived James Endell Tyler, the popular Rector of St Giles after whom Endell Street was named in the 1840s. **No.20** was home to the architect Edward P Warren before WWI, after which he worked on cemeteries in the Middle East. **No.22** has a blue plaque to the actor Sir Johnston Forbes-Robertson, who enjoyed almost 40 years of uninterrupted stage success. Upon his retirement in 1856 Sir Henry Ellis, Principal Librarian at the British Museum, moved into **No.24** and stayed until his death in 1869. Two years later, the architect Banister Fletcher was living here when he published *Model Houses for the Industrial Classes*. He later co-authored with his more famous son of the same name a history of architecture that was for long a standard text. The historian Sir George Prothero died here in 1922.

In the 1820s **No.25** was the home of lawyer Basil Montagu and his wife Anna Skepper, who hosted a literary salon at the house. Wordsworth and Coleridge were among their friends. Anna's daughter Ann Skepper married the poet 'Barry Cornwall' (Bryan Waller Procter) in 1824 and the newlyweds lived with the Montagus, whose household Carlyle recalled as a 'most singular social and spiritual menagerie'. Note that No.25 has a balustrade to mark the true start of the square **[18]**, while the two houses beyond, although numbered No.26 and No.27, are lower.

They flow into **BAYLEY STREET**, which was known as Bedford Street until 1878. Nos.6-10 form a terrace of 18th-century houses. **No.6** houses Ed Victor Literary Agents, for whom the writer Douglas Adams worked in the early 1990s. From 1897 **No.7** was leased by Arnold Dolmetsch, the early music revivalist, as his home and workshop; he moved out in 1901 but did not choose a sub-tenant wisely – it became a brothel and he was so heavily fined he was bankrupted. No.8 was the home of William Henry (1859-1928), an Olympic swimmer who founded the Royal Life Saving Society.

18 North-west corner of Bedford Square (photo: RichTea)

The Arts & Crafts architect Alfred Hoare Powell (1865–1960) and his wife Louisa (1882-1956) became celebrated as pottery designers for Wedgwood's, hand-painting many thousands of pieces themselves and training Wedgwood 'paintresses'. In their later years they were based at **No.9**. Percival Leigh, the satirist and deputy editor of *Punch* lived at **No.10** in the 1850s, when next door was the short-lived Mesmeric Infirmary opened by John Elliotson, whose supporters pioneered the use of hypnotism in medical operations. Charles Dickens was among his patients.

Beyond is **myhotel Bloomsbury**, a post-WWII rebuild in facsimile of the Victorian Bedford Corner Hotel on the corner with Tottenham Court Road ahead. In Bayley Street, this had supplanted several houses, including No.11 where the watercolour painter John Scarlett Davis died in 1845.

On the site of the large, anonymous Modernist building opposite (**No.3**) was No.3 Bedford Street, the house in which Henry Mayhew was living in 1851 when he first published his enormously influential *London Labour and the London Poor*. The Theatrical Ladies Guild (p 45) was based there in WWI.

The block turns the corner into **MORWELL STREET**. Look along it. The earlier, narrow Tavistock Mews provided stabling for the houses on the western side of Bedford Square. It was stopped up by the Bedford Estate in 1876 and the carriage houses, by then considered noisome, were demolished. This slightly wider street was built parallel to it, so none of the buildings here predate 1879 when Morwell Street was completed and named, after a Russell-family property in Devon. At this northern end there is a handful of Georgian-style houses, including **Nos.26&26A** and its neighbour on the corner, which date from 1996 and bear the letter 'B', for Bedford Estate. Properties it owned on the western side were sold off in 1960 to pay death duties.

Retracing our steps to **BEDFORD SQUARE**, walk down its **west side**. First, balustraded **No.28** is now home to the Nuffield Foundation but was the birthplace in 1900 of the author Frances Partridge, whose father was the architect William Cecil Marshall. Its neighbour **No.29** sports a flagpole and is the London office of the Turkish Republic of North Cyprus. In old age, the architect and developer Henry Harrison was living here in the 1850s and until 1864. **No.30** now houses Sotheby's Institute of Art, devoted to the study of art in its historical, contemporary and market contexts. It is one of the most prestigious degree-granting institutions of its kind, though not now owned by the auctioneers. At **No.31** the politician Sylvester Douglas, Baron Glenbervie was living 1789-94, when his son Frederick was born; the latter was likewise an MP and also a noted Classical scholar. From 1914 this was Edwin Luytens' home, where, after the war, he designed the Cenotaph; while living here he was appointed architect of New Delhi, for which he was knighted in 1919.

Many of the buildings on this west side are used by the Architectural Association's School of Architecture, which boasts a mock blue plaque announcing that 'Most Famous Architects 1847-2006 have been here sooner or later'. The AA School was formally established in 1890 and moved here in 1917. It attracts students and staff from all over the world. Its bookshop is at the central, pedimented, **No.32**.

No.35 bears two blue plaques: to the radical MP Thomas Wakley, founder in 1823 of *The Lancet* as a polemical medical journal; and to Thomas Hodgkin, another physician, reformer and philanthropist, after whom the glandular disorder is named. As on the north side, the house with the balustrade marks the true end of the square, and is followed by two lower houses, Nos.37&38. **No. 38** was the home of Dr Neil Arnott, reforming physician and friend of Bentham and in the 1870s of the stained-glass artist Alexander Gibbs, who collaborated with William Butterfield. **No.39** is a tall Victorian intruder, designed by the Bedford Estate surveyor Charles Fitzroy Doll and built in 1896.

On the **south side**, the numbering was changed in 1866 from the previous Nos.39-52 to the present Nos.40-53 after a No.39 (replaced by the present building in 1896) had been added to the west side. From 1850, balustraded **No.40** (then No.39) housed a homeopathic hospital known as the Hahnemann, but it closed within two years as the doctors running it quarrelled. From 1922 Albert Reckitt made the building the London HQ of his chemical company and lived here until his death in 1947. As a chemist he worked closely with bacteriologist W C Reynolds to develop the antiseptic liquid Dettol.

No.41 bears a blue plaque to Anthony Hope, author of *The Prisoner of Zenda*. The engineer John Braithwaite, who played an important role in the development of railways, lived here in 1841-54; and a later resident, in 1919-24, was the automotive engineer Frederick Lanchester. Another blue plaque, next door at **No.42**, records that the house was occupied in the 1820s by Sir John Bayley, the judge for whom nearby Bayley Street is named. It was home, from 1886 until his death in 1900, to William Butterfield, the Gothic Revival church architect who also designed Keble College, Oxford. Former Prime Minister H H Asquith moved in 1919 to **No.44** for a while, until his wife Margot, the diary writer, found the house too small for satisfactory entertaining. It had previously been the home of the literary hostess, and sometime lover of Bertrand Russell, Lady Ottoline Morrell. **No.45** was until 2015 the HQ of HM Courts and Tribunals Service; it was also the birthplace in 1863 of Margaret Frere, who helped develop the LCC's school care service. Her father Bartle Frere was still living here in 1881, when his first cousin and namesake, the colonial governor, was in disgrace, scapegoated for the British army's defeat at the hands of the Zulus at Isandlwana two years before. Along with No.44, the house is now occupied by the École Jeannine Manuel, which offers bilingual education 'to promote international understanding'. **No.46** is the Consulate General of the Republic of Angola.

No.48 has a green plaque commemorating Bedford College, founded here in 1849, as the Ladies' College, by the anti-slavery activist Elizabeth Jesser Reid. It was the first institution for female higher education in Britain, and its students included, in 1850-51, one Mary Ann Evans, later famous as George Eliot. It became a school of London University in 1880 and received a Royal Charter as Bedford College for Women in 1909. The name was retained when the College moved to Regent's Park in 1913, but was lost after its absorption into Royal Holloway in 1982. No.48 was earlier the home of painter and art collector James Orrock (1829-1913). Lord Leverhulme bought most of his collection, as well as one thousand of Orrock's own paintings, which formed the basis of the Lady Lever art gallery at Port Sunlight.

No.49 has a blue plaque to Ram Mohun Roy (1772-1833), Indian scholar and reformer, who campaigned against suttee (widow burning). Later residents included the entomologist Francis Walker and during WWII Cyril Connolly, whilst editor of *Horizon*; he let the attic to the biographer Peter Quennell, who shared it with Barbara Skelton, later Connolly's wife. The first occupant of **No.50** in 1777-79 was Serjeant John Glynn, an ardent supporter of John Wilkes. It was later home to the Quaker John Walker, with whom Robert Owen stayed during 1818-20, and now houses Bloomsbury Publishing. The house bears a parish boundary mark (St GF 1859) as does its neighbour at **No.51** (St GB 1823). The philanthropist John Passmore Edwards lived here from 1893 to 1905 and spent his publishing fortune endowing free libraries, hospitals, the Mary Ward Settlement and other public facilities.

No.52 was occupied in 1849-67 by Lewis Cubitt, the architect of King's Cross railway station and the 'Granary' goods shed behind. The poet and physician Robert Bridges lived here in 1877-81, often visited by his friend Gerard Manley Hopkins, whose works Bridges promoted when he became Poet Laureate in 1913. The south side ends at balustraded **No.53**. In 1884, this became the home of wealthy merchant and avid pornographic book collector Henry Ashbee and his wife Elizabeth, parents of the architect

C R Ashbee, and then of the actor Sir Seymour Hicks, when he founded the Hicks (now the Gielgud) Theatre.

The **east side** of Bedford Square was once considered the best side, as the houses backed on to the gardens of Montagu House. Worth a special look are the beautiful fanlights over several doors and the lamp-holder and link extinguisher outside No.4.

Balustraded **No.10** on the corner with Montague Place was the home of Charles Gilpin MP (1813-74), a great orator; and from 1879 to Agostino and Stefano Gatti, the entrepreneurial restaurateurs, who created an electricity company that by 1900 was supplying most of the City and West End. The house still has its early door blind, made by Deans of Putney, as has **No.9,** which is now part of the London School of Hygiene & Tropical Medicine. So, too, is **No. 8**, home in the later 19th century to publisher Frederick Warne. His company pioneered coloured picture books for children, including those of Walter Crane and Kate Greenaway, and from 1902 Beatrix Potter. His son Norman became Potter's editor and fiancé before his early death from leukaemia in 1905. **No.7** was the London home of the politician Sir Robert Harry Inglis (1786–1855). In 1820 he was given the unpleasant task of telling Queen Caroline at the doors of Westminster Abbey that she would not be admitted to the coronation of her husband, George IV.

No.6, in the centre with a splendid 5-bay temple front, is the largest house on the Square. It was completed by Leverton for the Lord Chancellor, Lord Loughborough, who lived here until 1798. Lord Chancellor Eldon, a notorious advocate of hanging for petty offences, then occupied No.6 until 1815, when the house was besieged by a mob during the Corn Law riots. The house was subdivided in 1880, and in the 1890s the publisher Leonard Smithers had rooms here; he published Aubrey Beardsley, launched the aesthetic journal *The Savoy*, and dared to publish Wilde's *Ballad of Reading Gaol*, when no one else would touch it. **No.3** was home to Dr Theophilus Thompson, who first promoted the use of cod liver oil. Until WWII the church architect Frederick Eden lived and worked at **No.2**. Finally, **No.1** was almost certainly designed by Thomas Leverton. A very satisfying composition, its entrance has a 'triumphal arch' containing the door, which unusually for the square is centrally placed. Author, artist and dramatist Weedon Grossmith, of *Diary of a Nobody* fame, lived here in 1903-19.

BLOOMSBURY STREET now begins. Most of its buildings pre-date Bedford Square, having been constructed from 1766. The street was called Charlotte Street before 1894, the part north of Great Russell Street at first being known as Charlotte Street, Bedford Square to distinguish it from Charlotte Street, Bloomsbury to the south (p 34). The two parts of the street were separately numbered. In what follows, we use the present numbering of Bloomsbury Street (east side, even numbers; west side, odd).

At **No.58** are the present offices of TACT (p 45). In the 1790s, **No.56** was home to the judge and politician Sir John Nicholl. The church architect John Dando Sedding established himself here in 1874, upon first moving to London. It became the HQ of the British Dental Hospital from 1931-46. The architect Geoffrey Ransom worked at **No.54** in the mid 1930s. **No.52** was home from the 1870s to the Dutch seascape painter Hermann Koekkoek. The controversial Egyptologist E A Wallis Budge lived for many years at **No.48**, where he died in 1934.

An early resident at **No.40** was George Keate, who died here in 1797: a writer and painter, he was a founder member of the Society of Artists. In the 1830s and '40s the house was leased by Alice Abbott, the long-term lover of the writer Thomas Love Peacock, who helped her and their daughter financially. A century later it was home to radio engineer and Labour MP Fred Cobb (1901-50). In 1890, Margaret Bright Lucas, who founded the British Women's Temperance Association, died at **No.34**, which from 1928 housed the showrooms of the Arts & Craft Exhibition Society (now the Society of Designer Craftsmen); it displayed the work of modern artists throughout the 1930s. The uniform terrace ends at **No.32**, once home of the architect Thomas Bellamy (1798-1876). Its entrance tiling used to sport the dolphin logo of Thames & Hudson, the art book publishers, who were here until 1999. **No.30** was home in 1911 to Daniel Angel, who ran the well-known firm of theatrical costumiers, founded in Seven Dials in 1840. The organist and composer James Hook, who played nightly at Vauxhall Gardens, was living at **No.26** in 1788, when his son, the writer Theodore Hook, was born. The latter became the editor of the scurrilous journal *John Bull.* Coleridge described him as being 'as true a genius as Dante'.

On the west side, **No.21,** now the side of a block of mansion flats, functioned in the early 20th century as the Palace Hotel. In the late 1930s it was renamed Bloomsbury House, the base for the Inter-Church Council for German Refugees which coordinated all efforts to resettle Jewish people who had fled Nazi persecution. The work was led by its Secretary, the Quaker Bertha Bracey (1893-1989). In 1942 the Council of Christians and Jews was set up at Bloomsbury House to promote mutual understanding; it moved to Doughty Street in 1950. The block now provides public sector offices.

Demolished to build the block and the Kenilworth Hotel (p 43) beyond, was a group of five houses, then numbered Nos.21-26 Charlotte Street. Bristol-born artist, John Muller, lived at the former No.22 from 1835 until he died in 1845. He was a member of the informal group of artists known as the Bristol School. He travelled on the continent and to Egypt and Alexandria, and also joined a government archaeological expedition to Lycia. At No.25 the sculptor William Groves lived 1834-71, while No.26 was the home from 1871 of the ornithologist and bird artist John Gould, who died here ten years later. Gould produced large illustrated volumes of bird paintings, greatly aided by his talented wife, who died at an early age in 1841. Edward Lear worked with Gould on the famous *Birds of Europe*; Gould failed to acknowledge his contribution in the finished volume.

Turn into **BEDFORD AVENUE** and walk westwards along it. This first stretch was until 1896 called Caroline Mews, a lane running past the coach-houses on the south side of Bedford Square, with constricted entrances at either end. In the 1890s the coach-houses were replaced by a uniform row of unusual 2-storey buildings, built in red brick with contrasting stone and terracotta detailing. Most of these function as offices for a variety of businesses but a few still provide rear access to houses in Bedford Square, including Bloomsbury Publishing (p 55). Enhancing this side of the Avenue is a line of mature plane trees, planted in 1896 after a subsidy from the first residents of the mansion flats on the south side. These form one of the two blocks called **Bedford Court Mansions**, built from 1891 (for the other see p 58). The block has a monumental frontage in an Arts and Craft style, with long wooden balconies painted white.

The mansion flats seem to have attracted many theatrical types. The music-hall proprietor and politician Walter De Frece was living here in 1911 at Flat No.23, with his wife Mathilda, better known by her stage name of Vesta Tilley and famous for male roles such as Burlington Bertie. At the same time another music-hall artiste Harry Relph, otherwise Little Tich, was at Nos.78-79, and the French silent-film actress Mathilde Comont (then Caumont) was at No.44.

Francis Jekyll, nephew of the landscape gardener Gertrude, lived at No.38 from 1908-13; he was a noted collector of folk songs. The chemist and explosives expert Sir Robert Robertson died in his home at No.51 in 1949; during WWI he had been responsible for the development of the manufacture and use of TNT. The American author and humorist May Isabel Fisk was living at No.60 in 1911, with her mother, the writer Belle Gray Taylor. The jazz drummer Carlo Krahmer, founder of Esquire Records, set up a studio in the basement of his flat at No.76, recording the early work of such artists as Ronnie Scott, John Dankworth and Cleo Laine. In 1957 he also founded here the short-lived

Starlite Records which focused on early Blue Beat or Ska. No.95 was home in 1911 to the Russian prince Vladimir Bariatinsky and his wife, an actress whose stage name was Lydia Yavorska. At the start of the 1930s, the stage and film actress Evelyn Laye was living at No.97, after divorcing her first husband Sonnie Hale because of his affair with Jessie Matthews. She was married again **[19]** to the actor Frank Lawton in 1934 until his death in 1969.

Cross over Adeline Place and continue into the western stretch of Bedford Avenue, first laid out in 1776 and until 1896 called Tavistock Street; none of its original

buildings remain. On the south side is the entrance to the St Giles Hotel, which occupies part of the YMCA complex. This lies over the site of No.3 Tavistock Street where lodged Samuel Standidge Boden, acknowledged as the best English chess player before his death there in 1882.

The north side is occupied by another block of **Bedford Court Mansions, Nos.122-142**, dating from the late 1890s, with a corner tourelle – and an impressive stone frontage round the corner in Adeline Place. The theatre and music-hall manager Sir Horace E Moss was living at Flat No.123 in 1901; No.128 was home to the publisher Jonathan Cape who died here in 1960; and the anthropologist Phyllis Kaberry died in 1977 in her home at No.142.

The flats cover the site of No.16 Tavistock Street, the office of the architect Charles Parker in the 1830s, when his Italianate domestic architecture was popular. Next door, No.17 was then home to John Orlando Parry, Welsh harpist and singer, who wrote and performed very popular entertainments in the 1850s at the Wornum Hall (p 96). In 1891, the printer Thomas Way was living at No.17; his encouragement of British artists to take up lithography led to a revival in the process.

At the west corner of the block is **MORWELL STREET**, which we first saw from its northern end. At the time of writing the roadway is blocked here, while a huge redevelopment, to be known as One Bedford Avenue, takes place beyond it to Tottenham Court Road, ahead.

ADELINE PLACE bisects Bedford Avenue. Renamed after the 10th Duchess of Bedford, and known before 1938 as Caroline Street, it was built in 1776 as a feeder road leading to Bedford Square. None of the original houses remain, but in its early years it was quite fashionable. Residents included the portrait painters Samuel Abbott (1761–1802), and Arthur Devis (1762-1822), who painted *The Apotheosis of Princess Charlotte* for the bereaved Prince Leopold; the sculptor and architect William Tyler (d.1801); and, before his move to a grander house in Great Russell Street, the actor John Philip Kemble. In the 1780s the street was home to Mrs Anna Laetitia Barbauld, then celebrated for her children's books, and to the orientalist writer William Marsden.

Past the immense YMCA building on the street's west side is the entrance to an underground car park. This is roughly on the site of No.3 Caroline Street, home in 1881 to Arthur Swanborough, manager of the Strand Theatre and husband of the noted actress Eleanor Bufton. On the east side **No.15** was the office in the 1950s of the town planner and architect Arthur Kenyon, closely associated with Welwyn Garden City. The sculptor Edgar George Papworth lived in the 1830s at No.16 Caroline Street. He was the nephew of the architect J B Papworth, who was listed as a Caroline Street resident in 1829.

19 Evelyn Laye with her second husband Frank Lawton, 1934

The street ends at **GREAT RUSSELL STREET**. Turn right, walking alongside the YMCA. Its site was first acquired in 1908, though the plan had been to build mansion flats on it, and houses had been demolished here at the end of the 1890s. Among them was No.112, home of the glass painter James Pearson (c.1740–1838) who played a significant role in the revival of English enamel glass painting. It then became one of a number of homeopathic pharmacies in London run by the Epps family in the 19th century. George Napoleon Epps had a homeopathic practice here in 1842-47. His brother James (1821-1907) ran the chemist's shop but also founded a great cocoa business associated with his name, fed by his cocoa plantation in Jamaica. Epps' Homeopathic Cocoa was sold from Victorian times until 1930. At No.114 the photographer William Jeffrey had a studio 1860-76, while No.115 was the home of hosier John Arthur Turnbull in 1879, the year he married; he went on to found with Ernest Asser the high-class outfitters Turnbull & Asser. At No.116 the prolific painter William Bigg lived from 1823 until his death five years later. Constable called him the most skilful restorer in London.

We soon reach Tottenham Court Road, having come full circle. Turn left to reach St Giles Circus and the Tube station on its far corner.

Route 4

Russell Square and adjacent streets

A circular walk from Russell Square Station

Russell Square is London's largest 'true' square, excepting the earlier and larger Lincoln's Inn Fields, which was not deliberately planned as such. The eponymous Underground station, where this walk begins, is actually in Bernard Street, close to but not on the Square. On leaving the station, turn left and cross Herbrand Street, named after the 11th Duke of Bedford, who was instrumental in the development of the hotel whose north side you next pass.

On reaching **RUSSELL SQUARE**, cross at the lights to the wide pavement on the garden side to look at the **Hotel Russell** and its red-brick and terracotta frontage. Erected in the closing years of the 19th century – note the '18' and '98' on either side of the main entrance – the hotel was designed by Charles Fitzroy Doll in a flamboyant 'super François Premier style, magnificently inflated to eight storeys' (Pevsner). The four life-sized female figures in costumes of different periods, standing above and beside the entrance, represent Queens Elizabeth I, Mary I, Mary II and Anne, after whom four suites of rooms were originally to be named. In a frieze above the first floor balcony are the coats of arms of various European royal and noble families, presumably displayed there in the hope that they would patronise the hotel. The Russell Group, of 24 leading UK research universities is so named because the informal meetings that led to its formation were held here.

A comparatively late arrival in Russell Square, the hotel covers the site of the earliest part of its development by James Burton after 1800 at the behest of the 5th Duke of Bedford. Those eight houses, at first known as Southampton Terrace, subsequently became Nos.1- 8 Russell Square (south to north). The numbering of Russell Square houses runs counter-clockwise, beginning and ending at the Guilford Street junction.

Looked down on by the aristocracy, 19th-century Russell Square was solidly upper-middle-class, occupied by families headed by professionals or City merchants. The barrister Richard Pankhurst moved with his family in 1886 from Manchester to Hampstead Road, and on again in 1888 to No.8 Russell Square, which was the northernmost house in the terrace. While he had come to London in search of a parliamentary career, his wife

Emmeline, and his then small daughters Sylvia, Christabel and Adela (later Adela Pankhurst Walsh) would eventually become far better known as suffragettes. The house was a hive of radical activity until the family's return to Manchester in 1893.

No.6, from about 1820, was the home and practice of Scottish physician George Darling (a partner of Dr Neil Arnott, p 54); he died there in 1862. F D Maurice, the founder of Christian Socialism and of the Working Men's College, lived at No.5 in 1856. Then living at No.2 was long-term resident Henry Shuckburgh Roots, physician to the St Pancras Infirmary and pioneering advocate of plastic surgery. No.1A was the birthplace in 1870 of diplomat Sir Francis Oppenheimer, and by 1891 home to Rev. Robert Bradley, vicar of St Peter's, Regent Square.

Walk along the pavement opposite the hotel, where worth noticing are the gardens' most mature specimen trees (holm oak and yew) and the perimeter railings with spearhead finials. At the next pair of pedestrian lights, cross to the south side of the Guilford Street junction. Here, set in the pavement outside the entrance to the corner building (present-day No.73) is a well-preserved old sign pointing to the Turkish Baths which once graced the basement of the original Imperial Hotel. We shall encounter its modern successor shortly, as we continue south. Meanwhile, look across at the Hotel Russell's south flank with its mixture of styles. The 'H' in the initials 'H R' at the top of the 'Dutch' gable might be interpreted as either Hotel or Herbrand!

Covering the site of former No.70, but with its entrance in Guilford Street, the **President Hotel** was opened in 1963; it supersedes an earlier, utilitarian-looking Premier Hotel at Nos.67-70 that had supplanted three houses built there in the 1840s on a thitherto undeveloped plot. Originally on this site was a large house erected long before Russell Square was laid out. At first known as Baltimore House (or No.26 Southampton Row), this had been built in 1759-63 for Frederick Calvert, the 6th (and last) Baron Baltimore, and was probably designed by John Vardy. Following Baltimore's trial for rape in 1768 and subsequent flight to Italy, Harry Paulet (or Powlett), 6th Duke of Bolton took over the lease of the house in 1770. He employed Robert Adam to make alterations to the interior and generally transform what was to become Bolton House (Adam's plans can be found at the Soane Museum).

After the duke's death in 1794, the lease was acquired by the Lord Chancellor, Alexander Wedderburn (Lord Loughborough and subsequently 1st Earl of Rosslyn). In 1803, he converted it into three separate houses. The smallest of these was at the rear of the site, with a garden accessed from Guilford Street. Becoming known as 'Bolton Gardens', the house was eventually numbered No.71 Russell Square. The architect Thomas Donaldson (p 16) lived here from about 1847-1861. Parish rate books affirm that Richard D'Oyly Carte, the Gilbert and Sullivan impresario, resided at 'Bolton Gardens' from 1881 (when his eponymous company opened at the Savoy Theatre) until 1886, the year after the death of his first wife, Blanche. A few years later, the National Union of Teachers became one of the first organisations to have a Russell Square address. From 1889 until its move to Mabledon Place in 1915, the union's headquarters occupied both Nos.71 and 67.

Porticoed No.67, facing the Square, was another part of the divided Bolton House. The judge Sir Vicary Gibbs, sometime MP and Attorney General, died here in 1820; his reputed sarcasm and general incivility had earned him the nickname 'Vinegar Gibbs'. Sir Thomas Noon Talfourd (p 65), friend of Dickens spent his last years there.

Former bow-fronted No.66, the third and largest division of Bolton House, has been identified with the home of the Sedleys in Thackeray's *Vanity Fair* (1847). In one episode, Amelia Sedley's suitor George Osborne walks to her Russell Square house along Southampton Row, expecting to see his girlfriend in her drawing-room window. This would make sense only if this was a bow window, and No.66 was the only house in the Square that had one. Installed there by the 1890s was the Royal

Photographic Society, later obliged to move to No.35 when the second phase of another grandiose building, the original Imperial Hotel, was built. This was erected in two stages, in 1907 and 1911 (the southern half first). It was designed like the Russell by Charles Fitzroy Doll, but in an even more extravagant style described in the current 'Pevsner & Cherry' as 'a vicious mixture of Art Nouveau Gothic and Art Nouveau Tudor' **[20]**.

The spectacular building was demolished c.1965 at the insistence of the GLC, who deemed its foundations to be inadequate, and the present **Imperial Hotel** was constructed. Pevsner & Cherry consider its 'tawdry saw-toothed' front to be 'entirely unworthy' of its position. Tastefully displayed, however, in the present hotel's interior courtyard, are various relics salvaged from the previous building. These include statues and statuettes that once adorned its exterior and a replica of the copper ship which topped its tallest tower. The clock here is modern. Not on display is the German-made clock once sited halfway up that tower, surmounted by a grotesque human head which on the hour rolled its eyes and poked its tongue out; there is no truth in the story that the insult was directed at the Duke of Bedford's statue in the Square. At first owned by Harold Walduck, the Imperial London Hotels Group is still a Walduck family business, its 'empire' having long ago expanded to embrace other local hotels, including the Premier/President next door.

The illustrious portraitist Sir Thomas Lawrence chose to live alone in one of Burton's houses here (No.65) from 1813 until his death in 1830. Here he painted his portraits of the Allies triumphant in the Napoleonic Wars, which hang in the Waterloo Room at Windsor Castle. Legend has it that when the Russian general, Matvei Ivanovich Platov was sitting for Lawrence, the house was guarded by Cossacks mounted on white chargers. The old Bedford Estate plaque reaffixed above Hertz Rent-a-car acknowledges the artist's residence nearby.

The first-built southern half of the old Imperial Hotel supplanted Burton houses at Nos.61 to 64. No.64 was the birthplace in 1825 of the genealogist and herald George Edward Cokayne (then called Adams) who was to write *The Complete Peerage*. Resident at No.62 by 1890 was William Swan Sonnenschein, the publisher a few years earlier of the first English edition of Marx's *Das Kapital*, of Shaw's *Unsocial Socialist*,

20 The Imperial Hotel soon after completion (postcard, c.1915)

and of *Women's Suffrage* by Mrs Maye Ashton Dilke. Living next door at No.61, for ten years from 1881, was the *anti*-suffragist novelist and social reformer Mary (Mrs Humphry) Ward, with her husband and their three young children; it was also the birthplace in 1887 of her nephew, the zoologist and philosopher Sir Julian Huxley. By the time she reluctantly left the Square in 1891, Mary had embarked on her social work in the local area that was to culminate in the founding of what became the Mary Ward Settlement in Tavistock Place, a centre which pioneered, *inter alia*, the children's play movement.

On 12 September 1933, a guest at the hotel, while crossing the road here to the other side of Southampton Row, came up with the idea of nuclear chain reaction. The Hungarian physicist Leo Szilard was in London for a British Association for the Advancement of Science (BAAS) meeting. He applied for a patent, but as he did not want it to become public, assigned it to the British Admiralty.

Immediately south of the present Imperial Hotel, between Nos.154 and 156 Southampton Row and behind a tall drainpipe, is a very narrow vertical band of brickwork, probably a relic of the Wards' Georgian house.

We shall return to Russell Square later, but for now continue southwards along the east side of **SOUTHAMPTON ROW**. A 'Row' originally denoted houses with an uninterrupted view of an open space – in this case, the Duke of Bedford's garden and Long Field. The poet Thomas Gray, of *Elegy* fame, took lodgings in a 'Southampton Row' cottage in 1759, in order to enjoy the pure air and the clear view northwards to Hampstead. For the next two years, he delved into the British Museum's manuscript holdings, partly to assist Horace Walpole with historical projects; he then returned to Cambridge.

No.109 opposite was designed in the 1970s by Richardson and Partners as small flats. To its left, the nondescript post-WWII flats of **Cranfield House** cover the site of the erstwhile West Central Hotel and of No.99, briefly a childhood home of the orphaned, American-born Edgar Allan Poe. The Allans, his foster parents, spent five years in Britain from 1815, lodging in Southampton Row. Soon after their arrival, his adoptive father, tobacco merchant John Allan, wrote of being 'by a snug fire in a nice little sitting parlour' at what was then No.47, with wife Frances and sister Nancy sewing, and a 6-year-old Edgar 'reading a little Story Book'. The family subsequently moved twelve doors south to the then No.39.

The east side of the road is characterised by late-Victorian and Edwardian buildings, with some long-established independent restaurants at street level. **No.154**, now occupied by the language school St Giles International, was previously home, for 96 years from 1896, to (Sir Isaac) Pitman's Central Secretarial College. **Russell Mansions**, at No.144, with its prominent iron balconies, is where Italia Conti, the actress and founder of the eponymous academy of theatre arts had a flat (No.6) in 1937. Adjoining it is a **Mercure Hotel**, which was built in 1903 as the Waverley Hotel, hence the Scottish heraldry over the entrance; it was then part of Robert Cranston's temperance hotel empire (p 43). Beyond it is the **Bloomsbury Park Hotel**, built shortly after and previously known as the Grand and then the Cosmo. Here a blue plaque recalls the birth in 1899, above a baker's shop in intersecting Cosmo Place, of Sir John Barbirolli, best known as the conductor of the Hallé Orchestra from 1943 until his death in 1970; the plaque records him as a Companion of Honour, indicating high achievement.

Cross to the west side of the street, where there was once a covered entrance that led into a stabling area behind called Southampton Mews. The present **Bedford Hotel** (part of the Imperial group, hence the ship logo) preserves the name of the street's oldest hotel. There, on 15 April 1840, Sir Francis Goldsmid and 23 other men met to sign a declaration marking the formation of Reform Judaism in Britain. The stepped entrance of the original Bedford Family Hotel is referred to on the bronze plaque to the left of the hotel car park entrance, stating that on 24 September 1917 twelve people were killed and many injured in one of the earliest ever night-time air raids. A German Gotha plane dropped a 110-lb bomb which exploded in the roadway.

A Starbucks café on the east side at **No.124** marks the site of former No.19, the workplace and home, from 1824, of Thomas Morson, the first quantitative pharmaceutical chemist in England and co-founder of the Pharmaceutical Society (p 17); in 1850 he moved house to nearby No.38 Queen Square. Although he was not a medical man, on his death in 1874, an obituary of Morson was unusually printed in *The Lancet*. Though he had moved his drug manufacture to laboratories in Hornsey **[21]** and later at Ponders End, his thriving family firm kept No.19 as their retail outlet until its demolition in 1900. Working as an assistant in the shop, in 1866-68, had been William Martindale, soon to be appointed pharmacist at University College Hospital, whose in-house pharmacopœia he edited. Further mansion blocks follow, with **Russell Square Mansions** at No.122 and **Ormonde Mansions** at No.110A.

21 Thomas Morson in his Hornsey laboratory (from a drawing by William J Müller)

No.73 on the west side is the street's sole Georgian survival. **No.69**, beyond, was previously a Post Office (built in 1902), but for some years has served as the HQ and auction rooms of the coin and collectables specialists Spink & Son. Two additional storeys in a matching style were added in 1999; high up on the south-facing wall there is a Bedford Estate ducal coronet.

Opposite is the **Bonnington Hotel** (with 'Double Tree by Hilton' over its entrance). Its founder was a Scotsman, John Frame, formerly a tailor and a temperance movement activist, who in 1884 had started a travel agency in Preston (Lancs.), promoting cheap railway tours for teetotallers. Moving to London, he first opened a temperance hotel at No.25 Bloomsbury Square and 1 Bloomsbury Place. By the 1900s he had a thriving travel business run from No.92 Southampton Row. Built on this site in 1911 was the present hotel, intended mainly to accommodate Frame's tourist clients. Named after Bonnington Linn, a waterfall in Lanarkshire, his native county, it was opened by the nonagenarian Lord Strathcona (the Scottish-born Canadian railway magnate and 'empire builder'). Frames Tours prospered and eventually had agencies in numerous cities worldwide, but was always based in Bloomsbury (with a later depot and coach station in Herbrand Street) until its demise in 2001.

Turn right into Bloomsbury Place (p 20) and then take the next right turn into **BEDFORD PLACE**. Both sides of this street have symmetrical, uniformly decorated terraces of four storeys with basements, and long cast-iron balconies at first-floor level. All but three of the houses are of yellow-brown stock brick, with stuccoed ground floor and basement. They were popular when first built in 1801-06 in the grounds of the recently demolished Bedford House (p 15), during a building slump occasioned by the Napoleonic wars. Remarkably, all their frontages survived WWII bombing and still form a pleasing ensemble.

In the late 19th century, widows and unmarried women began converting their homes into lodgings and boarding houses. In 1898 Booth's researcher updating the poverty map wrote that 'the Russell Square district passed out of the hands of fashion to the Jews, who in turn are making way for boarding houses'. **No.8** had become a commercial lodging house as early as 1881; it was called the Delmonico Private Hotel by 1925, and since about 1940 has been known as the Thanet Hotel. Today the street is dominated by a modern chain of small, 'boutique' hotels, with matching awnings.

On the west side, at **No.33**, is 'the Medical Research Council Unit for Lifelong Health and Ageing', and home to the MRC National Survey of Health and Development, the oldest of British birth cohort studies. It has gathered data since birth on the health and social circumstances of more than 5,000 men and women born in Great Britain in March 1946. **No.30** was where the dramatist Richard Cumberland, caricatured as Sir Fretful Plagiary in Sheridan's *The Rivals*, died in 1811. From August to October 1914, the poet T S Eliot lodged at **No.28**, before going to Merton College, Oxford; the poet Conrad Aiken, a friend from his days at Harvard, was already boarding at the same address, but was anxious to return to America, following the outbreak of WWI.

In the centre of the street's east side, **No.11** sports a trellis balcony with tented canopy. Richard Twining, a member of the tea and coffee dynasty, lived beyond with his family at **No.13**. His nine children included the physician William Twining, a writer on mental disability, who died in the house in 1848, aged 35, after ten years of paralysis. His elder sister Elizabeth, a talented botanical artist, helped found the Ladies' College in Bedford Square (p 55). Their younger sister Louisa lived at No.13 for some thirty years. Her many philanthropic endeavours included workhouse reform, her interest in which was first aroused by a conversation in 1853 with an old nurse at the Strand Union Workhouse; this led five years later to the founding of the Workhouse Visiting Society.

Mrs Mary Anne Clarke, mistress of Frederick, (the 'Grand Old') Duke of York, was living in 1818 with her mother at **No.14**; and for a year in 1806-07, **No.15** had been home to the smallpox vaccination pioneer Edward Jenner (p 48).

Built in a darker shade of brick, **Nos.21-23** at the end of the street project slightly forward, as do other houses which terminate the terraces. They are home to the Penn Club. Although not a formal Quaker institution, it has connections with the Religious Society of Friends and maintains Quaker values in the accommodation and services offered. The Club was established in 1920 with funds left over from the Friends' Ambulance Unit, active during WWI. The novelist John Wyndham lived and wrote at the Club in the 1940s and 1950s. Brought up with her sisters at No.21 was Jane Griffin (b.1792), the future second wife of Sir John Franklin, famously lost with his crew in 1847 on his ill-fated expedition to find the Northwest Passage. As a young woman, Lady Franklin had been introduced to her husband by a certain Dr Peter Mark Roget (p 45), to whom she was greatly attracted, describing him as the only man to have ever made her swoon.

We arrive back at **RUSSELL SQUARE** at the middle of its south side, the second part to be built. Turn right, past **Nos.52-53** on the corner, home since 2009 to the Chartered Institute of Public

Relations. In 1899 the properties had inappropriate terracotta added, at the insistence of Herbrand, 11th Duke of Bedford. George Grossmith, of *Diary of a Nobody* fame, lived at **No.55** with his family for about seven years from 1902.

The physician James Lind, who died in 1812 in his son-in-law's home at **No.56**; a friend of the poet Shelley, he had reportedly once saved him from being placed by his father in a private madhouse. By the 1830s No.56 was occupied by the writer, judge

22 George Edmund Street holding his plan for the Royal Courts of Justice

and politician Serjeant (later Sir) Thomas Noon Talfourd. His house became famous for the convivial dinner parties he held here, in the company of 'swarming children and numerous cats'. Charles Dickens and his circle of friends were regular guests, and Talfourd was the model for the idealistic Tommy Traddles in *David Copperfield*; while his children Frank and Kate lent their names to two youngsters in *Nicholas Nickleby*. Augustus De Morgan, UCL's founding professor of mathematics, was the London Mathematical Society's first president, hence the name De Morgan House for **Nos. 57-58**, its home since 1998.

Cross the road at the lights to the south-east corner of Russell Square Gardens (p 70). Turn back west outside them along the wide pavement, which we shall continue to follow clockwise around the Square. Facing Bedford Place is Sir Richard Westmacott's 1809 **statue** of Francis Russell, 5th Duke of Bedford. The decorations of the magisterial monument allude to the Duke's passion for agriculture: sheep on the rough stone plinth; bulls' heads on the corners; and cow, pig and horse in a frieze; with the Duke's right hand resting on a plough.

On the Square's south side, at **Nos.50-51,** is a 1960s office building bearing a plaque to Baron Thomas Denman, Lord Chief Justice of England, who lived at No.50, a house on this site; his son, the Rt Hon George Denman, a High Court judge, was born there 1819. The eminent publisher George Routledge died in the same house in 1888; by the time of his recent retirement, he had published 5,000 titles. The architect G E Street, resident at No.51 from 1862 until 1870, designed the Royal Courts of Justice **[22]** and many churches.

The architect James Knowles, who lived at **No.49**, and died here in 1884, had a thriving practice designing Italianate mansions for the rich and co-designed, with his eldest son (also James), the Grosvenor Hotel at Victoria Station. Opened by the present Queen in 1993 was the first home, at Nos.48&49, of the newly chartered Royal College of Anaesthetists (since relocated to Red Lion Square). The railway and public works contractor Sir Morton Peto and his family lived at **No.47** for a few years until 1853; as the country's leading Baptist layman, he was treasurer of the Baptist Missionary Society until his bankruptcy in 1868.

Montague Street (p 50) joins from the left, its houses merging with those of the Square's west side. Here is a run of houses which survive largely without external alteration. **No.43** was home to the conchologist and algologist Maria Gray, who died here in 1876; she assisted her husband John, a zoologist at the nearby British Museum, with his scientific work, and encouraged the study of algae in schools. By the early 20th century, as many houses in the Square were converted into offices, No.43 was named Chalmers House and in 1910 it became a homeopathic hospital as well as the headquarters and medical school for the British Homeopathic Association. On the outbreak of WWI, it became the HQ of the South East Mounted Brigade, which was sent to Gallipoli in 1915. A long-time occupant of the top flat at No.43 was Beryl de Zoete, a ballet dancer and dance researcher specialising in eastern dance. Her partner was the orientalist Arthur Waley, who lived with her here from the 1920s until her death in 1962. In WWII, he was a censor at the Ministry of Information (p 80), vetting letters and telegrams written in Japanese. Other interwar occupants of No.43 had included the London Federation of the League of Nations Union, and the Inter-Varsity Federation (an evangelical Christian group).

After Henry Shuckburgh Roots moved out to No.2 (p 60), **No.42** was home to Sir Chapman Marshall, a grocer and sometime Lord Mayor of London, recorded in the 1851 census as a widower (aged 67), with a housekeeper, cook, housemaid and coachman – occupants typical of houses in the Square in the 19th century. Later dubbed 'Marylebone House', No.42 was the headquarters of the Football Association from 1910 until 1929. After WWII it was used by a succession of publishers, mainly subsidiaries of Reed International, before housing the German Historical Institute (p 17) in 1977-82. At **No.41** the Australian novelist (Stella) Miles Franklin worked for the National Housing and Town Planning Council between 1918 and 1926. A major literary prize in Australia is named in her honour.

Charles Grant, East India Company director, MP and philanthropist, died in 1823 at his home at **No.40**, which today shares an entrance (labelled '39') with **No.39**, a building ravaged in the Blitz and later wholly rebuilt behind its original façade. Bombed out in this incident had been the British Museum's renowned conservation laboratory, established in 1920. All six houses at Nos.38-43 had been acquired by the BM in 1898-99, and have since accommodated a variety of museum departments. In 1817, a medical practice was opened at **No.38** by Helenus Scott, a former military surgeon, expert in the treatment of liver disease.

On the north corner of wide Montague Place and replacing Nos.31-37, 1980s **Stewart House** has a pleasing façade in imitation of Burton's houses at Nos.38-43. Designed by Gabriel Epstein of Shepheard, Epstein & Hunter for the Schools Examination Board, it now houses some of the University of London's administrative functions, and the 'London Deanery', an NHS-related initiative offering development courses for healthcare professionals. The building previously proposed for this site, an assembly hall for Senate House designed by Charles Holden, would scarcely have harmonised so well with its southerly neighbours.

Erstwhile No.37, on the site, was home to the judge Sir James Mansfield from at least 1808 until his death in 1821; when Solicitor General, he had participated in the prosecution of Lord George Gordon for high treason in 1781 following the Gordon Riots. A much later Solicitor General, Sir Edward George Clarke, lived at the same house with his second wife Kathleen; their son, William, an intelligence officer and code-breaker during both World Wars, was born there in 1883. Dr William Saunders, the first president of the Medical & Chirurgical Society, lived until 1814 at No.36.

At the entrance to Senate House's car park (the former east end of Keppel Street, p 80) is **No.30**, a heavy construction by Sir John Burnet, built in 1913-14 to house the Royal Institute of Chemistry (and still so labelled in Art Nouveau lettering). The Institute merged in 1980 with the Chemical Society to form the Royal Society of Chemistry, grandly housed at Burlington House, Piccadilly. The building replaced the house in which the diarist and journalist Henry Crabb Robinson lived from 1839 until his death in 1867. He worked for *The Times* for a few years from 1807 and claimed to have been the first modern war correspondent, having sent dispatches from the Peninsular campaign at La Coruña. In the 1820s, he participated in the founding of UCL, and his *Diary*, letters, travel journals and other papers are deposited in Dr Williams's Library (p 108), of which he was a trustee.

Since 2011, surviving **No.29** has been home to the Wiener Library for the Study of Holocaust & Genocide, an institution dating back to the 1920s; it also holds temporary exhibitions. No.29 was previously occupied by the Institute of Germanic Studies, founded in 1950 and now part of the Institute of Modern Languages lodged in Senate House (p 78). **No.28** was the home of Charles Abbott, Lord Tenterden, judge and Governor of the Foundling Hospital, who died here in 1832. The Licensed Victuallers' Central Protection Society of London was at **No.27** from 1904 until 1949, when the newly established Institute of Commonwealth Studies moved in. In repairs after WWII bomb damage, the building was furnished partly by gifts of Empire woods from universities and colleges throughout the Commonwealth; murals were painted by Henry Bird. Part of the University of London's School of Advanced Study since 1994, the Institute also occupied space next door at No.28 before moving into the Senate House building in 2006.

The scenery painter William Roxby Beverly lived with his family at **No.26**; two of his brothers died here, actor Henry in 1863, and actor and stage manager Robert three years later. Together with other adjacent properties, the house is now the base of Birkbeck's School of Social Sciences, History & Philosophy. Run from **No.25** in Edwardian times was the Ranyard Mission, also known as the London Biblewoman & Nurses' Mission, which combined evangelism in poor areas with district nursing; the house was then called Ranyard House, after its founder Ellen Ranyard, a writer of religious tracts. The Institute of Advanced Legal Studies (p 68), founded in 1947, moved into No.25 the next year, and was soon to expand into No.26. The Pears Institute for the Study of Anti-Semitism, founded in 2010, is also based here.

On an island in the Square's north-west corner stands a green **cabmen's shelter**. Captain G C Armstrong instigated the provision of refuges serving tea, coffee, bread and butter to horse-cab drivers, as an alternative to the ubiquitous, inebriating public house; and in 1874 the Earl of Shaftesbury established the Cabmen's Shelter Fund (run today by the Unite union). In 1914 there were 61 shelters; now only 13 remain. Though dating from 1901, the Russell Square shelter arrived here only after Leicester Square, where it previously stood, was pedestrianised. Two plaques on the door record its original funder, actor-manager Sir Squire Bancroft, and its restoration here in 1987.

The north side of the Square contains a few more remaining original houses at Nos.24-21, now part of SOAS (p 71). These were not built by Burton, but by other Bedford Estate contractors under orders to mirror his houses on the south side. The extensive terracotta ornament was added later. At **No.24**, the house on the left, a general publishing firm, Faber & Gwyer Ltd, was established in 1925. Its chairman, Sir Geoffrey Faber, used his own capital to transform the firm into Faber & Faber Ltd in 1929. As recorded by a brown plaque on the building's side wall (p 71), the poet, critic and dramatist T S Eliot worked here as literary editor and company director from 1925 until 1965, the year he died.

The very first occupants of **No.23** were the Swiss-born physician and chemist Alexander Marcet, known for his work on renal and urinary calculi (stones), and his wife Jane (née Haldimand), an author of popular science books; one of their children, François, became a well-known physicist.

Leila Rendel (1882-1969) spent many of her early years at No.23, the house of her grandfather, Sir Alexander Rendel, a Victorian radical. A social worker, she was to found a nursery in Cartwright Gardens in 1911, and then set up the Caldecott Community (named after the children's book illustrator Randolph Caldecott), giving therapeutic residential care to deprived children (and nowadays based in Kent). After WWI, the British Dental Association (founded 1879) established its headquarters at No.23. Lilian Murray (née Lindsay), the first woman to hold a British qualification in dentistry, moved with her husband Robert into the flat here in 1920, when he became the BDA's first Secretary; she built up a specialist library, and continued as honorary librarian until 1946, when she became the Association's first female president.

No.21, with its heavy 19th-century boot scrapers, bears a bronze Bedford Estate plaque naming Sir Samuel Romilly (1757-1818), law reformer and pioneer of the abolition of slavery, who moved here from No.48 Gower Street in 1803, taking the first 99-year lease on the newly built house. He committed suicide here in 1818, unable to bear the death of his wife, dying in the arms of his nephew Peter Mark Roget, then living nearby in Bernard Street.

To the right, an empty site permits an end-on view of the 1970s Institute of Education development (p 69). The Brutalist style is particularly evident in the reinforced concrete construction of **No.17**, home to the Institute of Advanced Legal Studies since 1976, and also known as Charles Clore House, after its main benefactor. In 1916, the original house at this address had been the New Zealand Soldiers' Club in London.

East of Bedford Way stands the huge block called **Russell Square House**. It was built on the site of Nos.9-16 in two halves, though the join is scarcely visible. The eastern half, intended as an extension to the Royal Hotel (p 69) and finished in 1941, was used as a hostel for US servicemen and then by the Ministry of Information before its move into Senate House; the Paymaster General's office moved in in 1947. Completed only after WWII, the western half was taken in 1955 by the Supplies Division of the Ministry of Health, which (as the DHSS and then Department of Health) remained here until 1995. There were physics laboratories in the basement, once used to test new types of medical equipment.

A blue plaque on the Russell Square façade commemorates Sir George Williams, founder of the YMCA, who lived with his wife Helen at No.13, on the site, from 1879 until 1905, when he died in a Torquay hotel. The house also served for a while as the YMCA's national headquarters. In 1825, Parliament awarded £6,000 to civil servant James Deacon Hume for consolidating customs legislation, reducing 1,500 Acts to 10; by the 1830s, the former No.15 was his family home and he had risen to be joint Secretary of the Board of Trade. No.12 was home to the Russian-born economist and early supporter of free trade Thomas Tooke; and later to his brother William, a lawyer and arts promoter, who died there in 1863, having earlier co-founded the Society for the Diffusion of Useful Knowledge and assisted in the foundation of UCL. No.10 was home to architect Horace Horne and his wife Hannah, whose architect, art collector and art historian son, Herbert was born there in 1864. His most substantial building, the Chapel of the Ascension on Bayswater Road, was bombed in 1940 and later pulled down. No.9 on the corner was the home of banker John Stevenson Salt, whose son William (1808-63), an antiquary, made many bequests to the British Museum; after his death, his widow was persuaded to donate his collection of Staffordshire topographical items to the county.

If you are still on the pavement outside the Russell Square Gardens, cross at the lights to the north side of the Square and walk straight ahead up the west side of busy **WOBURN PLACE**. On the other side of this road at No.2 is the long-established **Morton Hotel**. North of it, and dating from 1937, is **Russell Court** (Nos.3-16), built with single or older people in mind and containing small, mainly studio flats. The alternating wide bandings of Portland stone and brick, together with bay windows make for a plain but pleasing building; its northern end on the corner of Coram Street has a dramatic sweeping curve. When built, this was one of the biggest blocks of flats in London; the architects were (Val) Myer and Watson-Hart, whose most famous building is Broadcasting House.

To the north of Coram Street **Nos.19-29**, also of 1930s design, have now been converted from government offices into student accommodation. Today, no trace remains of the street's early-19th-century houses, or of the boarding-houses and small hotels that later colonised them. Further up the west side, where the Tavistock Hotel (p 103) now stands, the astronomer Richard Sheepshanks lived from 1824-41 at No.30; a small observatory was attached to his house. Samuel Warren, who lived a few doors to the south at No.35 in the 1850s, was consecutively a medical student, barrister, MP, 'Master in Lunacy' and writer of legal textbooks. He also wrote novels, and some of his ideas and images are said to have been borrowed by Charles Dickens (then living nearby, p 101). No.45 was the home of the brewer Benjamin Greene (of Greene King fame) after deciding to leave his native Bury St Edmunds, because of the furore over his pro-slavery views expressed in the local newspaper he had purchased. He had inherited a sugar plantation in St Kitts and had many slaves, for which like other owners he received compensation upon abolition. He died at No.45 in 1860. Born at No.47 in 1862 was Ada Ballin, a Jewish merchant's daughter who, having studied at UCL, went on to establish and edit two monthly magazines, a long-running *Baby* (on childcare), and a short-lived *Womanhood* aimed at the 'New Woman' of the 1890s.

Now lining most of the west side of Woburn Place is the (Imperial) **Royal National Hotel**, a long unlovely building which replaced two large, more distinguished hotels: the Royal here in Woburn Place, and the National behind in Bedford Way. Turn into the hotel's courtyard, through a gap that once gave access to 44 stables in an unusually long Woburn Mews West.

Walk across the courtyard and emerge into **BEDFORD WAY**. At first known briefly as Bedford Place North, and then as Upper Bedford Place, the street assumed its present name only in 1938. Nothing remains of the dignified terraces originally developed by John McGill

23 Dr Peter Mark Roget, c.1865

in the 1820s, and later monopolised by boarding-houses and hotels.

On the west side once stood No.18, to which Dr Peter Mark Roget **[23]** moved in 1843. Only six years later, when, aged almost 70, he retired from his medical, educational and scientific work, did he start work here on his famous *Thesaurus*, although he had been making lists of synonyms and antonyms since his youth. He died in the house in 1869. Thomas Donaldson, a founding father in 1834 of the Institute of British Architects (later the RIBA), a Professor of Architecture at UCL, and the designer of both the college's library and University Hall (p 108), died in his home at No.21 in 1885. An early resident at No.22 was the physician and chemist John Bostock, the first person to describe hay fever; his daughter Eliza, born in 1817, became a pioneer of women's education and was an early administrator of the Ladies' College, Bedford Square (p 55). No.25 was the home of architect Sir William Tite after his marriage to the wealthy Emily Curtis in 1832. He is best known for the Royal Exchange in the City and (locally) the now demolished 'miniature York Minster' that was the National Scotch Church in Regent Square. Twice president of the RIBA, Tite was also active in designing railway stations and as a member of the Metropolitan Board of Works.

The east flank of the **Institute of Education** (IoE) now occupies the entire length of Bedford Way's west side, except for UCL's Geography and Psychology Departments at the north end. The Institute was founded in 1902 by the London County Council in conjunction with the University of London as the London Day Training College, and open to 'duly qualified students of either sex who were engaged in, or intended to enter, any branch of the teaching profession'. Initially, classes were given at the London School of Economics in Clare Market; then at premises including those of the College of Preceptors (p 15) until 1907, when it moved into a new building in Southampton Row (the southern part of the former Central School of Art building). In 1909, the LDTC became a school of the University, and training for the MA in Education began in 1915. It became the Institute of Education in 1934. The present building in Bedford Way, designed by Denys Lasdun & Partners, was opened by the Queen in 1977. 'Notable' for its construction in reinforced concrete and use of anodised aluminium and glass, the entire range (including the IoE library extension of 1990-93) was given Grade II* Listing in December 2000. On 2 December 2014, it merged with UCL.

On Bedford Way's east side, No.40 was the home of church architect Richard Cromwell Carpenter and his family; he died there in 1855 from tuberculosis. Living with his family at No.46 in 1861 was the wine merchant and gin distiller (Sir) Walter Gilbey. Soon to move in was Henry Ashbee (pseudonym Pisanus Fraxi; p 55), a wealthy merchant and a bibliographer of erotica, who left his book collection to the British Museum. His son, Charles Robert Ashbee, who lived at No.46 from the age of two in 1865 until 1884, went on to be an architect, decorative artist, social reformer and founder of the Survey of London.

Walk south along the east side of Bedford Way, passing the entrance to Russell Square House, and cross at the lights into **Russell Square Gardens**. These were first laid out in 1805 by Humphrey Repton, with a wide perimeter path and broad diagonal walks under lime trees leading to a *reposoir* (shelter) in the centre, complemented by two narrower, winding walks. World War II saw the digging of trench shelters designed to sleep 2,000 people beneath the Gardens. When in 1941 the 12th Duke of Bedford objected to the removal of the surrounding railings to provide metal for making armaments, protestors daubed slogans on the base of his ancestor's statue with slogans such as 'Grandfather of a Quisling!' and 'Down with traitor and his railings'. The railings were removed but those in Bedford Square were spared, on account of their historical importance. On 23 June 1944, a V1 flying-bomb landed in the Square, wrecking the central pavilion. After the war the gardens became a venue for open-air concerts, both popular and classical. In 1959-60, Holborn Council re-landscaped the gardens, with a café in the north-east corner andthree fountains in the centre. The latest remodelling by Camden Council in 2001-02 restored the gardens to something like Repton's original layout, with lime trees and hornbeam hedging. In the centre is a new fountain, intermittently spurting.

Near the path on the north side is a walnut tree planted in 1991, with a plaque commemorating Hungarian patriot Gyorgy Krasso (1932–56). On the gardens' eastern side are two further commemorative trees. Quite close to the café is a young oak tree (with plaque) in remembrance of the bombing on a Piccadilly line train between King's Cross and Russell Square stations on 7 July 2005. In the next island bed beside the path is another oak in memory of the folk singer Ewan MacColl – 'folk laureate, singer, dramatist, Marxist' – planted by 'his communist friends' a year after his death, on 25 January 1990. Just inside the south-east gate is an Irish yew planted May 1996 in the presence of Mrs Valerie Eliot, in remembrance of her husband T S Eliot.

After exploring the gardens at leisure, return to the Underground station in Bernard Street or catch one of the many buses from stops in Woburn Place or on the north side of Russell Square.

Route 5

Around the University precinct

A circular walk from Russell Square

We begin this walk in the north-east corner of Russell Square, at its junction with **THORNHAUGH STREET**, so renamed in 1938 after an estate near Peterborough, brought into the Russell family by the wife of the 1st Earl of Bedford. Originally Upper Montague Street and stretching as far as Torrington Place, it was truncated, first by the development of Woburn Square, and then by the encroachments of university buildings.

In the pavement on the right-hand side, just outside the entrance to No.24 Russell Square is a coal-hole cover supplied by a local firm, West Bros of Marchmont Street. The building itself bears a plaque recording that T S Eliot worked here from 1925-65 (see p 67).

Immediately opposite is SOAS's **Brunei Gallery**, designed by Nicholas Hare Architects and completed in 1995 to exhibit art from Asian, African and Middle Eastern cultures. A plaque conveys the University of London's 'sincere apologies that the plans for this building were settled without due consultation with the Russell family and their Trustees, and therefore without their approval of its design'. The bricks, in the colours of hot desert sands, scarcely harmonise with those of its Russell Square neighbours. The building nevertheless received a Civic Trust Award in 1998.

Turn left through the gates topped by Art Deco lamps, dating from the 1930s and characteristic of the Senate House precinct, passing the Gallery's glass entrance on your left. On the right is the current main building of **SOAS**, the School of Oriental and African Studies. Established in 1916, the School of Oriental Studies, as it was originally known, was based in Finsbury Circus until the late 1930s, at which time it started to include African studies. Work on the building here in Thornhaugh Street, designed by architect Charles Holden, had hardly begun at the outbreak of WWII, a time of great demand for the School's services, particularly language training. The School's shield is carved in stone above the entrance.

Return to Thornhaugh Street, and make your way past the expanded SOAS Library building designed by Denys Lasdun and opened in 1973. Among its holdings is the UK's largest collection of missionary archives. In the grassed area outside are trees commemorating two young SOAS students: Bhavana Krishnamoorthy, murdered in 2004 by her paranoid schizophrenic boyfriend, and Alan Charles Sennitt, killed two years later in Washington DC while defending a friend. The turquoise bronze seated figure, of the Tamil poet and philosopher Thiruvalluvar, was donated in 1996 by the government of Tamil Nadu. Nearby is another tree, planted in memory of Elisabeth Croll CMG (1944-2007), the School's Vice-Principal and Professor of Chinese Anthropology, who had pioneered the study of Chinese women.

To the right of our path is the stepped west frontage of the UCL **Institute of Education** (IoE), also by Lasdun, the other side of which is in Bedford Way (p 69). Underneath the vast sloping paved area is its Logan Hall. In its Grade-II* Listing of the building, English Heritage described Lasdun's scheme as having 'preserved more of the Woburn Square and Bedford Way terraces than had earlier proposals'; and as having created a 'new square' between the 'spine building' and his SOAS pavilion. Obliterated in the IoE development was Upper Montague Mews (sometimes known as Upper Bedford Mews), a turning off to the right, which once ran east of and parallel to Woburn

Square, and which functioned as a mews into the early years of the 20th century.

On reaching **WOBURN SQUARE**, take the right-hand pavement, where on this east side **Nos.10-18** boast foot scrapers, railings with spear-headed finials, and elegant balconies. Most of these premises are now used by the IoE. The comic actor George Bartley died at **No.11** in 1858, eight years after the death of his thespian wife Sarah. Clement Scott, the *Daily Telegraph* drama critic lived at **No.15** and died here in 1904. Note the wrought-iron overthrow with two link snuffers, where the 'link boy' once hired for a farthing (¼d) to guide the house-owner home at night, on foot through ill-lit streets, would extinguish his flaming torch.

Turn left at the road ahead, and then shortly left again to enter the Square's garden, close to a wooden shelter. Once even more elongated, the Square may have been developed as an afterthought, having been built on the proposed line of Thornhaugh Street. It was originally intended to be called Rothesay Square, but instead was named after Woburn Abbey, the seat of the Dukes of Bedford. It was constructed c. 1829 by the Sim family of builders (James, James Jr and Robert), working to elevations specified by the Bedford Estate; they had previously developed neighbouring Torrington Square (p 74).

Woburn Square suffered bomb damage in WWII; and then in 1974, it lost more than half of its central garden and buildings to make way for the IoE and SOAS developments. Earlier residents on the east side of the Square included Thomas Pelham Dale, at No.5 in 1859-66; an Anglican clergyman and amateur scientist, he was a son of Rev. Thomas Dale (p 109). In 1898 the eminent Medical Officer of Health, (Sir) George Newman, set up home at No.2 with his new wife, the Quaker artist Adelaide Newman (née Thorp). At the time a part-time MOH for Holborn District Board of Works, George went on to become Chief Medical Officer at the Board of Education and then to the Ministry of Health. He was instrumental in important reforms to medical education in the fields of public health, and forensic and industrial medicine (a role that was to be taken on by the London School of Hygiene and Tropical Medicine).

Now walk south towards the children's playground. To the left is an emaciated sculpture of *The Green Man* (dated 1994) by Lydia Kapinska. Lent to the University by AlliedLondon, the figure is accompanied by extracts from Virginia Woolf's *The Waves*. The grassy space behind next to No.10 is the site of Christ Church, Woburn Square. Designed by Lewis Vulliamy, this had been built as a chapel-of-ease to St George's Bloomsbury in 1831-33 **[24]**, when the population of the parish was at its height. Notable for its soaring spire, it boasted stained glass added by Edward Burne-Jones and, also by him, a reredos in memory of worshipper Christina Rossetti. Damaged in WWII, the church was demolished in 1974.

Continue to the right, turning northwards along the Square's west side. Much of this was lost to bomb damage and/or university development. Dating from c.2007 is the **Henry Wellcome Building**, part of Birkbeck (p 75) housing its School of Psychology's BabyLab, or Centre for Brain and Cognitive Development.

Vanished No.41, to the south, was home to the widowed radical author G W M Reynolds, whose works outsold those of Dickens, and who died there in 1879. Born at No.31 in 1904 was the pianist Richard Addinsell, renowned as the composer of the *Warsaw Concerto*, and of film scores and songs for West End plays. From about 1853, (Sir) George Williams, founder of the YMCA, lived with his wife and children at No.30, before moving to Russell Square (p 68).

Nos.28-24, the only surviving Georgian houses on this side of the Square, have pretty balconies, and dark blue front doors surmounted by fanlights. They are now mainly occupied by parts of Birkbeck or the IoE, whose Thomas Coram Research Unit is at No.27. Charles Rieu, Keeper of Oriental Manuscripts at the BM and Professor of Arabic and Persian at UCL, lived at **No.28** and died there in 1904.

24 Christ Church, Woburn Square (demolished 1974)

The architect and civil engineer William Hosking, who had been involved in the genesis of the West London Railway, died in 1861 at former No.23. That house's last resident was Frederick George Donnan, Professor of Inorganic and Physical Chemistry at UCL in 1913. Drawn during WWI into the industrial production of 'synthetic' ammonia and nitric acid, he was later internationally known as a colloid chemist, and his theory of membrane equilibrium contributed to our understanding of the living cell. From 1928, Donnan was head of the Department of Chemistry at UCL. After his retirement in 1937, he continued to live at No.23 until 1940, leaving just twelve hours before it was destroyed by a bomb.

To the north of the Georgian houses, on the site of Nos.23-19 (and also Nos.1-6 Gordon Square) is an austere 1950s building by Charles Holden, its inartistic appearance belying its occupants' devotion to the study and appreciation of art. Behind the first door is the gallery where the Courtauld Collection of pictures was displayed until its move to Somerset House in 1989-90; more recently, it was home to a Study Centre for UCL's Slade School of Fine Art. Next door, up to the corner of Byng Place, is the **Warburg Institute**, part of the University of London's School of Advanced Study (p 80). The emblem above the entrance is based on a woodcut from a 1472 printing at Augsburg of

De Natura Rerum by St Isidore of Seville (died 636 AD); it refers to the interrelation of the elements earth, water, air and fire, the four seasons, and the four humours of man. Named after its founder Aby Warburg, the Institute is dedicated to the study of the classical tradition, and is concerned mainly with cultural history, art history and history of ideas, especially in the Renaissance. Among its previous Directors was the art historian E H Gombrich. If it is open, enter the foyer area: preserved there is the panel depicting the nine muses, which formerly graced the side elevation of No.1 Gordon Square (p 106).

Turn left to reach Byng Place (p 107) and then left again into **TORRINGTON SQUARE**. From the last quarter of the 17th century, 'Montague Fields' (behind Montagu House) became a haunt of duellists. Hereabouts was the apocryphal 'Field of Forty Footsteps', the subject of an eponymous melodrama by Percy Farren, first staged at the Tottenham Street Theatre in Fitzrovia in 1830. Supposedly, two brothers fought a duel with pistols after a major falling-out, with fatal consequences for both. Their footsteps left impressions on the ground where no grass would grow. Robert Southey went in search of them, finding them to be 500 yards east of Tottenham Court Road. The 40 had now become 67, a change the poet attributed to God's displeasure at the 'horrid sin' of duelling. In the 1790s and until 1805, the land here was rented by the Toxophilite Society for the less lethal pursuit of archery.

Torrington Square was named after Viscount Torrington (the father of Georgiana Byng, first wife of Francis Russell who was to become 5th Duke of Bedford). Very little remains of the elongated Square as originally developed by James Sim and his family in 1821-28; **Nos.27-32** on the east side are all that is left of its dignified Georgian terraces. The residence of 'poetess' Christina Rossetti is marked by a Bedford Estate bronze plaque on **No.30**, into which she moved in 1876 (from Endsleigh Gardens, p 114). Here she lived until her death in 1894, with two very elderly aunts and largely as an invalid, but continuing to produce many of her celebrated poems. The antiquary Joseph Hunter had died in the same house in 1861.

Much of the rest of the Square was lost in the 1930s: the London Squares Preservation Act 1931 was intended to protect the central gardens of the capital's squares, but named Woburn and Torrington Squares as exceptions, in order to permit the University precinct's development.

Erstwhile No.23 on the east side was by 1859 the home of lexicographer Charles Richardson. William Sandys, a solicitor and antiquary, and reviver of traditional Christmas carols, lived in retirement at No.10, where he died in 1874. Mid-19th-century residents at the far end included, at No.1, the artist and lithographer George (Johann) Scharf, father of Sir George the first director of the National Portrait Gallery; and the actor-manager Charles Kean, then busy introducing focused limelight to the London stage, who lived at No.3 with his actress wife Ellen (née Tree).

No.70 on the west side was the birthplace in 1894 of code-breaker John Hessell Tiltman, eventually Chief Cryptographer at the Government Code & Cypher School, Bletchley Park. Alfred Cellier, a composer and conductor of comic operas, lived with his wife Harriet at No.69, dying there in 1891. The next year another, more famous composer stayed in the house when he was conducting a season of Wagner's operas at the Royal Opera House: Gustav Mahler. The Square was the final home of at least two astronomers: of Thomas Galloway, also a mathematician, who died in 1851 at No.45; and Frederick Simms (d.1865), also a civil engineer, at No.50. Here, too, were the final lodgings of pioneer physiologist William Sharpey (d.1880). No.46 was home to the future travel agent (Sir) Henry Simpson Lunn (p 114); born there in 1889 was his son Hugh, better known under his pen-name as the writer Hugh Kingsmill.

South of No.27 stands Birkbeck's **Clore Management Centre**, a building designed by Stanton Williams, and although dating only from 1996-97, it seems to blend in. A newish footway, known as the 'Woburn Link', leads off towards Woburn Square and the later, but matching,

Henry Wellcome Building (p 72).

Next along Torrington Square's east side is the SOAS main building (p 71), while dominating the west side is the eastern frontage of **Birkbeck,** 'London's Evening University' which, having long faced onto Malet Street, has now turned to face east. Softening the utilitarian appearance of the original building and providing a more welcoming main entrance is the glass-fronted extension of 2001-03, an £18-million project incorporating a new library and four basement lecture theatres.

Near the end of the modern version of the Square's central garden is an 'armillary sphere sundial', unveiled by the Princess Royal in 2008 to mark the University of London's 150th anniversary. At the foot of steps beyond, work was in progress in early 2016 to extend and develop the north wing of the Senate House building (p 78) for occupation by SOAS.

Descend the steps, and turning right go out through the gates into **MALET STREET**. Northwards on the east side is the erstwhile front of Birkbeck College, completed in 1951 by Adams, Holden & Pearson and officially opened the following year by University Chancellor, Queen Elizabeth the Queen Mother. Inscribed above the first doorway are two other key dates in the College's history: 1823, when it was founded by Dr George Birkbeck as the Mechanics Institution, for the education of working men (its first women students were admitted seven years later); and 1885, when it moved from its earlier home in Southampton Buildings (off Chancery Lane) into nearby Breams Buildings. The Institution changed its name to the Birkbeck Literary & Scientific Institution in 1866, becoming Birkbeck College in 1907 and officially part of the University of London in 1920. Also above the door, the motto *In nocte consilium* (study by night) denotes the college's promotion of evening study, as do the heraldic owl and oil lamps to be encountered further along the frontage.

Facing us across Malet Street is the east side of the London School of Hygiene and Tropical Medicine (see p 78), surmounted by a frieze honouring, in large letters, six of the great and the good in public health. The frieze continues round the building's south and west sides (to be viewed later), where a further 17 names are displayed. Among the 23, not one woman is included: some say Florence Nightingale was rejected because her surname was too long to fit, though room was evidently found for Max von Pettenkofer, a rather obscure Bavarian apothecary with an equally lengthy name.

Malet Street was developed only in 1906-07, sweeping away Keppel Mews North, whose line it followed, and parallel Little Torrington Street and Torrington Mews to the east. The new street was named after the diplomat Sir Edward Malet (d.1908), who had served as ambassador in Berlin; he was the husband of Lady Ermyntrude Russell, daughter of the 9th Duke of Bedford (and sister of Sackville and Herbrand, the 10th and 11th Dukes respectively).

Next along the west side, sporting three tiered balconies of different sizes and design, is the imposing rear elevation of Warwickshire House, dating from 1912. It was built as a hostel for women employees of the former Oxford Street department store Bourne & Hollingsworth. Facilities provided for the residents included a library, ballroom and swimming pool. The building is now accessed only from its other side, in Gower Street (p 76). The hostel was damaged in the severe air raid of 16/17 April 1941.

Likewise extending through to Gower Street, the **Royal Academy of Dramatic Art** (RADA) next door was a victim of the same Luftwaffe attack, and was rebuilt in the 1950s. In 2001, Avery Associates Architects completed the latest remodelling of RADA's interior (including the Vanbrugh Theatre) and replaced the previous Malet Street frontage with a stylish opaque glass bow front.

North of that is the University of London's **College Hall,** where Lady Lockyer, one of the founders of its previous incarnation in Byng Place (p 107), laid its foundation stone in 1931; the architect was W J Walford. The building cost £65,000 and had accommodation for

165 female students. For the duration of WWII, College Hall was leased to the King George & Queen Elizabeth Victoria League, (founded in 1901 as the Victoria League for Commonwealth Friendship), which during WWI and WWII ran clubs for overseas servicemen in London. The Club here, apparently opened originally with funding by the Nuffield Trust, could accommodate up to 400 men; facilities included a barber's and a tailor's shop. 350 Canadian soldiers were sleeping in the Club when, in the aforementioned air raid, it was struck by a parachute bomb and 17 people lost their lives. ARP Warden Graham Greene helped rescue the survivors.

According to a stone atop the building, adjacent **Dilke House** was erected in 1914. It was named in memory of Sir Charles Wentworth Dilke (d.1911), a noted Liberal and Radical politician, and a champion of the trade union movement. For much of its existence, it was home to the National Amalgamated Union of Shop Assistants, Warehousemen and Clerks (now USDAW, the Union of Shop Distributive & Allied Workers, since relocated in 2012 to TUC Congress House (p 43) and subsequently to Manchester. Pevsner describes Dilke House, by Lander, Bedells & Crompton, as 'a well-proportioned classical front skilfully coping with seven storeys'.

The last building on the east side of Malet Street, next to Birkbeck and by the same architects, is what was originally known as the University of London Union. Founded in 1921, this intercollegiate students' union moved here in 1958. In 2013 the University announced that it was to be abolished. Removed from student control and now staffed by the University, the building has been revamped and rebranded as **Student Central**.

On reaching Torrington Place (p 90), turn left beside Waterstones, and then left again into **GOWER STREET**. This took its name from Lady Gertrude Leveson-Gower, the wife of the 4th Duke of Bedford, and a daughter of the Earl of Gower. The street was entirely renumbered in 1864, such that no house retained its original number. We now walk south along part of its now even-numbered east side (for the rest of the street, see pp 83-95).

Dating from about 1787, the surviving houses at **Nos.80-74** are of fairly uniform design with fanlights. The archaeologist Sir Charles Newton lived at No.74 with his artist wife Mary (née Severn), who painted portraits of Queen Victoria's children; she died here in 1866. By the 1880s the house was home to the Bedford Estate architect Charles Fitzroy Doll (incidentally the designer of the flamboyant Waterstones building we just passed). At demolished No.72, beyond, was the Ladies' Embroidery Teaching Guild run by Mary E Cutts, a Sister of Mercy of the Community of John the Baptist.

The remainder of the range southward to Keppel Street is entirely of the 20th century. At **Nos.62-64** we find the Gower Street entrance of RADA (p 75), adorned on either side with Masks of Comedy and Tragedy by Alan Durst. It was to a Georgian house at No.62 that RADA moved in 1905, having been founded the previous year by Sir Herbert Beerbohm Tree at His Majesty's Theatre in the Haymarket. Nos.62-64 were later replaced by Geoffrey Norman's 1927 building, with a donation of £5,000 from Bernard Shaw towards the cost.

Warwickshire House at Nos.56-58 preserves the name of the former Bourne & Hollingsworth staff hostel (p 75), but occupies only a 1920s extension to its large premises. Later becoming a nurses' home, the original 1912 block (at Nos.44-54) is now named **Bonham Carter House**, after Richard Bonham Carter, the pioneering paediatric cardiologist (at UCH, 1948-66). The building continues to serve as a residence for hospital staff, while also housing the Bloomsbury Healthcare Library and the 52 Club, the sports and social club for UCLH NHS Trust employees, with an inherited basement swimming pool. Walk along to its imposing stepped entrance where there is an Association of Anaesthetists plaque stating that the first (ether) anaesthetic was given in a house on this site on 19 December 1846. It was administered for a tooth extraction by dentist James Robinson (p 95) at No.48 (ex-No.24), the home of his friend, American physician and botanist Francis Boott. A few days later Robert Liston, professor of surgery at UCH, was to give the first *public* demonstration of an operation under anaesthetic at the hospital up the road.

The first house at No.54 was home to the eminent surgeon Luther Holden until his retirement around 1880, and then to Alexander Stuart Murray, Keeper of Greek and Roman Antiquities at the BM. No.52 was shared by photographer Alice Mary Hughes, who opened a portrait studio there in 1891; and her father, portrait painter Edward Hughes, who lived in the house until his death in 1907. The Irish genealogist John Burke (of *Peerage* fame), who died in 1848, lived latterly at No.50 (ex-No.25).

Houses at Nos.42-22, pulled down in 1911, in the wake of demolitions connected with the formation of Malet Street, included No.36, the home from 1856 of genre painter Abraham Solomon (**[25]** shows an example of his work). A 'Shakespeare Memorial Theatre' was proposed for the cleared site, to open in 1916 (the tercentenary of the Bard's death), but WWI intervened and the plans were shelved. Instead, the site was offered rent-free to the YMCA, who erected a 'Shakespeare Hut' of mock-Tudor design for the entertainment and reception of soldiers in transit. This stretch of Gower Street is now lined by the west side of the London School of Hygiene and Tropical Medicine.

Cross **KEPPEL STREET,** turn left along its south side. The now short street originally continued east to meet Russell Square. It was at first called New Store Street (appearing thus on a Bedford Estate map of 1795), but by 1800 had been renamed after Elizabeth Keppel (d.1768), the mother of the 5th and 6th Dukes of Bedford. Building began in 1807, but the small houses erected by the developer Thomas Lewis were not of the highest standard. It had a somewhat lurid reputation by late Victorian times. PC French, who accompanied Booth's researcher in 1898, told him there were no brothels, but the 'romantic actresses and music hall artistes' who stayed there often brought men home. When the leases

25 *'First Class – The Meeting'* by Abraham Solomon, 1862

fell in a few years later the entire street and the turnings off it were swept away.

Stand with your back to the long wall of the sunken garden on the right to view the front of the world-renowned **London School of Hygiene and Tropical Medicine** (opposite at No.1, now the street's only address). Founded in 1899 by Sir Patrick Manson in the London Docks, the London School of Tropical Medicine moved in 1920 to Endsleigh Gardens (p 111). The Rockefeller Foundation made a gift of $2 million for a building on the Keppel Street site, which was purchased for £52,000. A competition for the design of the School building was won by Morley Horder and Verner Rees. The foundation stone was laid on 7 July 1926 by the Minister of Health, Neville Chamberlain (whose father, Joseph, had been involved in founding the School). The building was opened by the Prince of Wales on 18 July 1929. With its Portland stone facings, it was one of London's first steel-framed buildings, although this did not prevent the destruction of one sixth of it in an air raid on 10 May 1941.

Over the entrance is a carving of two Greek gods associated with health, Apollo and Artemis, riding a chariot; this symbol, based on a Sicilian coin struck in 466 BC and designed by sculptor and medallist Allan Gairdner Wyon, is also used as the School's seal and logo. On the first-floor balconies are representations in gilded bronze of vectors of disease: louse, rat, bedbug, mosquito, flea, snake, tick and fly. High up on the façade is a continuation of the frieze encountered earlier (p 75), with the names of ten further pioneers of tropical medicine or public health, including Jenner, Chadwick, Lister and Pasteur. Added in 2004 to the building's interior was a new lecture theatre named after John Snow, who famously confirmed the link between cholera and a contaminated Soho water pump. Low down near the School's south-east corner is the 1926 foundation stone.

Once standing hereabouts was a wine and spirit shop established in 1860 at No.41 Keppel Street and trading there until its demolition. Two doors east of No.41, and so buried beneath Malet Street (p 75), is the site of No.39, the home from 1809 of the French-born draughtsman and artist Auguste Pugin; born there in 1812 was his only child, architect Augustus Welby Northmore Pugin, who became the leading figure of the Gothic Revival. They later moved to Great Russell Street (p 42). Facing their house was the former No.1, where the landscape artist John Constable lived with his wife Maria, and had a studio, from 1817 to 1822. Next door, in the early 1850s, No.2 was home to Charles James Richardson, Surveyor to the 5th Earl of Harrington and a former pupil of Soane. He designed many houses in Belsize Park but is chiefly remembered for his books on Tudor and Elizabethan architecture.

Near the base of the wall on the south side of the street is a boundary stone which reads 'SGB SGF 1823, refixed 1896' and marks the old parish boundary between St George's Bloomsbury and St Giles-in-the-Fields. Behind the wall, at basement level, is a large sunken garden. By 1914, the original long, individual back gardens of Nos.2-20 Gower Street (p 94) had been combined to form a communal area. Acquired by the University in 1951 as its own private garden, it features in John Wyndham's novel, *The Day of the Triffids*, which was published that year. With an entrance on the east side and named **Malet Street Gardens**, the secluded haven is now open to all, although only on summer weekdays from 11am to 3pm.

Cross over **MALET STREET** and following the former line of Keppel Street eastward, pass through the gates of **Senate House**. To our right, on the corner of one wing, is a bronze plaque to Mary Prince. Of African descent and born a slave in Bermuda, Mary was later brought by her owner to England, where slavery was no longer legal. Helped by the Anti Slavery Society, and having escaped her master's clutches, she worked in 1829 as a servant to Mrs Forsyth at No.4 Keppel Street. Mary's influential autobiography (1831), a first-hand description of the brutalities of enslavement, was the first account of a black woman's life to be published in the UK. A subsequent resident at No.4, from

1837 until his death in 1873, was Thomas Lupton, an innovative engraver who introduced the use of steel in mezzotinting.

Possibly the earliest building in old Keppel Street was a Particular Baptist Chapel, with seating for 500, built in 1795 for a congregation of Strict Baptists from Grafton Street (Soho). Set back from the north side, and backing onto the south side of Little Torrington Street, it was eventually accessed through an archway and along a narrow passageway beside No.34. That house was the home of the actress Maria Foote, who performed every season at Covent Garden from 1814 to 1825. She successfully sued a gentleman who had offered her marriage for breach of promise and was awarded £3,000 damages. The case made her even more famous and she played to packed houses until 1831, when she married the dandy 4th Earl of Harrington and retired from the stage. Living at No.34 in 1851 were physician Robert Davey and, in his care, John and Elizabeth Dickens. Census night that year (on 30 March) saw the presence, as visitors, of their son Charles and seven other Dickens family members and friends. Unrecorded in the Census was John Dickens who, having recently undergone a gruesome operation without anaesthetic, died before dawn.

It would be hard to miss the tower of Senate House which, at 209 feet, is regarded as London's first skyscraper. Since 1937, when the building opened, most of the tower has housed the University of London Library. Four storeys are accessible to readers, with eleven floors of book storage above.

To your left, at the foot of the tower is the foundation stone laid by King George V and Queen Mary on 26 June 1933. However, the University's plans for a purpose-built main building in Bloomsbury go back to before WWI, when Edwin Lutyens prepared a design embodying an open courtyard opposite the British Museum's new King Edward VII Galleries entered from Montague Place, to be surrounded by buildings on a New Delhi scale. Another design was suggested by Charles Fitzroy Doll. WWI interrupted these plans, and it was not until 1927 that land was purchased from the Bedford Estate with the aid of a grant from the Rockefeller Foundation. Appointed as architect in 1931 was Charles Holden, whose first plan **[26]** was for a colossal spinal building stretching north

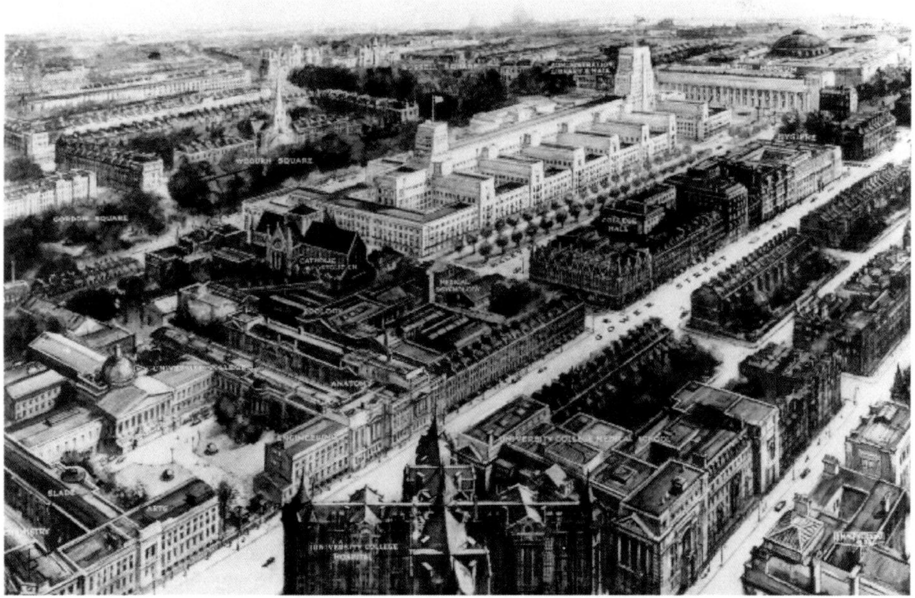

26 Bird's eye view of Bloomsbury, showing the original design for Senate House and the University precinct (*Illustrated London News*, 21 January 1933)

from a huge tower in Montague Place as far as Torrington Place and wholly wiping out Torrington Square. It was intended to house all University of London colleges. Holden's revised 1932 plan for a building occupying a much smaller space was necessitated both by a shortage of funds and by Birkbeck's demand for a separate building. Even so, the use of grey Cornish granite and Portland stone on the exterior suggests that little expense was spared in the materials used in its construction.

During WWII, Senate House was occupied by the Ministry of Information, the government department responsible for wartime propaganda. The building is said to have inspired Graham Greene, who briefly worked here for the MoI, to write *The Ministry of Fear* (1943). It is also thought to be the model of the Ministry of Truth in George Orwell's *1984*; Orwell's future wife Sonia Brownell, was employed in its Censorship Department. It was rumoured that Senate House was spared by the Luftwaffe because Hitler had earmarked it as a post-invasion HQ for his Nazi party; however, the building did sustain damage in an air raid on the night of 7/8 November 1940.

Enter the vestibule area of Senate House. The door on the right leads to the library, administrative offices and two large halls, one of them named after William Beveridge, University Vice-Chancellor (1926-28), who devised the 1940s welfare state reforms. The left-hand door led to the School of Slavonic and East European Studies until 2005, when it moved to its own premises in Taviton Street (p 111). Since a major remodelling of the building begun the next year, most of the Institutes of the School of Advanced Study have moved here from addresses nearby. Among them is the Institute of Historical Research; also here is the Human Rights Consortium and the Institute of Modern Languages.

Running north-south somewhere under Senate House is the line of former Torrington Street. An 1819 map suggests that this was meant to continue north as far as present-day Torrington Place, but was truncated when Torrington Square (p 74) was built. The satirical novelist and poet, Thomas Love Peacock lived at No.1 Torrington Street in the 1840s. Following the large-scale demolition of Keppel Street, Keppel Mews South and the surrounding area in the early 1900s, a new wide road was constructed. British Museum Avenue, partly on the line of Torrington Street, and linking Torrington Square with Montague Place, was intended as a grand northerly approach to the newly extended British Museum. A mooted further northward expansion of the museum failed to materialise, and the short-lived Avenue was never more than a roadway lined by hoardings covered with posters **[27]**.

Leave the Senate House foyer by its east door to continue along the old course of Keppel Street. A rectangular plaque on your right records the births of two brothers at a house 'on this site': in 1810 of the writer Thomas Adolphus Trollope, later to marry the sister of actress Ellen Ternan, Charles Dickens' mistress; and in 1815 of the novelist Anthony Trollope. Although the family moved out early in Anthony's life, Keppel Street and nearby Bedford Square are major settings in his novel *Lady Anna*. The plaque is wrongly positioned, as the Trollopes' home at No.16 was actually further along the street, near where erstwhile Russell Mews intersected. Later lodging in the house, in the 1880s, was the Irish politician Charles Stewart Parnell. His fellow lodger, Irish author Augustus Moore wrote of how Parnell, on coming home from Parliament 'armed with a pistol', would relax by playing with a toy train set.

More correctly sited is a second, Anglo Finnish Society, plaque to the social anthropologist Edward Westermarck, who lived at No.12 from 1897 to 1900. An earlier resident here was Lazarus Lee (formerly Levi), a dealer in ostrich feathers, with two industrious children: Elizabeth Lee, born in the house in 1857/58, a biographer, translator, and contributor of many articles to the *Dictionary of National Biography*; and (Sir) Sydney Lee who, as the dictionary's second editor, employed his elder sister as the only woman in an editorial team of ten.

Not quite opposite, No.27 Keppel

Street was home to the architect Robert Abraham, who in 1818 designed the now demolished county fire office at the top of Lower Regent Street. That year his wife Eliza, a noted flower painter, died at home aged only 40.

Finally, along on the left, we can take a closer look at the former Royal Institute of Chemistry building at No.30 Russell Square (p 66), and over its entrance the thoughtful seated figure, sculpted by Gilbert Bayes, of the father of British chemistry, Joseph Priestley (1733-1804). We have come almost full circle as we emerge into the Square. From here a short walk along the north side of Russell Square takes us to Bernard Street and the Russell Square Underground Station.

27 British Museum Avenue in 1919, looking north and lined by advertisements; in the foreground, a WWI tank presented to the Borough of Holborn

Route 6
Gower Street and UCL

A linear walk between Euston Square and Goodge Street Underground stations. For University College Hospital (UCH) and north-westerly turnings off Gower Street, see *Streets of Fitzrovia*.

We begin at the south exit from Euston Square station, at the north end of Gower Street. This walk will focus on that thoroughfare and on the institution that dominates its northern reaches, University College London (UCL).

First, though, we walk east along the south side of **EUSTON ROAD**, which forms Bloomsbury's northern boundary. Originally known as Euston Place, the Georgian houses built here beside the New Road (p 9) with their substantial front gardens, included No.215, the London base from 1916 of the Quinton Polyclinic (or Sea Water Dispensary). One of 69 free clinics in Europe and North Africa opened by French biologist René Quinton, it claimed to alleviate many different conditions by injections of his 'isotonic marine plasma', diluted plankton-rich seawater. The houses were supplanted by 20th-century buildings, among them a handsome, 'Arts & Crafts' Unity House, headquarters of the National Union of Railwaymen until its demolition in 1980; an unremarkable replacement Unity House of 1983 was short-lived. Covering its site today is the hi-tech glass-fronted **Gibbs Building**, by Hopkins Architects (2004), the administrative HQ of the Wellcome Trust. Named after Sir Roger Geoffrey Gibbs, the Trust's late Chairman, it has eight storeys at the front and four at the back, and a curved glazed roof enveloping a generous atrium.

Beyond it stands the earlier **Wellcome Building**, with emphatic Ionic columns on its elegant classical façade. It was built in 1931-32 by Septimus Warwick to house the laboratories and collection of medically-related objects of Sir Henry Wellcome (d.1936), co-founder of the pharmaceutical company. Between 1947 and 1989 it was also the headquarters of the firm (confusingly called the Wellcome Foundation). In 1986 it became the HQ of the Wellcome Trust, the medical charity into which all the profits of the company (since merged into GlaxoSmithKline) were poured. The building still houses the Wellcome Institute (now the UCL Centre) for the History of Medicine and the Wellcome Collection, with its museum and world-famous Wellcome Library of medical history.

On this site, at No.191, John Westland Marston, poet, playwright and friend of Dickens, died in 1890. His son, the poet Philip Bourke Marston, formed a literary club called 'The Vagabonds', which met monthly in the house.

Turn south along Gordon Street, and then shortly return westward along **GOWER PLACE**. This street's north side is now wholly lined by the backs of the Wellcome buildings old and new. Living here at former No.44 from 1825, and still working hard at his writing, was the septuagenarian political philosopher William Godwin along with Mary Jane (his second wife), his library and a servant called Jane. He left in 1833, when the onetime scourge of the Establishment was appointed Yeoman Usher of the Exchequer and given a small stipend by the Whig government, together with chambers at Westminster.

Dating from the early 19th century, the street's 3½-storey houses were still tinted on Charles Booth's 1898 poverty map in a 'fairly comfortable' pink. In the autumn of 1878, George Gissing had lodged with Nell Harrison in a single room at No.31, until obliged to leave for Huntley Street (west of Gower Street) 'in consequence of some unpleasantness'. In his later novel *Workers in the Dawn*, Arthur Golding and his girlfriend, the prostitute Carrie Mitchell, similarly move house between the same two streets.

No.3 on the south side is on the site

of a Hawarden Castle pub, named after Gladstone's north Wales estate. Here today is UCL's Health Centre (Farrell Grimshaw Partnership, 1972). This spans the entrance to **Gower Court**, the modern-day successor to erstwhile Little Gower Place. When, as man and wife, George and Nell Gissing returned to Gower Place in 1882, taking three rooms on the south side at No.15, they enjoyed not only the luxury of a 'proper kitchen' but also a view onto one side of UCL, across the near-slum that was Little Gower Place – coded a 'poor' light blue on Booth's map, and described in his notebook as occupied by 'costers and casuals', and characterised by 'broken windows, doors open, bread and vegetables left lying about, chickens and barrows'.

South of here was the site of an earlier, and most unusual, example of working-class housing, that was an important local landmark in the late 18th century. Mortimer's Folly was a row of twenty back-to-back cottages with small front gardens, aligned north-south near the eastern edge of the meadow called Bromfield, and with no apparent access road. A local watchman, giving evidence in court in 1792, described them as 'them little huts'. They had been speculatively built by Hans Winthrop Mortimer, the MP for Shaftesbury (who had bought up most of the houses in that town to secure his election), and who was the owner of Bromfield for some forty years until his death in 1807. (He was also the developer of Mortimer Market on the west side of his property, off Tottenham Court Road.)

The building now lining much of the south side of Gower Place, with a handsome classical façade, was designed by F M Simpson and opened in 1913 as the UCL chemistry laboratories. It was much later renamed the **Kathleen Lonsdale Building**, after the pioneer crystallographer who in the 1920s first applied Fourier analysis to X-ray images from crystals to elucidate molecular structures; she was Professor of Chemistry at UCL 1946-68 and the first woman elected (1945) to the Royal Society. Converted in 1985 with a new top floor, the premises now house a variety of college departments.

The large door beyond, marking the site of a second covered entrance into Little Gower Place, is part of an unusual Flemish-style building at **No.23**. Grade-II-Listed for its curiosity value, this late-Victorian beershop, the Barley Corn, has now been recycled as 'The Huntley', a student bar.

Reaching **GOWER STREET**, glance along to the right. The present exit here from **Euston Square Station** dates only from 2011. Its predecessor was set in the ground floor of No.140 Gower Street, an anonymous red-brick office block on the Euston Road corner. Officially opened on the Metropolitan Railway in January 1863, the station could claim to be the world's first completed railway station that was wholly underground. In the days of steam operation, the platforms were ventilated by shafts emerging in the front gardens of houses along Euston Road. The station was initially known, more accurately, as 'Gower Street'. The railway company ran a horse-bus 'feeder' service to it from Camden Town, and it may have been to this that Oscar Wilde alluded in *The Importance of Being Earnest* (1895), when Miss Prism recalls the upsetting, 'in younger, and happier, days', of 'a Gower Street omnibus'. The one-way motorbus service down the street itself dates only from the 1960s. Though lying at some distance from Euston Square, the station assumed its present name in 1909. Its surface buildings have been remodelled several times.

Until 1864 this northernmost end of Gower Street, on the southern edge of Lord Southampton's Tottenhall estate, was known as Gower Street North – not to be confused with modern North Gower Street beyond the Euston Road, at that time called George Street. The earliest building in Gower Street North, on the west side, was the Gower Street Chapel, erected in 1820 by 'seceding members' from William Huntingdon's Providence Chapel in Gray's Inn Road. From 1854 it was home to a Strict Baptist congregation, which remained here until 1917 when the chapel, one of the few buildings to survive the eastward expansion of Maple's, was sold to the company for £250. The Baptists moved to Shaftesbury Avenue, where their 'Gower Street Memorial Chapel' still stands, now a Chinese church.

Adjacent No.2 Gower Street North was home to the librarian (Sir) Anthony Panizzi from 1828 to 1837, when he was appointed the British Museum's Keeper of Printed Books. In the autumn of 1823 the family of Charles Dickens had taken a neighbouring house; his feckless father John was on the run from his creditors, while Mrs Dickens had the idea of opening a private school here. Young Charles was sent out to deliver circulars to local houses in the hope of attracting pupils, but none came and the project was a failure. John Dickens was arrested and imprisoned in the Marshalsea, and Charles was sent to work in a blacking warehouse.

On the south corner of Gower Place, No.136 (p 82) is UCL's **Lewis's Building**, which houses a students' union café. Lewis's medical bookshop was founded here (as noted on the plaque) in 1844 by Henry King Lewis, whose bust adorns the doorway of the shop's later rebuild of 1931-32. For over a century Lewis's was *the* source of books (and skeletons) for UCL medical students, until it was absorbed as a department of Dillon's down the road (p 91).

A little distance along the west side of Gower Street lies the entrance to the main campus of **University College London** (see map, **[28]**). Enter the Main Quad. The college occupies part of the land

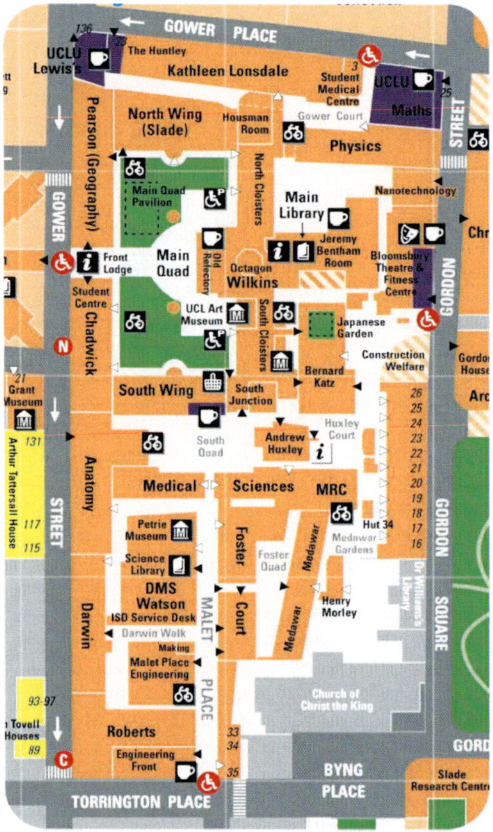

28 Map of the main campus of University College London

variously known in the 18th century as Bromfield or Brickfield, and owned for four decades by Hans Winthrop Mortimer (p 83). On his death in 1807 the land was bought by Sir William Paxton, a Scottish-born sailor and businessman, and sometime MP, with interests in South Wales. Plans were made for a residential development on the east side of his Bloomsbury property, to be called Carmarthen Square, but Paxton died in 1824 and the square was stillborn.

Its proposed 7½-acre site was acquired by a banker, David Bevan. But within a year three benefactors – Benjamin Shaw (MP and chairman of Lloyd's) and bankers John Smith and Isaac Lyon Goldsmid – had bought the land as a site for the proposed University of London. Here, unlike at Oxford or Cambridge (then the only universities in England), neither teachers nor students would be required to declare Anglican faith. Of the three benefactors, Goldsmid was Jewish and Shaw a Baptist. There was to be no teaching of theology, causing the institution, often referred to simply as 'Gower Street', to be nicknamed the 'Godless College'. The 'University of London' was founded as a limited company in 1826. Among its founders, all men of liberal and radical political views, were Henry Brougham and George Birkbeck, each already active in the foundation of Mechanics' Institutions.

Despite opposition from the clerical establishment, and the establishment of a rival King's College on the Strand, which 'preserved traditional values', the foundation stone of the university was laid on 30 April 1827 by the Duke of Sussex, the only son of George III who could be considered as having liberal leanings. Opened to students in October 1828, the University offered classes not only in such traditional Oxbridge subjects as mathematics, philosophy and classical languages, but also in newer subjects, including science and modern languages.

Despite their rivalry, in 1836 King's College and the Gower Street institution agreed to co-operate in the formation of an examining and degree-awarding body to be called the University of London, of which King's and the renamed University College would be constituents. William IV signed its charter on 28 November 1836.

The first architect of UCL, selected after public competition, was William Wilkins, whose later National Gallery was much derided. As originally designed, the main block facing Gower Street, predominantly in Portland stone, was to have two projecting wings, but these materialised only later, and not to Wilkins' designs.

The building of UCL was distinctly fitful, and the imposing portico of the **Wilkins Building** had nothing much behind it until the Main Library was built there in 1849. The dome and much of the central block were badly damaged in WWII and were afterwards rebuilt by Sir Albert Richardson (1880-1964). He was UCL's Professor of Architecture for 27 years, designing many of its buildings. A president of the Royal Academy, he had a passion for all things 18th-century, including art, clothes, candles (he eschewed electricity at home) and the sedan chair. He was the founder of the Georgian Group.

The rotunda under the dome was restored in the 1990s. Flaxman's St Michael was brought into it out of the cold of the portico where it had languished for many years, and his sculpted plaques depicting various acts of charity, which are set in the plaster of the wall, were cleaned. The grand façade of the Grade-I-Listed Wilkins Building has featured as a backdrop in numerous TV programmes and films, memorably posing as the entrance to St Swithin's Hospital in *Doctor in the House* (1954) and its sequels. In *The Mummy Returns* (2001) it masquerades as the British Museum, while in *Gladiator* (2000) the quadrangle serves as ancient Rome.

The present **South Wing**, at right angles to Gower Street, was finally built in 1869-76 to house University College School (UCS). This was founded in 1830 by some of University's proprietors, to provide a classical education for boys (day pupils, not boarders), preparing them to go on, at age 16, to attend the University itself. The school's principles were similar to those of the college, with admission open to the sons of parents of any religion or none. There was to be no religious teaching, nor, unusually, any corporal punishment. The school, first opened with 136 pupils in a house at No.16 Gower Street and known as 'London University School' moved into the University in 1832, occupying rooms behind the portico, and with a playground on a large plot of still undeveloped land fronting Gower Street to the south. When the University's name was changed four years later, the school followed suit, briefly becoming the Junior School of University College and then UCS in 1838. This moved to Frognal, Hampstead in 1907.

Behind the white 'Main Quad Pavilion' (a semi-permanent venue for miscellaneous events), the north wing of UCL houses the prestigious **Slade School of Fine Art**, founded following a bequest from Felix Slade and built in 1871-81. By 1891 the south wing had made a 90° turn and was edging north along Gower Street, some early-19th century houses being demolished to make way for it. The new building, the south-west wing, erected for the Department of Engineering, begun in 1891 and completed 1923 by Richardson, is now the **Chadwick Building**, named after the sanitary reformer Edwin Chadwick. The north-west wing, built in 1913-14 by F M Simpson for the new Bartlett School of Architecture, is now called the **Pearson Building**, after the statistician Karl Pearson. In 1984-85, both of these wings were extended towards the lodges by Sir Hugh Casson, so ingeniously that the extensions are scarcely perceptible as being of a later date.

Walk over to the **UCL Art Museum**, to the right of the main portico. It houses over 10,000 prints, drawings and other artworks dating from the 1490s to the present day, and is open to the public on weekday afternoons. From here, a right turn and a few further steps will lead you to UCL's oddest possession – the 'auto-icon' of Jeremy Bentham, the Utilitarian philosopher often regarded as the founder of UCL, but whose influence at the age of 78 was more spiritual than practical. When he died in 1832, he left careful instructions regarding the dissection of his body and its preservation as his auto-icon. Previously in the custody of Southwood Smith and kept in Percy Street, Fitzrovia, it was offered in March 1850 to Henry Brougham, the President of University College Council. Smith's offer was readily accepted, and so UCL became the effigy's unintended final resting place. Here, seated in a glass-fronted cabinet, in a pose suggestive of deep thought, is Bentham's skeleton, padded with straw, dressed in his own clothes, and with a wax model of his head. An inscription declares the head itself to have been placed in the college safe. The head was preserved by being desiccated, somewhat unsuccessfully, and is now kept in controlled atmospheric conditions at UCL.

Back in the Main Quad, observe the twin domed, octagonal, long disused Observatories (of 1905-07), before returning to **GOWER STREET**. Opposite on the west side here is the unusual Neo-Gothic edifice in red brick and terracotta known today as the **Cruciform Building**, originally built as University College Hospital (see *Streets of Fitzrovia*). Turning left down the east side, note the elaborate **plaque** on the wall of the Chadwick Building, erected in 1933 by the Trevithick Centenary Memorial Committee. It states that '*Close to this place Richard Trevithick..., Pioneer of High Pressure Steam ran in the year 1808 the first steam locomotive to draw passengers'*. The Cornishman's intention was to demonstrate that transport by rail could be faster than by horse. Laying down a circular track within a circular palisade, he charged a shilling for admission to his 'Steam Circus', which included a ride behind his engine, named *Catch Me Who Can* **[29]**. But the trackwork proved weak, and a lack of public interest led Trevithick to abandon railway locomotion. The exact location of the event has been controversial, some sources placing it 'near Lady Southampton's Nursery', and thus nearer to what became Euston Square; but other evidence suggests that it was indeed close by, on the UCL site.

The section of Gower Street southward to Torrington Place was known as Upper Gower Street until 1864, when the whole length of modern Gower Street was radically renumbered, with odd numbers on the west side and evens opposite. For most of the 19th century the street remained residential, home to a host of academics, artists, architects, doctors and lawyers. The character of the street changed radically in 1892, when UCL's rights over the roadway were bought by St Pancras Vestry for the colossal sum of £15,000, and the bar-gates marking it as a private road were removed.

On the west side, and on the corner of University Street, are the east face of the former UCH Medical School, and the pretentiously grand (hardly ever used) entrance to its library. This part of the building now houses the UCL **Grant Museum of Zoology,** established by Robert Edmond Grant in 1828 as a teaching collection. It contains 67,000 exhibits, including a quagga and a dodo.

Demolished houses on this site included No.29 Upper Gower Street (UGS), home in 1856-69 to a close friend of Charles Dickens, the solicitor Frederic Ouvry, whose neighbour at No.30 was the genre and portrait painter Emily Osborn. This house had earlier been occupied by the barrister Edward Ryan, later FGS and FRS and knighted, until his appointment in 1826 as a judge in Calcutta. Back in England in 1843 he became a privy councillor, railway commissioner and in 1871-74 Vice-Chancellor of London University. In February 1898, Eleanor Marx (p 48) lodged at erstwhile No.135 while her partner Edward Aveling was in UCH for an operation.

All the original houses on the east side of the street are long gone, having gradually been replaced in the 20th century by a succession of extensions to UCL. On your left, with a busily ornamented classical front, is the **Anatomy Building**, designed by Richardson and opened in 1923 by King George V. On this site lived the art patron Lewis Pocock FSA (p 50), who died here at No.126 (No.20 UGS), aged 80 in 1882. A true polymath, and a friend of the scientist Michael Faraday, Pocock patented in 1852 a scheme for 'electric lighting combined with the production of colour and power', and another for purifying sea water.

29 Trevithick's 1808 'Steam Circus' on the UCL site; also showing (upper right) the back-to-back cottages of Mortimer's Folly

Surviving on the west side is a long terrace of original houses, some much altered. The first eight, of four storeys plus basement and with cast-iron balconies, were built in 1811-19 on Sir William Paxton's land, the former Mortimer estate. Now occupying nine houses at Nos.115-131 is **Arthur Tattersall House**, UCL student accommodation named after a former Secretary of the college who died in 2005.

Living at **No. 129** (No.32 UGS) in 1844-46 was Henry Wylde, the composer and conductor who later founded the London Academy of Music. The same house was the refuge in 1858-59 of Lajos (Louis) Kossuth, the Hungarian patriot, who lived in England for eight years after his failed attempt to make Hungary independent. He had been much fêted on his arrival in England in 1851, soon after which some 12,000 'respectable artisans' had formed a parade in Russell Square to march to Copenhagen Fields in Islington and hear him speak. Since 2015 the house has borne a blue plaque to Sir Victor Horsley, who lived here from 1882 to 1885. He is widely regarded as the world's first neurosurgeon and took a leading role in eradicating rabies from Britain. He also campaigned for women's suffrage and temperance.

Edward Turner, UCL's first Professor of Chemistry, lived at No.38 UGS in 1829-32, as three decades later did the organ builder William Hedgeland. By 1903, as **No.117**, the house was the base of the Upholsterers' Club, a social club with 130 members, maintained (according to the Fabian Sidney Webb) 'by the sale of beer and a billiard table'. Housed at **No.115** in the 1930s was the Bureau of Human Heredity, founded in 1933 by a group of eugenicists to collate information about human genetics.

On the east side, houses at Nos.106-112 were replaced in the late 19th century by a large building owned by Shoolbred's, the Tottenham Court Road department store, containing dormitories for some 300 company employees and provided with a library and a billiards room. In the 1930s it became a YMCA hostel for Indian students. This building, together with a range of houses bomb-damaged in 1941, in turn gave way to a further UCL extension. Now lining the street, with a plain white-stone façade, is the Biological Sciences Building, built in 1959-64 by Richardson's practice and now known as the **Darwin Building**.

On this site, No.15 UGS (later No.116 Gower Street) was home in 1827-32 to an elderly Francis Douce, antiquary and Keeper of Manuscripts at the British Museum. His morbid fear of being buried alive led him to leave £200 to an eminent surgeon on condition that either his head be cut off, or his heart removed, to ensure he was dead. Living at No.14 UGS (later No.114) for 28 years until his death in 1858 was John Pritt Harley, an actor and singer, renowned for his portrayal of Shakespearean clowns. Exceedingly thin, he was satirically nicknamed 'Fat Jack'.

No.10 UGS (No.106) in 1866-67 was successively home to two painters, first to Simeon Solomon and then to Sir Edward John Poynter, soon to become the first Slade Professor at UCL, and later Director of the National Gallery (1894) and President of the Royal Academy.

Living for thirty years from 1836 at No.9 UGS was Thomas Chitty, a member of the family of lawyers and legal writers who lent their name to Chitty Street in Fitzrovia. The same house, as No.104, housed (1874-75) John Rylands, the philanthropic textile manufacturer and merchant, whose widow founded the eponymous library in Manchester in his memory. He was followed in 1877 by the civil engineer Edwin Clarke, who worked with Robert Stephenson on his Menai Straits Bridge, patented telegraph equipment and designed boat lifts, including the well-known surviving example at Anderton (Cheshire). A later resident was the art collector Isaac Falcke, whose collection of Wedgwood ware was one of the largest ever assembled in Britain, and who died at No.104 in 1909.

An early resident at No.12 UGS (later No.110 Gower Street) was Leonard Horner, factory inspector, educational reformer and geologist, appointed Warden of UCL in 1827. But the house's greatest claim to fame was as the first marital home of Charles Darwin (see the LCC commemorative blue plaque). Darwin moved in before his wedding, on 29 January 1829, followed after it by his bride Emma Wedgwood. The couple nicknamed their furnished let 'Macaw Cottage', on account of its yellow curtains, garish blue walls and red plush furniture. Their two eldest children were born here. Ever plagued by digestive problems, Darwin was often unwell during his time in Gower Street; even so, he was able to write, before taking his family to live at Down House (Kent) in September 1842, an unpublished 35-page sketch of his theory of evolution.

In 1871, and for seven years, the house became a Polish Catholic chapel, under Rev. Emeric Podolski, while exactly opposite Darwin's plaque, on the west side of the street and signalled by a Papal flag, is Newman House, the University's Catholic Chaplaincy at **No.111**. This was previously a girls' hostel of the Sisters of Mercy of St Vincent de Paul, and earlier still (1875-77) home to the artist John Surtees. It is part of a range of houses erected on land owned by Lord Southampton, extending east from Tottenham Court Road and called the Tottenham Court Six Acre Close.

Resident at next-door **No.113** (No.40 UGS) in 1827-49 was the Staffordshire-born landscape painter Peter De Wint, and living on in the house until her own death was his wife Harriet, whose brother, the painter William Hilton RA, had died here in 1839. By the end of the century, Nos.107-113 had become the Mills University Hotel.

No.107 (No.43 UGS) was home in 1856-61 to the Scottish genre and history painter Alexander Johnston. A later lodger here, in 1907, was 'Chicago May' Churchill, an Irish-American thief and blackmailer, whose *modus operandi* was to pick up a respectable man in a hotel bar, spike his drinks and then bring him in a stupor to her bed. There he and May would be 'surprised' by her accomplice (and lover), posing as her husband, who would threaten to pursue the poor fellow in the courts unless a large sum of money was handed over.

Much altered **No.105**, now a private students' residence, was for six decades the headquarters of the Royal National Institute for the Deaf (now Action on Hearing Loss). A rectangular black tablet recalls its opening in 1936 by King George VI 'while Duke of York'. In 1971, the charity expanded into Nos.101&103, so becoming landlord to the Magic Circle in their hideaway at the rear of **No.103**, where they stayed for two decades from 1968. This house, which had latterly served as the Queen's Court Hotel, had been home in 1861-85 to the landscape painter Alexander Davis Cooper.

A wrought-iron lamp standard is preserved outside **No.101**. Here in 1791-95 (at No.46 UGS) lived William Marsden, orientalist and numismatist, who had been with the East India Company in Sumatra, of which he wrote a history; he later became First Secretary of the Admiralty and vice-president of the Royal Society. In 1846 the house witnessed the death of the physician George Man Burrows, who much earlier had founded the Association of Surgeon Apothecaries and was instrumental in the passing of the Apothecaries Act, 1815. Retiring from general practice, he had written on insanity and established two lunatic asylums. Much later residents at No.101 were stained-glass artists Horace Wilkinson and Arthur J Dix, who lived here c.1939.

No.99, now housing the *Chinese Weekly*, a newspaper targeting the Chinese community in the UK, was for half a century home to *The Spectator.* But the house had a murkier past, as a 'Temple of the Occult'. Lodging here in 1901 were two religious fraudsters, Frank Dutton Jackson and Edith Loleta Jackson, *alias* Theo Horos and Edith Swami **[30]**, of the spurious Theocratic Unity & Purity League. Dressed as Eastern mystics, they lured impressionable young women to a dimly lit room stuffed with religious paraphernalia, where they were seduced with a promise that the children they conceived would be 'divine', and relieved of their money and valuables. Both swindlers were eventually arrested, tried and convicted, receiving lengthy prison sentences.

Across yet another old estate boundary, Nos.87-97, with their pleasing doorways and fanlights, were built c.1789 on the

30 Edith Loleta Jackson, aka Edith Swami, bogus 'Eastern mystic'

Duke of Bedford's Cantlowes Close property. Nos.93-97 now form **John Tovell House**, further UCL student accommodation. Living at **No.97** (No.48 UGS), for 17 years before his death in 1841, was another polymath, Rev. Thomas Rackett, FSA, FRS, FLS, antiquary, draughtsman and musician, and student of astronomy and conchology. He was succeeded here in 1842 by John Royle, FRS, a surgeon, naturalist and collector of oriental plants.

An accountancy firm now occupies **No.91**, where a blue plaque recalls the immensely influential architect George Dance the Younger, who as Surveyor to the City of London designed a new Newgate Prison and, locally, the original Alfred Place. Also an artist, he was a founding member of the Royal Academy. On his death here, at what was No.51 UGS, he was buried in St Paul's Cathedral. At **No.89** (No.52 UGS), in 1827–1832, lived Rev. William Agutter, Chaplain and Secretary to the Asylum for Female Orphans in Lambeth. He was famous for his sermons, many railing against the slave trade. The house is now occupied by the Institute of Measurement & Control.

Every vanished house on the east side of the street could boast residents of some note. No.100 (No.7 UGS) was the intermittent home from 1838 of Dr Frederic Septimus Leighton, lately appointed lecturer in forensic medicine at the Middlesex Hospital; and of his son Frederic, the future painter (Lord) Leighton, who was enrolled aged about eight at University College School, which he sporadically attended when the family was not travelling abroad. The house was later the long-term home of the historian Mary Anne Everett Green (née Wood), author of the scholarly *Lives of the Princesses of England*, and editor of 41 volumes of state papers. Moving here with her parents in 1841, four years later she married the artist George Pycock Green. In 1851 she signed (along with Dickens, Carlyle and Macaulay) a petition in support of free access to public records for literary researchers. Her grandson, the classical scholar Andrew Gow, was born in 1886 at No.100, where Mary remained until her death in 1895.

Living at No.98 (No.6 UGS) in 1789–1836 was barrister William Bentham, a collector of topographical books and prints, and noted for the nectarines that grew on three trees in his back garden. Joint tenants in 1873 were George Cook, artist in stained glass, and the designer Bruce James Talbert, regarded as one of the pioneers of the Aesthetic Movement.

The barrister James Parke, later a senior judge and ennobled in 1856 as Baron Wensleydale, lived for twelve years at No.96 (No.5 UGS) after his marriage in 1817. Subsequent occupants were the eminent mathematician and historian Augustus de Morgan, who lived here for six years from 1831 before moving south to today's No.35 (p 93); and the Danish botanist Nathaniel Wallich, FRS, who died in the same house in 1858.

No.94 (No.4 UGS) was home to the philologist Hensleigh Wedgwood, grandson of the potter Josiah and cousin of Charles Darwin, until his death there in 1891. Inhabitants at No.92 (No.3 UGS) included the topographer and legal writer William Dickinson Rastell in 1789-92, and in 1847-51 serjeant-at-law William Ballantine, renowned for his brilliant powers of cross-examination. Much later, No.90 housed two of the last private residents in this part of Gower Street, serving for many years as the townhouse of the politician Sir Alfred Duff Cooper (1st Viscount Norwich) and his wife, the actress and society hostess Lady Diana Cooper. When the couple were bombed out in 1941, murals painted by Rex Whistler were removed from the house and installed in a dining room at UCL.

On reaching **TORRINGTON PLACE**, turn left along its north side. This part of the street began as an easterly extension of Francis Street, assuming its present name in the 1830s. The large bookshop on the south side (strictly, No.82 Gower Street) is now a branch of **Waterstones**. The building it occupies was erected in 1908 as a co-operative venture between private developers and the University of London, which owned the site. Its design in red brick and terracotta was by Charles Fitzroy Doll, and its kinship with his flamboyant Russell Hotel (p 59) is immediately apparent. With its gabled skyline and sweeping decoration, and numerous gargoyles depicting mythical beasts, the block was described by English Heritage, with some restraint, as in 'elaborate Franco-Flemish-Gothic style'. The block originally contained a variety of small shops, and into one of these, in 1956, moved the entrepreneurial bookseller Una Dillon. Transferring her stock from Store Street (p 96), and in partnership with the University, she opened here the eventually world-renowned Dillon's University Bookshop. This thrived and gradually expanded to occupy the entire block, as well as spawning branches at many other universities, but the chain was sold in 1977 to the Pentos retail group, who advertised the Bloomsbury shop with a cheeky poster in a Charing Cross Road bus shelter right opposite its rival, Foyles: 'Foyled again? Try Dillons'. Waterstones, who took over Dillon's in 1995, have named their café Dillons Coffee.

Looming over the street's north side is the 11-storey **Roberts Building**, housing UCL's Department of Engineering. Designed by Professor Hector Corfiato and opened in 1961, it takes its name from the engineer Sir Derek Roberts, who twice served as Provost of UCL. It is now largely masked by its 'Engineering Front' (Grimshaw Architects, 2008) which, with its ground-floor café, is intended to add a 'public face' to the UCL campus, many of whose buildings look inwards.

Beyond it is the imposing entrance to **Malet Place**. Extinguished as a public 'highway' in 1983, this now serves as a 'public gateway' into UCL's main campus, of which it is an integral part. Assuming that at least the side gate is open, make a short detour north along it; the campus map (p 84) will aid navigation.

Originally a stabling area for houses in Gower Street, and known as Upper Gower Mews, the former street was later colonised by Shoolbred's, who erected several buildings here for the manufacture and warehousing of its furnishing products. After the closure of the Tottenham Court Road department store in 1931, most of its premises here were soon acquired by UCL. **Foster Court**, on the east side of Malet Place, also served during WWII as a Civil Defence depot, but on its wall is a reminder of an earlier conflict. Facing 'Darwin Walk', an inconspicuous black stone tablet bears a now hardly legible list of residents of University College Hall who lost their lives in WWI; the memorial was brought here after that residence (in suburban Ealing) was closed in 1948.

Further along, in a covered entry, a plaque records the naming of Foster Court in 1933 after Sir T Gregory Foster, UCL's first Provost from 1904-29. The passageway leads to the 'Foster Quad', on the far side of which is the **Medawar Building**. Set at an angle, reflecting a kink in the old estate boundary, this was bought by UCL in 1933 to house the Zoology department. Sir Peter Medawar, the Nobel Prize-winning immunologist, was Professor of Zoology here in 1951-62. The building had been Shoolbred's bedding factory, and the courtyard once had a glazed roof to protect mattresses in transit from the rain. Surmounted by an 18th-century lantern, its entrance also boasts a fine pair of door handles cast in the image of Adam and Eve, while overlooking them from across the Quad is a Georgian clock turret, with a handsome timepiece inscribed '1937'. Known as 'Richardson's follies', all were trophies of Sir Albert Richardson, who salvaged artefacts from demolished buildings elsewhere in London in order to embellish UCL. In the 2005 film *Batman Begins*, the exterior of the Medawar Building serves as that of the Gotham City police department.

Back in Malet Place, the footway northward burrows beneath a range of buildings erected in 1909 and 1912 for the Departments of Physiology and Pharmacology, and known today as the **Medical Sciences Building.** On the sites of this block, and of the 'South Quad' beyond it, lay the old playground **[31]** of University College

School (p 85). Do not venture through the tunnel, but turn back south.

The small 2-storey building on the west side of Malet Place is a former Shoolbred's stable block (a horse ramp is preserved within), but whose basement once contained a mineral water factory. Here today is the **Petrie Museum** of Egyptian Archaeology, housing some 80,000 objects, including antiquities sold to UCL in 1913 by the Egyptologist Flinders Petrie, another former UCL professor. It contains a large collection of mummy portraits (1st to 3rd centuries AD) from Roman Egypt.

Next door, and now housing UCL's Science Library, is the **DMS Watson Building**, named after palaeontologist David Meredith Seares Watson, once the college's Jodrell Professor of Zoology and Comparative Anatomy. The 5-storey block once contained more Shoolbred's stables and further dormitories for the firm's employees (cf. p 88). It later housed both the headquarters of the Library Association (named Chaucer House), and the National Central Library, forerunner of the British Library Lending Division, whose upper floors were destroyed by enemy bombing in April 1941, along with half of its vast book stock. Both bodies moved to the Store Street area in the 1960s (p 96).

South of 'Darwin Walk', UCL's Malet Place **Engineering Building** (of 2005, by Grimshaw) stands on the pre-WWII site of the Tavistock Institute of Medical Psychology (p 103), which

31 University College and school playground, 1833

included a lecture theatre and canteen, and a playroom for child patients.

From the Torrington Place gateway, retrace your steps to **GOWER STREET**, cross over to its west side and continue south. (For the east side here, see pp 76-77.) Named after Lady Gertrude Leveson-Gower, the wife of the 4th Duke of Bedford, and a daughter of the Earl of Gower, the street was begun at its southernmost end around 1780. From the start it was criticised for its plainness, and to help relieve the monotony the Bedford Estate subsequently added some stuccoed doorways. The houses underwent a radical renumbering in 1864.

The austerity of **Nos.85-51** is relieved somewhat by their doorways and railings. Today's small family-run hotels are successors to the boarding-houses that opened here in the late 19th century. An earlier resident was William Morice, a Church of England clergyman who served the Society for the Propagation of the Gospel for 51 years, for many of them as its Secretary; he died at No.67 (when No.53) in 1819.

Beyond Chenies Street, Nos.49 to 15A are of a more traditional and unadorned Georgian style. Much of the brickwork has yet to be rid of the blackening caused by 150 years of soot from coal fires. **No.49** (ex-No.62) was the birthplace of jurist John George Phillimore in 1808; although he wrote extensively on jurisprudence, he was unpopular both among the legal profession and as a Liberal MP for Leominster from 1851, such that in 1857 the Liberal chief whip (Sir William Hayter) stated a preference for a Tory instead of so 'inconvenient' an MP. **No.43** (ex-No.65) is known to be home to the actor John Bannister and his actress and singer wife Elizabeth (née Harper): he died there in 1836, she in 1849. In the basement of **No.31** the young Joe Orton took lodgings when he first came to London in 1951 to join RADA; a few months later he moved in with Kenneth Halliwell. Present-day **No.35** (ex-No.69) was the second Gower Street home of the eminent mathematician and historian Augustus De Morgan **[32]**; born here in 1839 was his son, the potter and novelist William Frend De Morgan, who was to become well known for his ceramic tiles. Since 1970 this has been the London Study Centre of the Florida-based Eckerd College. At the end of this stretch **Nos.17-21** have decorative fanlights.

Just past Store Street, and now part of the Staunton Hotel, **No.13** (when No.80) was home from the 1830s to the conchologist Hugh Cuming, for much of the time as an invalid; he had spent the previous decade as a sail-maker in Chile (where his mistress bore him two children). In his 'Cumingian Museum' at No.80 he kept the vast collection of shells he had amassed on voyages to Polynesia, South America and the Philippines. Although he was elected a fellow of the Linnean Society and his specimens were widely used by eminent zoologists, others regarded his work as a shell dealer with disdain. After his death in 1865, his collection was purchased for the nation for £6,000.

Jonathan Cape opened his book publishing firm at **No.11** in 1921, moving to Bedford Square four years later (p 58). Later living and working here (1943-73) was the writer and literary agent Robert Aickman who, with his wife Ray, and Tom (L T C) and Angela Rolt, founded the Inland Waterways Association and campaigned vigorously to revive and preserve Britain's canals (witness a recently erected plaque).

Past **No.9** is the narrow entrance into **GOWER MEWS**. Originally developed in

32 Augustus de Morgan, mathematician and historian

the 1770s, this was one of three streets of coach houses and stables for coachmen and horses belonging to residents of Bedford Square (p 51). The south side of the Mews retains its original buildings, though garages have replaced stables. The flat at **No.19** on the left was the early scene of a decade-long affair between theatre costume and set designer Dorothy Glover and novelist Graham Greene: they were both air raid wardens. On 14/15 October 1940, a high-explosive bomb wrecked the west end of the Mews. Lining its north side are **Gower Mews Mansions**, of 1930s origin; the freeholder was Percy Hill, a Holborn Councillor and twice Mayor (1929-31) – hence the existence, to this day, of an organisation called the Hill Tenants Association, covering properties here and in neighbouring Store Street (p 95).

Back in **GOWER STREET**, no fewer than nine window openings, in brick, enliven the side wall of both houses flanking the entrance to the mews. South of this the theatrical genre painter and engraver George Clint lived at **No.7** (ex-No.83) for at least twenty years from 1817; his studio here became a meeting-place of the leading actors and actresses of the day. Living in the same house with his parents, from 1844 to 1854, was the young (Sir) John Millais. A child prodigy, he had first exhibited at the Royal Academy in 1840, aged only eleven. After studying at Sass's Academy (p 34), he progressed to the RA Schools, where he met Holman Hunt and Rossetti; and as the blue plaque on No.7 recalls, the Pre-Raphaelite Brotherhood was founded here in 1848.

An early occupant of **No.3** (ex-No.85) was the actor William Farren; he lived here for some nine years until his death in 1795, when his actor-manager son Percy (p 74) was also resident. Occupying separate floors here in 1916, in a house then owned and lately vacated by John Maynard Keynes (p 105), were the writer Katherine Mansfield with her lover John Middleton Murry, and the painters Dora Carrington and Dorothy Brett. Katherine did not enjoy her year-long stay at No.3, accusing Dora of spying on her friends.

The southernmost house on the east side of Gower Street is **No.2**, where a blue plaque records the residence here, until her death in 1929, of the author and suffragist Dame Millicent Garrett Fawcett. She had moved here with her daughter Philippa after the death in 1884 of her supportive husband, the (blind) Liberal MP Henry Fawcett. He and Millicent had been co-founders of Newnham Hall (later College) in Cambridge, where Philippa studied mathematics. Already installed in the house was Millicent's sister and fellow suffragist Agnes Garrett, a skilled interior designer, who ran a flourishing decorating business from No.2. Her equally talented cousin, Rhoda Garrett, had been her business partner until her untimely death in 1882; Agnes lived on in the house until 1935. Nowadays, the recently refurbished No.2, together with No.11 Bedford Square (p 51), is part of the central London outpost of Egham-based Royal Holloway University of London (founded by Thomas Holloway, p 39).

The houses at Nos.4-18 are now occupied by various parts of Birkbeck College. The journalist and politician Vernon Bartlett was living at **No.6** before he emigrated to Singapore in 1954. Living at **No.8** (ex-No.4) from 1810 was Luke Hansard, the printer to the House of Commons, whose name is now synonymous with the verbatim records of both Houses of Parliament. Later on, from 1876, the house was home to the postage-stamp dealer Stanley Gibbons.

An early resident at **No.10** (ex-No.5) was the physician and magistrate Sir Richard Ford. Living with him was the actress Mrs Jordan (real name, Dorothy Phillips), who as his mistress bore him two daughters, and a son who died at birth. In 1790 she transferred her affections to the Duke of Clarence, later King William IV, and moved in with him at Roehampton. The literary hostess Lady Ottoline Morrell must have been delighted to have had such a predecessor at her home. Having previously lived in Bedford Square (p 55), and then at Garsington, she and her husband Philip moved to No.10 Gower Street in 1928. In her salon here, and at tea parties in the communal garden behind (p 78), Ottoline, though by then in poor health, continued to entertain the literati of the day. Her circle of friends included W B Yeats, T S Eliot, the Huxley brothers and Virginia Woolf; and she also sought to cultivate friendships with younger women such as Dilys Powell, Charlotte Mew and Elizabeth Bowen. A blue plaque records her residence at No.10 until 1938, when she died in Tunbridge Wells after incorrect medical treatment for a mysterious illness.

The architect Joseph Kay, who died in 1847, lived out his last years at **No.12** (ex-No.6). Though best known for his work in Greenwich, in 1814 he had been appointed surveyor to the Foundling Hospital and superintendent of its estate in eastern Bloomsbury, where he was responsible for the houses on the east side of Mecklenburgh Square. **No.14** (ex-No.7) was home (1784-89) to the renowned actress Sarah Siddons. However, the blue plaque records the residence here, from c.1841 until his death in 1862, of the dentist James Robinson. It was he who had administered the first anaesthetic at No.48 further up the street, whose site is similarly marked by a plaque (p 76).

No.18 is where Nikolaus Pevsner began work in 1946 on his *Buildings of England* series. At his office here he also worked for Penguin Books on their 'King Penguins'; and when a garden party was held behind No.18 in 1949 to mark the publication of the 50th book in that series, some penguins from London Zoo were among the guests, and one of them inevitably misbehaved. The William Morris Society held its committee meetings here. Pevsner described Gower Street as comprising 'long, almost wholly unadorned brick terraces, even, soothing, dignified, and with a sense of overall planning, although certainly without much imagination'. His relatively benign assessment may have been a deliberate rebuff to John Ruskin, his *bête noire*, who had so despised the thoroughfare, branding it the '*nec plus ultra* of ugliness in street architecture'.

STORE STREET, running west from Gower Street, was sometimes known in its early days as Great Store Street. An early resident, for fifteen months from September 1791, was Mary Wollstonecraft. During her time here, she first met her future husband William Godwin, was painted by John Opie **[33]**, and wrote and published her controversial *Vindication of the Rights of Woman*, which she had dedicated to Talleyrand. When the French statesman called on Mary at her 'commodious' Store Street apartment, he was amazed to be served wine in a teacup. Auguste Pugin and his family (p 78) moved in 1819 to a house in the street, using its well-lit attic rooms as drawing-offices.

Store Street has retained its historical role as a shopping street. Only one building, **No.43**, is original but it is followed by an early-20th-century re-creation of a Georgian terrace, unified by pilasters. It houses a parade of small independent retail outlets and cafés, refurbished in the early 2000s with attractive uniform shop fronts and fascias. There is an admirable musical instrument display at **No.41**, now home to Foote's Music Shop, founded in 1920 and specialising in drums. The café at **No.34** was opened in the 1930s by the Olivelli family, who from 1961 also ran a small hotel patronised by theatrical folk. At **No.32** is the Store Street Gallery of contemporary art. The second Dillon's bookshop (cf. p 91) was run by Miss Una Dillon at **No.33.** With loans from her father and friends, she had established her

33 Mary Wollstonecraft, by John Opie

first shop in 1937 at No.9 on the street's north side, but had moved her business across the road after wartime bombing.

These days, the north side is dominated by modern development, covering the sites of No.9 and the pre-WWII Gower Arms public house. The main building at **No.14** of the private-sector University (formerly College) of Law was erected for the National Central Library, previously in Malet Place (p 92) and later to be absorbed by the British Library on its inception in 1974. Just beyond it to the west, the **College Arms** at No.18, previously known as the University Tavern (1972-2002), has preserved its Victorian 'console brackets', sporting two enigmatic female faces. The pub was first opened in 1861 as the Camden Arms (an intriguing name, given that only a century later would this area become part of the present borough of Camden).

Hereabouts, at former No.16, was the entrance to the premises of piano makers Robert Wornum & Sons, who arrived here in 1830. Two years later, the company's founder was the inventor of the 'low upright or cottage piano'. The factory extended north to Little Britain (see below), embracing within it the Wornum Hall, opened in 1832 'expressly for Morning and Evening Concerts', and seating up to 1,000 people. Similar public concert rooms would later be established by such better-known firms as Bechstein and Steinway. In 1868 the Wornum Hall was the venue for the first British performance of George Tolhurst's *Ruth*, regarded by many as 'the worst oratorio ever'. The hall was also used for non-musical events, including in November 1888 a meeting chaired by William Morris to mark the first anniversary of 'Bloody Sunday' (when a socialist demonstration in Trafalgar Square was violently suppressed).

Another piano manufacturer, John Hopkinson, advertised at Nos.6-7, claiming that his pianos were up to 40% cheaper than other first-class instruments. Other piano makers filing patents from Store Street addresses were James Marsh (at No.13 in 1855) and John Henry Schucht (in 1867 at No.14).

Byron, the upmarket burger restaurant at **No.6** on the corner of Ridgmount Street is a sympathetic renovation of a former much-loved local landmark, the art deco Bloomsbury Petrol Station, opened in 1926. Depicting this former use is a colourful tile mural by Brian James, surmounted by the word 'PETROL'. On the same end wall a capital 'B' surmounted by a ducal coronet and dated '2012' indicates its construction by or for the Bedford Estate.

RIDGMOUNT STREET was known as Little Store Street until renamed in 1877 after Ridgmont (*sic*), a village of the Duke of Bedford's Woburn estate. At **No.8** on the east side is the Ridgmount Centre, housing the Child & Family Practice, a private mental health facility. Dating from 1963-66, and designed by Sir Giles Scott & Partners to house the Library Association, **No.7** (opposite) has since 2003 been home to its successor body, the Chartered Institute of Library & Information Professionals (CILIP). In the same building, but with a separate entrance is the prestigious Institute for Fiscal Studies.

Until 1938, the turning now named **RIDGMOUNT PLACE** was known as Little Britain. This short cul-de-sac was once a hive of industry, with a piano factory on its south side (see left). On the north side (but actually No.6 Ridgmount Street) were the soap factory, warehouses and offices of Yardley and Co., who moved here from Vine (now Grape) Street in 1883. After their departure for Stratford in 1904, the premises became the base of A Escoffier Ltd. As a sideline, the celebrated hotel chef had started a business, run by his son, marketing pickles and sauces that were bottled and sold with smart labels bearing the Ridgmount Street address. The building subsequently became the first local base of the perfumers Delafine, before their later expansion into other premises nearby (p 97). Based on the site in the 1960s, in the unlabelled post-WWII building at **No.2**, were the Modernist furniture makers Knoll International.

At the end of Ridgmount Place is **Rossetti Court**, originally built for the Soho Housing Association as a mixture of workshops and flats. This pleasing modern development in pale yellow brick occupies the footprint of the pre-

WWII 'Dallas Building'. The firm John E Dallas & Sons manufactured banjos (trademarked 'Jedson'), guitars, drums and other instruments, and also published sheet music. Founded in the Strand, the peripatetic company moved in 1937 into a purpose-built 5-storey factory here in Little Britain. The building was hit by an incendiary in the air raid of 16/17 April 1941. Early on the scene that night was ARP warden Graham Greene (p 94), who recalled in *Ways of Escape* 'behind every window in every floor a wall of flame blowing up ....' Nine people perished in the factory's basement shelter. The gutted building was abandoned by the company.

Part of the University of Law occupies the building on the corner of **RIDGMOUNT STREET**. Most of its west side is occupied by nondescript commercial buildings of the 1950s and '60s. No.15 was home in that decade to the short-lived Pig Industry Development Authority (PIDA) and then known as PIDA House; its responsibilities were taken on in 1967 by the Meat and Livestock Commission, which was based here for a few years. A fortunate survival of WWII is the beautiful frontage at **Nos.19-21**. An air raid on 14/15 October 1940 reduced what was then another part of Delafine's perfume factory to a shell, but the façade was rescued after the war, and the building is now occupied by a language school. The east side of the street is lined by **Nos.10-40**, a residential terrace development of c.1972, on whose northern rectangular gable end is another dated Bedford Estate monogram.

Across Chenies Street lies **RIDGMOUNT GARDENS**. Originally developed in the late 18th century, this street began life as a southern continuation of Chenies Mews. After the stables' leases fell in, the present imposing mansion flats – with pediments bearing striking shell motifs (the scallop being a Russell family symbol) – were erected in 1889, to house 'other than the artisan or labouring classes'. When Booth's researcher visited the area in 1898 accompanied by a policeman they discussed the new policy of the Bedford Estate of doing away with mews so that the roadways were lined on one side with mansion flats facing gardens on the other. The gated gardens here are private, but are usually opened as part of the Open Squares weekend in June.

Eustace Miles and his wife Hallie lived here from at least 1911, first at **No.22** then at **No.10**. He played real tennis, winning English and world titles, and a silver medal at the 1908 Olympics. They were both prolific writers on diet, health and exercise, their output including twenty books on vegetarian food. Eustace started the Eustace Miles Restaurant Co. Ltd, opening his first West End restaurant in 1906, and then expanded his business into health food shops, an idea ahead of its time. He was declared bankrupt in 1934, after which he and Hallie moved away.

Born at **No.30** in 1906 was the senior police officer Sir Ranulph Bacon, who rose to head the Criminal Investigation Department of the Metropolitan Police; he was to hit the headlines in 1964, when he urged the public to 'have a go' if they saw an armed robbery. A blue plaque on the block at **Nos.25-46**, erected by the Nubian Jak Community Trust in 2006, commemorates Bob Marley, the Jamaican pioneer of Reggae music, who occupied **No.34** in 1972 when he first came to England. In the same block the music hall star Sam Mayo, properly Cowan, was living at **No.30** in the mid-1930s when he went bankrupt. In old age the feminist and writer Mary Bright, better known by her pen name George Egerton (1859-1945), was living at **No.57**.

W J Locke was at **No.90** in 1904, shortly before becoming really successful as a novelist and playwright. **No.97** was the home from 1957-80 of Hylda Baker, the music hall, cabaret and TV comedienne. These flats are in the final block, which is entered from Torrington Place.

Turn left along the latter's western portion (known until 1938 as Francis Street, see *Streets of Fitzrovia*). On reaching Tottenham Court Road, cross to its west side and turn left again to reach Goodge Street Station and the end of this walk.

Route 7
Cubitt's Bloomsbury

A sinuous circular walk
from Euston Station
via Tavistock and Gordon Squares

Here we explore the last part of Bloomsbury to be fully built up. It is a neighbourhood which, though never fashionable, was always respectable, and almost wholly coloured a 'wealthy' gold on Booth's 1889 poverty map. A major player in its development after 1820 was the master builder Thomas Cubitt. Revolutionising the London building industry, Cubitt was the first contractor to organise contracts as a whole, to employ all the builders and craftsmen directly, and to have a central builder's yard from which materials were supplied (in the case of Bloomsbury, not far away on the Gray's Inn Road). He was assisted in all this by his younger brother Lewis Cubitt (p 55), who later designed King's Cross Station and probably also many of the houses attributed to his more famous brother. Also involved was Lewis Vulliamy, the architect of Christ Church, Woburn Square (p 72), who designed certain houses, as we shall see.

Leaving the Euston Station concourse through Exit 2 (by the ticket hall), walk straight ahead past Robert Stephenson's statue, to reach Euston Square Gardens and finally **EUSTON ROAD**. Remaining on its north side, look across to the south side, which lies on Bloomsbury's northern border.

Euston Square was laid out in c.1811, near the southern edge of Lord Southampton's estate, in a field called Murrells which had latterly been occupied by nursery gardens. The high-class housing that was to surround the square was very gradually developed by Thomas Cubitt. At twice their present size, its central gardens once extended on both sides of the New (later Euston) Road, and the square was thus unusual in having a main thoroughfare bisecting it. When in the 1920s the leases of the surrounding houses began to fall in, they were bought by Sir Alfred Butt, a theatrical impresario and property developer, who made it a condition of resale that the buyers should have no rights over the gardens, on which he would thus be free to build.

Despite protests, the south-western part was sold to the Society of Friends, who had outgrown their Houndsditch headquarters. A competition for the design of a new **Friends' House**, which was confined to Quaker architects, was won by Hubert Lidbetter. His plain but dignified design, graced by stately Doric columns (over to the right), won the 1926 RIBA award for best building of the year.

The ground to the east was sold to the London County Council (LCC), who erected a Weights and Measures office, and to the GPO. The red-brick neo-Georgian building at **Nos.165&167**, formerly housing Euston Post Office, still contains BT's Euston Telephone Exchange. The refusal of St Pancras Council to intervene to preserve an open space here caused an outcry, and the eventual setting up of a Royal Commission on London Squares. In due course the LCC acquired statutory powers to veto any such developments in future.

Walking east, cross straight ahead at the next crossroads, and from in front of the fire station view the north side of **St Pancras New Church**, opposite. This was built in 1819-22 on land bought from Lord Southampton, to cater for the growing population of a neighbourhood which could no longer be accommodated in the medieval church in Pancras Road. The (St Pancras-born) architects were William Inwood and his son Henry, and the 'Greek Revival' design, in brick faced with Portland stone, was based, with what was considered scrupulous attention to classical detail, on parts of the Erechtheion in Athens. Henry Inwood visited Athens – no light undertaking in those days – to make drawings of both the Erechtheion and the Tower of the Winds, renderings of which form the two lowest stages of the steeple. This is surmounted by a cross instead of a Triton weathervane, in a belated affirmation that this is a Christian church, not a pagan temple. The curious wings flanking the apse at the east end are mirror-image versions of the south porch of the Erechtheion, but with only four caryatids instead of six. They are made of a kind of terracotta akin to Coade stone, and the sculptor Charles Rossi, who had once worked for Mrs Coade, has succeeded in making them look more Roman than Greek. It is said that they were made too tall to fit the St Pancras porticoes, and had to have their midriffs removed, resulting in sets of rather dumpy matrons. They carry ewers and inverted torches, the latter symbols of death (appropriately enough, as the wings give access to the burial vaults). The church was consecrated by the Bishop of London on 7 May 1822. Summerson considered it 'the parish church par excellence of Regency England', though some contemporaries thought it improper to use a pagan temple as a basis for a Christian church. Damaged during WWII, it was extensively restored in 1951-52 and is now Grade-I-Listed. Each year, around the 12th of May – St Pancras Day – the church hosts the London Festival of Contemporary Church Music, founded by Christopher Batchelor in 2002.

Cross Euston Road to reach the church entrance. The imposing interior repays a visit. To the south of the church, in grounds never used for burials, is an onyx sculpture by Emily Young, entitled Archangel Michael and installed 'in memory of the victims of the 7th July 2005 bombings [p 102] and all victims of violence'.

The 1920s office block opposite the church, in red brick and stucco, in what was once the undeveloped south-east corner of the Euston Square garden, is former Nettlefold House, once occupied by the wholesale ironmongers Nettlefold & Sons, hence the letter 'N' in the first-floor ironwork.

Now continue south of the church, along **UPPER WOBURN PLACE**, which was laid out by Thomas Cubitt from 1820. We pass **Central House** (modern No.14)**,** an honestly classical office-block, now part of UCL's Bloomsbury Campus. It was erected on the site of a much-loved building called Woburn Lodge **[34]**, built by the Inwoods in 1820 as their own residence and pulled down in 1930. Alongside stands the **Ambassadors Hotel** (No.12), dating from 1900 but refurbished in the 1960s,

34 Woburn Lodge, built by the Inwoods as their residence in 1820, demolished 1930

and incongruously sporting a baroque pediment above a modern entrance canopy.

On the west side, turning the corner into Endsleigh Gardens (p 114) stand the last surviving Cubitt houses, now much altered and combined to form the **Hilton London Euston Hotel**, known latterly as the Euston Plaza and previously as the Cora Hotel. In 1934 travel agent John Frame (p 63) died here, aged 86, in his own hotel where, when not globetrotting with his wife Elizabeth, he had lived for many years.

The porticoed corner house began as a one-storey extension but was later built up to the height of the buildings it linked. The splendid façade facing Upper Woburn Place boasts confident Corinthian pilasters in the so-called Tivoli order. Here, at the then No.12 in 1854-56, lived Herbert Brown, a novelist, barrister and writer on law, whose *Legal Maxims* became an established text-book. No.13, next door, was the family home of William Bradbury, the printer and publisher associated both with *Punch* and with Dickens' *Household Words*, who died here in 1869. Dickens wrote of the house that it 'looked grim and dry, with all the blinds down, brooding in a hot, dusty, tearless, frozen kind of way, at the unsympathetic street'.

Turn left into wholly pedestrian **WOBURN WALK**, a Regency gem with a Grade-II* Listing. Built by Cubitt in 1822 as a street of shops with wooden bow windows, it was tucked away in a corner of the Bedford Estate so as not to disturb its wealthy residents. Known as Woburn Buildings until 1939 and having deteriorated into a fairly parlous state, it was restored to its original purpose by St Pancras Council in 1959. In 1974 Woburn Walk won the Cleary Prize for the best shopping street in London. Today, with its eclectic choice of upmarket small shops and eateries, and filled with tables, chairs and sunshades for al fresco refreshment, it has gained a fresh vibrancy.

A rectangular black plaque on **No.5** recalls the residence here, from 1896 to 1917 – in two rooms at what was then run-down No.18 Woburn Buildings – of the Irish poet and dramatist William Butler Yeats. Fellow poets who attended his 8pm meetings here on Monday evenings included T S Eliot, a then unknown Ezra Pound, and John Masefield, who described Yeats' sitting-room as 'the most interesting in London'. Often seen walking around the neighbouring streets, wildly swinging his arms, Yeats was referred to by locals as 'the toff wot lives in the Buildings'.

Opposite, as recorded by a Marchmont Association plaque at **No.6** (former No.2), three rooms were occupied in 1905-06 by Dorothy Richardson (p 114), then a journalist but later the author of *Pilgrimage*, regarded as England's first 'stream of consciousness' novel. Though never on speaking terms with Yeats, she recalled seeing him standing at his window on hot summer evenings, 'breathing the parched air'. Woburn Buildings she described as a 'flagged alley' that was 'a terrible place to live'.

Next door, at **No.4**, the elegant canopy above the first floor was erected by George Jacob Holyoake. From 1850 to 1861 the atheist radical orator, and founder of the co-operative movement, lived here with his family at the then No.1. It is said that from his first-floor window Holyoake once addressed an audience assembled in the street below. Lodging with the family throughout their tenure was Holyoake's friend, the picture restorer, art critic and novelist Henry Merritt. Further along, at **No.14** (then No.6), the writer Thomas Carlyle lodged in 1831 with George Irving, brother of Rev. Edward Irving (p 107). With its Listed Windsor-style lamp-posts, it has served as a location in many a 'period' movie and TV drama. In the 1997 film *Keep the Aspidistra Flying*, **No.12** posed implausibly as the (Hampstead) bookshop where George Orwell once worked.

Return to **UPPER WOBURN PLACE**. Here was the boundary between the Southampton and Bedford Estates, and one of the four gates that once closed off the Bedford Estate from the north, each manned by a gatekeeper housed in a lodge alongside. Drays, carts and waggons were barred from entering, as were omnibuses and empty cabs. Only gentlemen's carriages, riders on horseback and cabs with fares were allowed in, estate residents being provided with silver discs called 'tickets' entitling them to enter. These impediments to traffic, particularly resented so near to three mainline railway termini, were finally banished by the London Streets (Removal of Gates) Acts of 1890 and 1893.

South of here is the plain façade of the **County Hotel** (1940), and facing it a huge apartment block of 1935 named **Endsleigh Court**, on whose site at vanished No.18 the church architect William Milford Teulon lived with his wife in the 1870s. The singer, theatre manager and later journalist Emily Soldene (stage name, Miss FitzHenry) died at No.21 in 1912. Residents of Endsleigh Court itself have included the actor Denys Blakelock (1901-70), an intimate friend of Laurence Olivier, and his brother Alban, also an actor; and from 1956 to 1959 the comic actor Kenneth Williams.

Demolished Cubitt houses on the east side included No.6, home in 1830-37 to William Essex, enamel painter to Queen Victoria and Prince Albert; and No.5, where Sheldon Amos, Professor of Jurisprudence at UCL, lived from 1887 with his wife Sarah, a political activist who campaigned on women's issues and against the regulation of prostitution. Notable residents at No.1 included the law reformer James Humphreys, who died there in 1830 after falling from his horse; Peter William Clayden, *Daily News* journalist and Liberal St Pancras alderman, until his death in 1902; and finally the actor-manager Harry Brodripp Irving, son of the illustrious Sir Henry, with his actress wife Dorothea Forster, creator of the roles of Trilby in George du Maurier's play of that name and later (in 1904) of Mrs Darling in *Peter Pan*. Born there that year was their daughter Dorothea, later Lady Brunner, who became an actress but also in 1955 founded and headed up the Keep Britain Tidy Group.

These houses gave way to **Tavistock House North**, one of two red-brick office blocks fronting **BMA House**, whose main entrance we shortly encounter on arriving at **TAVISTOCK SQUARE**. A little to the right of the entrance a Dickens Fellowship blue plaque recalls the residence of Charles Dickens in a house 'near this site'. A driveway once ran eastward from this point (to Burton Street), bounded to the south by a grand house with an enormous back garden. It was erected c.1801 by the builder James Burton (p 9), who named it Tavistock House and lived there himself for six years. It was later divided into no fewer than three large houses, Nos.1-3 Tavistock Villas. Nearest to the square was No.1, retaining the 'Tavistock House' name, but now with only eighteen rooms. From 1851 to 1860 this was the last and largest of Dickens' London family homes. Here he wrote *Bleak House*, *Hard Times*, *Little Dorrit* and *A Tale of Two Cities*. The large schoolroom in the house he converted into what he billed as 'The Smallest Theatre in the World', and here many of his amateur theatricals were performed. The house also witnessed the break-up of Dickens' marriage in 1858.

Dickens' next-door neighbour was the solicitor John Bate Cardale, also the first 'Apostle' of the Catholic Apostolic Church (p 107), who lived at No.2 ('Bedford House') with his wife and fourteen children. 'Russell House' at No.3 was occupied by the artist Frank Stone, who had moved out of No.1, making way for his friend Dickens. By the 1880s No.3 had become a home for lady students run by Elizabeth Cail, while No.1 housed the peripatetic Jews' College (see below). All three Tavistock Villas were demolished in 1901.

The lease of the site was sold to the Theosophical Society in 1912 and Edwin Lutyens (whose wife Emily had Theosophist leanings) was engaged to design for it a combined headquarters and college. Work began in 1914, but WWI intervened and the completed half of the building was acquired by the War Office. Though offered in 1920 to the Society of Friends (p 98), it was eventually taken over by the British Medical Association (previously based in the Strand) and completed in 1929. From the barred gateway may be glimpsed Lutyens' wrought-iron 'memorial screen' and gates of 1926, and beyond them – in 'Wrenaissance' style (English Heritage)

– the main block, whose grand Council Room was meant to be the Theosophists' temple. In the inner courtyard is a further war memorial, of 1954, by James Woodford and S Rowland Pierce: four statues set around a pool, representing Sacrifice, Cure, Prevention and Aspiration.

On the railings outside **Tavistock House South**, just past the plaque to Dickens, is a simple plaque in memory of the thirteen commuters who lost their lives on 7 July 2005 when, in one of four attacks on the London transport network, a bomb was detonated on a double-decker bus (on diversion through the square) by a suicide bomber. Doctors at a meeting in BMA House rushed to the scene to treat the injured.

The east side of Tavistock Square was originally developed by James Burton in 1803, and his terraced houses survived until bomb-damaged in WWII. After the war they were replaced by two further office blocks, **Lynton House** and **Tavis House**. The latter initially housed the Paymaster General, and later offices of several other government departments; it is now home to the charity Age UK.

Original houses here included No.19, home in 1854-55 to the novelist Elizabeth Rundle Charles (born in Tavistock, Devon!) and husband Andrew, part owner of a Wapping soap and candle factory; he ran a ragged school in the house on Sundays, while she taught at the Servants' School in Great Ormond Street. At No.18, Adolf Neubauer, the Hebrew scholar, died in 1907. No.15 was the long-term home of Eleanor Grove, a pioneer of women's education and the first principal of College Hall (p 107); she died here in 1905. 'Stoke House' at No.6 was the residence from 1827 of anatomist Joseph Swan, who converted the billiard room into a dissecting room; and later, until his death in 1880, of Edward Kenealy, a barrister who founded his own mystical religion. Living briefly at No.3 was the singer and theatre manager John Braham, whose eldest daughter Frances, the future political hostess Countess Waldegrave, was born here in 1821. Braham had previously had a 20-year relationship with the diva Nancy Storace. John Hull, botanist, obstetrician and advocate of caesarean sections, died in 1843 at No.1, the home of his son, the liturgical writer and hymnologist William Winstanley Hull.

The north side of Tavistock Square was developed by Thomas Cubitt in 1825-26, two decades after Burton's work on the east side. All his houses have now gone. On the corner is a new grey oval plaque in memory of two Auxiliary Firemen from 'Station 73 Euston', who died from injuries resulting from enemy action 'near the site' on the night of 16/17 April 1941. The plaque is affixed to the wall of **Woburn House** (No.20), now let as offices but built in 1932 as a centre for Anglo-Jewry. It housed Jews' College (precursor of the London School of Jewish Studies) for 25 years until its move to Montague Place; later, as Adler House, it housed the Jewish Museum (until its removal to Camden Town in 1995) and the Court of the Chief Rabbi. In 1906-09 a flat on this site at erstwhile No.22 was the first marital home of the radical poet Anna Wickham. The original No.24 was the London home in the 1840s of the Barbados-born merchant Jacob Levi Montefiore, whose company helped finance the growth of New South Wales.

Funded by a wealthy Baptist businessman, Robert Wilson Black, **Tavistock Court** (No.27) was built in 1934-35 as the headquarters of the National Free Church Council (p 111), which became the Free Church Federal Council in 1940, and is today known as Churches Together in England. Two of the reliefs on the façade depict the legend of St Eustace, a Roman general who, while hunting a stag in Tivoli, saw a vision of a crucifix lodged between the stag's antlers and was immediately converted. (Eustachius, or Eustace, is the patron saint of Tavistock.) Much of Tavistock Court is rented out as flats.

The railings surrounding **Tavistock Square Gardens** were removed during WWII, but afterwards reinstated. In 1965 the gardens were taken over by the newly-formed Camden Council. In the north-west corner stands a large memorial stone dedicated to conscientious objectors, unveiled in June 1994 by Sir Michael Tippett as a calculated response to that year's D-Day celebrations. Just to its south, beside the middle pathway, is a cherry tree planted in August 1967 in memory of the victims of the atomic bombing of Hiroshima. Centre stage in the square, and often bedecked with floral tributes, is the fine statue of Mahatma Gandhi sculpted by the Polish-born Fredda Brilliant and unveiled by Prime Minister Harold Wilson in May 1968, the £10,000 cost having been met by public subscription. A move in the 1980s to rename the square 'Gandhi Square' came to nothing. Continue along the central path, past two other notable trees – one planted in memory of Sir John Barbirolli (born locally, p 62); and the second, a copper beech, presented to St Pancras Council in 1953 by Pandit Nehru during a visit to London to discuss its offer of a site for a Gandhi memorial, which was only to come to fruition fifteen years later.

In the south-east corner of the gardens is a double bronze bust by A G Walker of Dame Louisa Brandreth Aldrich-Blake, one of the first women surgeons in this country, and dean of the Royal Free Hospital Medical School in 1914-25. The plinth and stone seat below it were designed by Lutyens.

The square's south-west corner features a bust of Virginia Woolf, installed by the Virginia Woolf Society in June 2004. From 1924 the writer and her husband Leonard lived just across the road, on the south side of the square on the top two floors of No.52. In the basement were a hand-press on which were printed the first publications of their Hogarth Press, and a writing-room where Virginia wrote several of her major novels. Disturbed by the noise of nearby building work, the couple moved to Mecklenburgh Square in 1939, only to be bombed out of their new abode the next year.

Founded in 1920, next door at No.51, had been the Tavistock Clinic for Functional Nervous Disorders, later to move (as the Tavistock Institute of Medical Psychology) to Malet Place (p 93). At No.54 was 'Les Lilas', a French-speaking boarding house where the poet Wilfred Owen stayed in the autumn of 1915, having just enlisted locally in the Artists' Rifles Officers' Training Corps. He wrote to his mother that 'Tavistock Square is a replica of every other Bloomsbury Square; wadded with fog; skeletons of dismal trees behind railings; but the usual west-end pervasion of ghostly aristocracy'.

A much earlier resident next door at No.55 was Lewis ('Turnpike') Levy, a rich 'farmer of tolls' described in 1832 as 'the master of nearly all the toll gates within 15 miles of London', who died there in 1856. Most of the south-side houses were destroyed by bombing in WWII and replaced in 1951 by the 8-storey (rebuilt and extended) **Tavistock Hotel**, designed by C Lovett Gill & Partners and containing some amusing Art Deco interiors.

The west side of the square is the only part to survive the ravages of WWII, and even here only the magnificent façade is intact. Dating from 1825-26, it is certainly the handsomest of the surviving terraces locally and is Grade-II*-Listed. The seventeen houses, Nos.49-25, were built by Cubitt in 1824-27 but his design was greatly enhanced by Lewis Vulliamy with the addition of two pairs of 2-storey Ionic columns flanking the slightly projecting central house, **No.37**. The 4-storey houses are of stock brick, with a basement protected by cast-iron railings, continuous cast-iron balconies, and stuccoed ground floor. Many of the front doors have been swept away by UCL's remodelling.

At Nos.45-36 is **Connaught Hall**, an intercollegiate University hall of residence. Jessie Pigott (née Kemp), daughter of a rich Baptist flannel manufacturer, was born at **No.43** in 1851, becoming a missionary to China and anti-slavery campaigner; Sir John Joshua Platt, Baron of the Exchequer, lived at **No.39** 1832-46, and William Frend, reformer and religious writer (and father-in-law of Augustus de Morgan), died at **No.36** in 1841. A later occupier of the same house was Sir John

Simon **[35]**, a Liberal MP and barrister (and only the second Jew to be called to the Bar), who in 1871 founded the Anglo-Jewish Association, and who lived at No.36 from that year until his death in 1897. His wife Rachel was a sister of Charles K Salaman, the composer. Later, between the two World Wars, Hotel Monopol occupied **Nos.44&45**, while **Nos.37-40** housed the Tavistock Residential Club.

The northern half of the terrace is now wholly occupied by various departments of University College (UCL). At **No.35** is the Jill Dando Institute of Security and Crime Science, founded in 2001 in memory of the murdered BBC Crimewatch presenter. Thomas Beale, novelist of the East End and author of *Living in Bloomsbury*, lived in the 1930s at **No.33**, but the brown Camden Council plaque commemorates Ali Mohammed Abbas, who worked tirelessly for the creation of a separate state of Pakistan and presided here over a kind of informal Pakistani embassy before the state was formed. Edward Ball Knobel, chemist, astronomer and managing director of Ilford Films, died in 1930 at **No.32**, which houses Birkbeck College's School of Social Sciences. **No.31** was the pre-WWII headquarters of the Society for Psychical Research, founded in 1882 to promote scholarly investigation into psychic phenomena. **No.29**, on the corner, now UCL's Rubin Building and housing its Department of Political Science, was the 1850s home of the wealthy civil engineer and railway contractor Edward Betts, partner in the well-known firm of Peto & Betts.

Other Tavistock Square residents have included Alexander McDonnell, the first great British chess player, who lived for many years in a boarding-house here until his death in 1835. He had been a sugar planter in the West Indies and at his death was awaiting compensation for the emancipation of 300 slaves he owned there. The history painter Edward Armitage, was born in the square in 1817, as in 1833 was Horace Waller, missionary to Africa and slavery abolitionist.

35 Sir John Simon (*Vanity Fair*, 25 Sep 1886)

Turn left along Endsleigh Place (p 112), a short street linking Tavistock and Gordon Squares and lined on the south side by an elegant screen between the end houses in each. The latter, **No.36 Gordon Square**, was home in 1878-81 to the barrister Charles Darling, who later presided as judge over the Crippen and Casement appeals, and was created Lord Darling. This house, which served as the Greek Consulate between the wars, is now occupied (along with Nos.37&38) by the London International Development Centre. In the film *Tom and Viv* (1994), based on the relationship of T S Eliot and his first wife Vivienne Haigh-Wood, No.36 masquerades as the Russell Square offices of Faber & Faber (p 67), where the poet works.

The east side of **GORDON SQUARE** was used in August 2000 for the late-night filming of a sequence in another movie, *The Mummy Returns*. In this, a bus is seen swerving to avoid an oncoming car, before crashing into another car and veering round the corner into Endsleigh Place – actually, no buses serve Gordon Square. Surviving on this east side is a terrace of eleven early,

4-storey, Cubitt houses, some endowed with Corinthian pilasters, all with iron balconies, square-headed doorways, fanlights and panelled doors. It has many associations with the unconventional Bloomsbury Group. The painter Vanessa Bell lived at **No.37** in 1920-22. The same house was later home to the author Kate O'Brien. The barrister Charles Phillips, a friend of Henry Brougham, died in 1859 at **No.39** two years after writing a pamphlet urging the total abolition of the death penalty. The later occupation of this house by the National Union of Women Teachers in 1922 marked the beginning of the conversion of this side of the square from residences to offices, and later to university use, a process almost complete by the 1950s.

The psychoanalyst and translator James Strachey (younger brother of Lytton, see below) lived at **No.41** from 1919 to 1956 with his wife Alix, sometimes joined by his writer friend Ralph Partridge, whose lover, the painter Dora Carrington, also lodged here in 1920-23. An earlier resident, in 1840-41 at **No.42**, was Thomas Gordon Hake, a physician who attended Dante Gabriel Rossetti in his frequent illnesses, and a poet whose verse Rossetti admired.

Now occupying Nos.39-47 is the Birkbeck School of Arts, with its 90-seat Birkbeck Cinema. Between 1938 and 1956, **Nos.44&45** housed Charles Ogden, the originator and promoter of Basic English, and the Orthological Institute that he founded. **No.46** was the London home of the economist and Bloomsbury Group member John Maynard Keynes, from 1916 until his death in 1946; and from 1925 of his devoted wife, the Russian ballerina Lydia Lopokova **[36]**:

What a marriage of beauty and brains,
the fair Lopokova and John Maynard Keynes.

But the blue plaque to Keynes on No.46 tells only half the story. It was to this house that the four children of Sir Leslie Stephen moved on the death of their father in 1904. Virginia, pleased to be escaping from the 'mummified humbug' of Kensington to the respectable but unfashionable Bloomsbury, lived here with siblings Vanessa, Adrian and Thoby till 1907, and it was then that the Bloomsbury Group can be said to have begun. The 'Thursday evenings' here, of conversation and recitals, were attended by Thoby's Cambridge friends, including Leonard Woolf (Virginia's future husband), Lytton Strachey, Clive Bell, David Garnett, Duncan Grant, Keynes, Roger Fry and Saxon Sidney-Turner. Vanessa Stephen's 'Friday Club' for artists led to her friendship with the art critic Clive Bell, and in 1907 to their ill-fated marriage. The couple lived on at No.46 for another ten years, each of them engaging in extramarital affairs; and born here were their sons, the poet Julian Bell and Quentin, the potter and art historian. According to a famous witticism attributed to Dorothy Parker, the Bloomsbury Group 'lived in squares, painted in circles and loved in triangles'.

After his early success here in Bloomsbury, Thomas Cubitt moved on to Pimlico and Belgravia, only too successfully competing with himself and making it difficult to sell his later Gordon Square houses. The larger houses Nos.47-53 at the southern end of the east side were built by Cubitt & Co. only in the late 1850s, and in a heavier

36 John Maynard Keynes and his wife Lydia Lopokova

Italianate style. Thomas's original design of the whole of the east side had been abandoned, for admirable social reasons (offering more room and better sanitary arrangements for ever larger families) but with unhappy aesthetic consequences.

Living in 1896-99 at **No.47** was the author and journalist Henry Duff Traill, and Brandon Thomas, the actor and playwright best remembered as the author of *Charley's Aunt*, died in the same house in 1914. Various academic departments of UCL now occupy Nos.48-51. The toymakers Paul and Marjorie Abbatt lived in a flat at **No.49**, where they held an exhibition of their toys in 1932. It was such a success they were able to set up a shop at No.29 across the Square.

Today, the basement at **No.50** contains one part of the UCL Day Nursery. The house was the post-WWII home of Arthur Waley (p 66), the Oriental scholar and translator, until his retirement to Highgate in 1962. Coincidentally, it now houses UCL's Centre for Translation Studies. The brown plaque here, erected by Camden Council, belatedly informs us, rather vaguely, that 'Here and in neighbouring houses during the first half of the 20th century there lived several members of the Bloomsbury Group, including Virginia Woolf, Clive Bell and the Stracheys'. Vanessa Bell moved into No.50 in 1920 and then out again (to No.37) in 1922, when her estranged husband Clive moved into No.50. A blue GLC plaque next door at **No.51** more precisely records the residence of Lytton Strachey, the critic, biographer and author of *Eminent Victorians*, who lived here from 1909 to 1924, for much of that time in a strange ménage à trois with Dora Carrington and her husband Ralph Partridge.

Sir Charles Whetham, chairman of the London & Blackwall Railway Company and Lord Mayor of London, died at his home at **No.52** in 1885. Rounding the corner and with a south-facing portico, **No.53** served for many years as a convent of the Poor Servants of the Mother of God. It was later home until 2007 to the Percival David Foundation, comprising a library of Chinese art and the finest collection of Chinese ceramics outside China, presented to the University by Sir Percival David in 1950 and now removed to the British Museum. The house is at present home to the Doctoral School of SOAS.

Across the road and stretching to Tavistock Square to the left is a fine Cubitt terrace of c.1824, numbered as part of Gordon Square. The ground floor of **Nos.55-59** has been remodelled, eliminating the original front doors, and the block now houses parts of UCL's Institute of Education and further premises of the UCL Day Nursery. **No.55** was once Miss Peters' private school for girls, which receives a mention in the diaries of Virginia Woolf: the school took younger children of both sexes, and her nephews Julian and Quentin Bell both went there. **No.57** was the interwar home of the Finnish Consulate. **No.59** housed the Heraldry Society from 1960 until its eviction by the University nine years later. Its surviving west-facing portico gives access to whole block.

Turn right along the pavement lining the south side of the square's central garden, past a refreshment kiosk that was once the gardener's hut. Opposite, on the corner of Woburn Square, stood No.1 Gordon Square, pulled down, together with Nos.2-6, to make way for the Warburg Institute (p 73). Charles Fowler, the architect of Covent Garden Market, established his practice at No.1 in 1830. A subsequent occupant, some two decades later, was Henry Seymour Westmacott, the Gray's Inn solicitor out of whose North Wales property the fantasy village of Portmeirion eventually evolved.

Thomas Graham, pioneer of physical chemistry and formulator of Graham's Law of Diffusion, died in 1869 at No.4. William Davies, the Welsh singer and sculptor known as 'Mynorydd', lived at No.5, where in 1857 his daughter Dilys (later Mrs Glynne-Jones), the promoter of Welsh female education, was born. The house was next home to the architect Edward Welby Pugin, the eldest son of A W N Pugin (p 42), who lived here with his widowed step-mother, and who designed over 100 Roman Catholic churches before his early death in 1875, aged 41.

37 Church of Christ the King, side chapel, detail of a photo by Joaquim Alvar Gaspar, Lisbon

Beyond the gardens continue to the broad expanse of **BYNG PLACE**, which took its name from Georgiana Byng, the first wife of the 6th Duke of Bedford. The roadway here has recently been paved over to create a so-called 'Shared Space' where, in theory at least, pedestrians, cyclists and cars can mingle happily together. The plain stucco classical building on its west side at **Nos.1-3** was erected by Cubitt in 1832, originally as three houses but, because they did not sell, quickly converted to house Coward College, a residential training establishment for Protestant theological student ministers. Founded under the will of merchant William Coward (d.1738), this was a forerunner of New College at Swiss Cottage, to which it moved in 1850. Later opened at No.1, in 1882, was College Hall, providing accommodation for female students at UCL (and the London School of Medicine for Women). Four years earlier UCL had become the first British university to admit women on equal terms to men. Eleanor Grove, the Hall's first Principal, worked there without a salary. Having progressively expanded into Nos.2&3, the Hall moved to Malet Street (p 75) in 1932. For some forty years from 1964, the building, renamed William Penn House, served as the International Centre of the Society of Friends. Nos.1-3 today contain serviced apartments let to students and tourists.

Once obstructing the roadway to their left was another of the gates controlling access to the Bedford Estate, this time from the west. In the wide space on the right, on the site of a Victorian cab rank, and behind new public tables and chairs, are three Grade-II-Listed telephone kiosks, two of which are of Giles Gilbert Scott's famous K2 design.

Behind them, and looming over Bloomsbury like a beached whale, is the **Church of Christ the King [37],** built by Raphael Brandon in 1851-54 as a central place of worship for the Catholic Apostolic Church (CAC). Its congregants were often inaccurately described as 'Irvingites' after the charismatic minister Rev. Edward Irving, the sect's reputed founder, though the CAC was, in fact, established by his followers only after his death. Governed by leaders styled 'Apostles' and local bishops known as 'Angels' (and eventually with offshoots worldwide), the CAC was noted for its elaborate ritual and its prophecies of an imminent millennium. When the Second Coming failed to occur, attendances fell and after the last Apostle died in 1901, the sect went into terminal decline; today (in Britain) it is all but extinct. Built on a cathedral scale in Bath stone, with an Early English exterior and Decorated interior, the Gordon Square church was never completed: only five of the projected seven bays of the nave were built, and a planned 300-ft spire, which would have challenged St Paul's, did not materialise. Taken over by the University's Anglican Chaplaincy, the building was known from 1963 as the University Church of Christ the King. Held here in 1983 was the memorial service for Sir Nikolaus Pevsner. In 1992 the CAC, still a legal entity, leased part of the property to Forward in Faith, a traditionalist group within the Anglican church. The 'English Chapel', at the eastern end, is open for prayer during the week; it has a highly polished tiled floor and one can glimpse many of the church's beautiful internal features from here.

Now turn north along the west side of **GORDON SQUARE**, past the present church entrance and **The Cloisters**, a Gothic-style structure in stock brick with limestone dressings, originally erected as flats for the CAC clergy. At 2nd-floor level, between ogee windows, is a carving of a Green Man.

At Nos.14&15, described by Pevsner as 'domestic battlemented neo-Jacobean on a ridiculous scale', is **Dr Williams's Library**. Its intrusion into a sober residential square reflected the financial desperation experienced by both Cubitt and the Bedford Estate as Cubitt's houses failed to sell. The building, now toned down by a century's soot, has five storeys, some of its tall windows running through two floors. It was built in 1848-49 by Thomas Donaldson (then UCL's Professor of Architecture) as University Hall, founded by a committee of (mainly Unitarian) Dissenters as the first hall of residence for male students. Few of them came, many probably deterred by the Unitarian connection. Manchester New College (MNC), a nonconformist academy, was therefore persuaded to move south to share the building, and this they did from 1853. Though flourishing by 1880, University Hall was still failing to pay its way, and it was agreed that MNC should assume full control over the building's finances. When nine years later the college decamped again, to Oxford, it sold the lease not to University Hall as expected but to Dr Williams's Library. Ironically, while women students had their College Hall there was now no such accommodation for the men.

Nos.14&15 were converted in 1890 to house the library of Rev. Dr Daniel Williams, who in 1729 had provided in his will for the establishment of a library of books relating to the nonconformist movement. This had had a series of homes before moving here from Grafton Way off Gower Street. The library trustees promptly let some of the rooms to Mary (Mrs Humphry) Ward, in which to establish her proposed 'Settlement', which was to be run by socially-conscious middle-class educators for the benefit of the local poor. This was very soon to resettle in nearby Tavistock Place, in what is now Mary Ward House, purpose-built premises designed by two former University Hall residents, Cecil Claude Brewer (p 114) and A Dunbar Smith. Next to rent space at Nos.14&15 Gordon Square was a private girls' high school, known by the 1920s as the Gordon Hall School of Pharmacy for Girls.

Dr Williams's Library still flourishes here today. The main collections relate to English nonconformity but there is also an impressive collection of medieval manuscripts, including a psalter made for Philippa of Hainault, wife of Edward III. A blue plaque commemorates Dr Robert Travers Herford, a Unitarian minister and 'interpreter of Judaism', who 'lived and worked' here as librarian in 1914-25.

Ahead on the west side, at Nos.16-25, is a terrace of stuccoed Italianate Cubitt houses dating from the mid-19th century, the stucco unusually unpainted. All are now occupied by UCL and accessed from within its campus at the rear. Resident at **No.18** in 1880-85 was Sir Frederick Treves, the eminent surgeon who befriended Joseph Merrick, the 'Elephant Man', helped found the British Red Cross, removed Edward VII's appendix and gave appendicitis its name. In the same house, in 1944-45, Graham Greene and Dorothy Glover (p 94) rented top-floor rooms let to them cheaply because they were vulnerable to bombing; and living here a decade later was Theodore Komisarjevsky, the Russian theatrical director and designer, whose creations included the interior of the Phoenix Theatre in Charing Cross Road.

Gordon Square Garden, in contrast to Tavistock Square Garden, is informal in layout, traversed by winding paths and awash with daffodils in the spring and roses in the summer, making it the most picturesque of London squares. John Russell, 6th Duke of Bedford, personally supervised the (initially formal) design and planting of the gardens, naming the square after his second wife, a daughter of the 4th Duke of Gordon. In 1920 the Bedford Estate agreed to sell the site to the Government for the proposed building of the University of London. Remaining for some time for keyholders' private use, the gardens were eventually opened to the public. In 2007 they were formally reopened by the Princess Royal after a seven-year restoration project.

Near the gate, a bronze by Shenda Amery unveiled in 2011 by the Prince of Wales, is the head of the Indian philosopher and poet Rabindranath Tagore, the first non-European to win the Nobel Prize for Literature, who in 1879 had briefly studied law at UCL.

In the garden's north-west corner a sarsen stone was installed in 2012 to mark the 75th anniversary of the Institute of Archaeology, which occupies the north side of the square. In the north-east corner, unveiled by the Princess Royal in November 2012, is a bronze bust of Noor Inayat Khan. Moscow-born, and of Indian and American extraction, but brought up in the square, Noor served as an agent of the Special Operations Executive. In 1943, codenamed 'Madeleine', she was the first female radio operator to be flown into occupied France to aid the French Resistance. Betrayed and arrested, she was sent to Dachau concentration camp, where, aged thirty, she was shot by the SS in September 1944. Britain's only Muslim war heroine was posthumously awarded the George Cross and the French Croix de Guerre.

The **Institute of Archaeology** is housed in a bland 7-storey building opened in 1958, replacing a whole row of Cubitt houses, the first to have been erected in the square. Here, from east to west, No.35 was home (1843-64) to Peregrine Bingham the Younger, a legal writer who edited Bentham's *Book of Fallacies*; later for some twenty years to James Martineau, the Unitarian Principal of Manchester New College (p 108), who died here in 1900; and later still (1933-40) to the newly formed pioneering, though now defunct, Institute of Sociology. No.33 was the second base of David Gourlay's Wayfarers Travel Agency (p 112), catering here for the travel needs of various Bloomsbury Group members and home in the late 1920s and early 1930s to the journalist Ivor Brown, drama critic at *The Observer*. No.32, in 1844-52, housed John (later Baron) Romilly, the second son of Sir Samuel (p 68) and the first Master of the Rolls to grant students free access to the public records. In the 19th century No.31 served as St Pancras Vicarage, housing a procession of notable vicars. This included the popular Rev. Thomas Dale, also Professor of English at UCL and creator of the St Pancras church extension scheme, which divided the old parish into thirty smaller units, each with its own new church; Rev. William Weldon Champneys (later Dean of Lichfield); and Anthony Wilson Thorold, who became Bishop of Winchester.

In the north-west corner of the Square stands a late-Victorian cast-iron lamp-post, now disused but retaining its original 'cradle-type' carbon arc lamp fitting, the last remaining example in London of its kind. **No.29** Gordon Square, with a modern façade in Regency style, is named Gordon House and occupied by UCL. The original No.29 was the 1920s headquarters of the mystical Sufi Order of the West, established here by Hazrat Inayat Khan, a poet and musician of Indian royal descent. Brought up here with her siblings was his daughter, SOE agent Noor Inayat Khan (see above). The house later contained the pre-WWII headquarters of the Historical Association.

On the west side, Nos.27&28 Gordon Square were pulled down to make the back entrance into the main UCL campus, but **No.26** still stands. In 1852 this was the second home in the square of Rev.

Christopher Heath, the first 'Angel' of the Gordon Square CAC (p 107). At now demolished No.28 lived (1864-68) the art amateur and polymath Lewis Pocock (p 50).

North of here **GORDON STREET** begins. Laid out in the 1820s, but only slowly developed, this was originally to be called Wriothesley Street. Cubitt objected, claiming that every one of his builders would need to be taught how to pronounce the name. Instead it was briefly known as William Street, probably after young William Russell, the future 8th Duke of Bedford. Soon assuming its present name, the street was later radically renumbered in 1874.

Dominating the west side is UCL's **Bloomsbury Theatre**, containing both a 535-seat auditorium and a Fitness Centre. Designed by Fello Atkinson of James Cubitt [*sic*] & Partners, it opened in 1968 as the Collegiate Theatre, assuming its present name in 1982. Supported by an arcade of tall concrete spines, the blank, brick-faced top storey overhangs so as to neatly hide the fly tower behind. Alterations took place in 1987, with interior design by Gerald Scarfe, who also created the theatre's logo. The building stands partly on the site of UCL's war-damaged Memorial Hall, a conversion in 1928 by Richardson of All Saints' Church. Designed by Thomas Donaldson and consecrated in 1842, this was declared redundant and closed in 1909, its short-lived parish being merged with that of St Pancras New Church.

On the theatre site at No.11 (later No.3) Mark Lemon, editor of *Punch* and friend of Dickens, was living in the 1850s. Resident at No.7, from 1880 until his death there in 1903 was Professor Thomas Roger Smith, the designer of laboratories for UCL and of Mount Vernon Hospital in Hampstead. In 1888 Frederick Mew, an architect's assistant, moved his family into No.9, where they lived in 'genteel near-poverty'; his children included Charlotte Mew, the future poet.

On the opposite side, after his marriage in September 1931 to Ernestina Corvaja, the travel writer Norman Lewis lived at No.4 with his in-laws and ran his photography business from this address for a number of years. The physician and medical statistician William Augustus Guy, author of *Principles of Forensic Medicine*, died at No.12 in 1885. Living at No.16 in the 1920s was a coterie of four female psychoanalysts, including Ella Sharpe and Mary Chadwick, and referred to by James Strachey (p 105) as the 'ladies' of the 'Gordon Street ménage', as they shared not only lodgings but also a 'certain position on psychoanalysis'.

Another house in the street was rented in the 1880s by the surgeon and zoologist John Bland-Sutton. A small man resembling Napoleon but with a strong Cockney accent, he rose from poverty, as one of nine children of an Enfield stock slaughterer and amateur taxidermist, to receive a knighthood in 1912.

Much of the east side of Gordon Street is now taken up by the uncompromisingly brutalist façade of UCL's **Christopher Ingold Building**, chemistry laboratories built by Architects CoPartnership. Coming second in a list of 'Best Buildings of 1970' drawn up by Camden Council, it was named after the theoretical organic chemist (and UCL professor) Sir Christopher Ingold, FRS, in whose memory it bears a hexagonal blue plaque. Beyond it is **Wates House**, by the same architects, funded largely by the Wates Foundation and opened in 1975. This 'unappealing' block (Pevsner) ironically houses 'The Bartlett', home to UCL's Faculty of the Built Environment and Bartlett School of Architecture.

Opposite, the street's last surviving Cubitt houses have finally given way to a glassy new building, designed by Feilden Clegg Bradley Studios as the Bloomsbury premises of the **London Centre for Nanotechnology**, launched in 2003 as a joint venture of UCL and Imperial College. Living on this site, at old No.4 (later No.17), from 1857 until his death in 1865, was the Quaker Samuel Lucas, merchant, educational reformer and editor of *The Morning Star*, the radical paper that had recently been started by Richard Cobden and John Bright. His wife, Bright's sister, was the temperance activist and suffragist Margaret Bright Lucas.

Passing on the west side the back of Richardson's **Physics Building**, rebuilt in 1954 after wartime damage, we now re-cross the old Bedford-Southampton estate boundary, where once stood another of the Bedfords' controversial gates. The part of the street to the north of this gate was at first known as Upper Gordon Street, where, at No.1 on the left, William Morris and Edward Burne-Jones rented rooms during August 1856 before moving together to Red Lion Square.

Here today is a 9-storey red-brick Victorian building that began life as the Endsleigh Palace Hotel, numbered 23 Endsleigh Gardens. During WWI it was requisitioned to serve as a Red Cross hospital for officers. As recalled by a blue plaque of the Seamen's Hospital Society (SHS), next to move in, in 1920, were the Hospital for Tropical Diseases (founded 99 years earlier) and the London School of Tropical Medicine (founded 1899), both offshoots of the Greenwich-based SHS, and each previously more appropriately located in the Royal Albert Dock. Nine years later the School moved on to Keppel Street (p 78), and the hospital was evacuated to Greenwich on the outbreak of WWII. After several further moves, the latter has become part of University College Hospital, providing outpatient services in Mortimer Market off Tottenham Court Road. Damaged by a landmine in May 1941, the Gordon Street building was acquired by UCL in 1959 and now houses **UCLU**, its students' union.

Diagonally opposite, on the corner with Euston Road is **Drayton House**, the western end of Friends' House (p 98), let out by the Quakers as offices and now occupied by UCL. George Fox, the founder of the Quaker movement, was born in 1624 in the Leicestershire village of Drayton-in-the-Clay (now Fenny Drayton).

Turn right into **ENDSLEIGH GARDENS**. Originally forming the south side of Euston Square (p 98), the street was renamed in 1880 by order of the Metropolitan Board of Works, after a Devonshire property of the Bedfords (see p 113), although it actually lay on the former Southampton Estate.

Pass the northern side of Wates House. Here formerly, at Nos.15-22, stood the large Endsleigh Hotel. James Winstone, the trades unionist and Welsh miners' leader, died in 1920 at No.21. From 1876 until his death in 1911, No.18 was home to Sir Percy Bunting, barrister, social reformer, editor of the *Contemporary Review* and co-founder of the (Methodist) West London Mission; the National Free Church Council (p 102) was founded at his house in 1891. The chemist Charles Loudon Bloxam, deviser of an electrolytic test for arsenic, died at No.16 in 1887.

Ahead, beyond Taviton Street, is a short row of original houses, with substantial Doric porticoes and balconies above, built by Cubitt in 1829 under contract with Lord Southampton. Here at **No.14**, the comparative anatomist Charles Stewart died in 1907. **No.13** (as No.48 Euston Square) had earlier in 1854-68 housed Rev. James Hamilton, Presbyterian minister of the Regent Square Church, and before him (1846-52) Rev. Thomas J Judkin, hymn writer, painter and minister of the Anglican Somers Chapel in Eversholt Street, who subsequently moved next door into No.49 Euston Square, now **No.12**. This house, which by the end of the century contained the Home for Young Women Employed in Houses of Business, later became part of a YWCA 'Hostel for Girl Workers' at Nos.12-14. All three houses now serve as a St Mungo's hostel for the homeless.

Return and proceed along the east side of **TAVITON STREET**. Laid out in the 1820s, this was initially named Georgiana Street, after Georgiana Byng, second wife of the 6th Duke of Bedford. The take-up of building plots here was exceedingly slow, and this was the very last of the local streets to be fully built up: as late as 1840 only the gatekeeper's lodge had been built, and five years later only four other houses were occupied. By this time the street had been renamed after Taviton, a Devonshire estate given to the 1st Earl of Bedford by Henry VIII.

On the west side, the only surviving houses are **Nos.20-24**, now UCL's Campbell House West. They are somewhat plainer than the usual Cubitt style and probably completed by his executors after his death. The Scottish composer-conductor Sir Alexander Mackenzie died at **No.20** in 1935.

Surviving opposite on the east side is a handsome symmetrical terrace of twelve houses built by Cubitt and all now owned by UCL. Unusually, there are Art Nouveau stained-glass panels in the door of **No.1**. Here lived the writer Jane Ellen Panton, daughter of the painter William Frith, who when her husband, the brewer James Panton, died in 1921 after 52 years of marriage, lined his coffin with her wedding dress; two years later she herself died in the house. **No.4** was once home to the widowed mother of war heroine Noor Inayat Khan (p 109), and it was from here that in 1943 her daughter set off on her fateful mission to France.

Nos.5-10 now together form the student accommodation called Campbell House East. A blue plaque at **No.6** recalls its earlier occupation, in 1888-1902, by the Methodist minister Hugh Price Hughes, editor of the *Methodist Times*. Taviton Street was popular with clergymen, and with actresses too: Dame Madge Kendal and her theatre manager husband William Hunter Kendal had a house in the street in the 1860s and '70s; Ellen Terry lived here in 1875 while separating from her husband; and Sidney Bateman, the American actress and playwright died at **No.7** in 1881. **No.8** was the interwar base of the London College of Physiology. Emily Faithfull, an activist for women's rights, was living at **No.10** in 1863 when she set up the Victoria Press, a women's publishing company.

Much of the opposite (west) side of the street has been sacrificed to academe. In the 1920s, vanished No.19 was variously home to a bookshop run by David ('Bunny') Garnett (p 105) with his boyfriend and fellow pacifist, Francis Birrell; to the Wayfarers Travel Agency co-founded in 1921 by David Gourlay; and to the latter's girlfriend, Janet (later Dame Janet) Vaughan, who became an eminent haematologist and radiobiologist. Also lodging here at the time, in a remarkable assemblage of talented people, were the sculptor Dora Gordine, the interior designer and urban reformer Elizabeth Denby, the popular novelist Anne Sedgwick, and the sinologist and photographer John Hope Johnstone. The site of No.19 is now covered by the hideous rear elevation of the Christopher Ingold labs.

Beyond this on the corner, the University's post-WWII Examination Halls have given way to the new home of **SSEES**, the School of Slavonic & East European Studies. Inaugurated in 1915 by Tomáš Garrigue Masaryk, later President of Czechoslovakia, the School was located for ninety years within Senate House, becoming part of UCL in 1999. The foundation stone of its new Taviton Street building was unveiled in May 2004 by the President of Poland, Aleksander Kwaśniewski, and at the opening ceremony in October 2005 the keynote address was given by Václav Klaus, President of the Czech Republic. Behind its most unusual brick façade with its interplay of windows, somewhat marred by two large entrance gates, Short & Associates' environmentally-friendly building employs an innovative system of 'natural ventilation', using 'downdraught cooling' to avoid the need for air conditioning in warm weather, a process in which the four prominent white 'chimneys' are presumably involved.

Living on the SSEES site, in 1866-77 at now demolished No.17, was the Dowager Viscountess of Sidmouth, daughter-in-law of the former prime minister. Lewis Foreman Day, the decorative artist, industrial designer and specialist in stained glass, died in 1910 at No.15.

Passing **No.12**, outside which once stood the Taviton Street gate, turn left into **ENDSLEIGH PLACE**. Dating from 1827, and known until 1937 as Gordon Place, the handsome terrace on its north side at Nos.1-7 was designed by Lewis Vulliamy for the builder James Humphries. Today all the houses, bereft of all but two of their round-arched doorways, serve as **Passfield Hall** of residence for students of the London School of Economics. By 1900 now unmarked **Nos.1-3** had together been transformed into the Balmoral and the Osborne, two hotels. **No.5** was home in 1856-60 to the barrister Alexander Pulling, one of the last surviving members of the Ancient Order of Serjeants-at-Law, of which he wrote a

38 Nancy Price, CBE (1880-1970)

history, *The Order of the Coif*. Living there in 1936 was the actress Nancy Price **[38]**, also author, theatre director and co-founder six years earlier of the resolutely non-commercial People's National Theatre, animal-rights campaigner and all-round 'good egg'. **No.6**, home in 1924-25 to the art critic Raymond Mortimer, contained a mural painted by Duncan Grant. **No.7**, which in 1888-93 housed Rev. G J Blomfield, father of the architect Sir Reginald Blomfield, later became between the two wars a Convent of Mercy.

Noting the pretty frieze on the latter's eastern end (there is a twin on the west wall of the terrace), turn left again along the west side of **ENDSLEIGH STREET**, another Cubitt street laid out c.1825 but completed much later, its name being taken from Endsleigh Cottage, the 6th Duke of Bedford's then newly-built holiday retreat near Tavistock.

Still standing near its south-west corner is the bay-windowed gatekeeper's **lodge**, sporting a stuccoed ducal coat of arms with the Russell family's Italian motto, *Che sarà sarà* ('What will be will be'). The gates in Gordon and Taviton Streets were removed by Act of Parliament in 1890, but this one – some meters south of the estate boundary – was reprieved until 1893. The previous year, excavations to deepen the local sewers had unearthed parts of mammoth tusks, which were described in a paper read by Henry Hicks to the Geological Society; other remains were uncovered in neighbouring streets.

Beyond the lodge is an attractive terrace in variegated stock brick, with square-headed doorways, patterned fanlights and studded doors. The engineer Samuel Seaward, a designer of marine engines, died at **No.13** in 1842. **No.14** sports an iron trellis and tented canopy; it was the home from 1905 of Dr Jessie Murray, suffragist and consultant physician at the Quinton Polyclinic (p 82), who in 1913 co-founded here, with teacher Julia Turner, the Medico-Psychological Clinic, the first public clinic to offer psychoanalytical therapy and training in psychoanalysis. The next nine houses combine to form the John Adams Hall (of residence) of the Institute of Education, their disused doors now numberless. **No.15** (identified in its fanlight) served as the HQ of the Anti-Apartheid Movement in 1960-64. In the 1920s, **No.17** housed the London Artificial Sunlight & Colour Therapy Clinic. **No.18** was once home to Asher Asher, the Jewish physician and community worker, who died here in 1889. Attracted to the street by its proximity to three railway termini, with convenient services to various parts of his diocese, Rev. John Wogan Festing, Bishop of St Albans, lived at **No.21** until his death in 1902. Behind the lower end of the Hall's access ramp is a stone bearing two coronets and the letters 'B' and 'S', marking the actual old border between the Bedford and Southampton Estates.

On the east side, **Winston House** is a routine block of post-WWII council flats thrown up by St Pancras Council on a bomb-damaged site, where No.9 had been the birthplace in 1871 of Cecil Claude Brewer, the co-architect of Mary Ward House. The future novelist Dorothy Richardson lodged from 1896 at No.7, with landlady Keziah Baker, while working as a dentist's assistant in Harley Street. In *The Tunnel*, part of *Pilgrimage*, her 13-volume autobiographical novel, Endsleigh Street becomes 'Tansley Street'. After a spell in Woburn Buildings (p 100), Richardson returned to the same lodgings c.1907, in the wake of a brief affair with H G Wells, a pregnancy and a miscarriage, remaining there for four years.

Four original Cubitt houses survive at **Nos.3-6**. For some ninety years until 2013, No.3 was the headquarters of the National Union of Students, hence the name of its offshoot, Endsleigh Insurance, founded here in 1965. A flat at No.3 was home for a year in 1933 to the bisexual David Garnett (p 112) and his first wife, the illustrator Rachel (Ray) Marshall. In the attic was impecunious and deeply disturbed young Welsh writer Dorothy Edwards, offered board and lodging by the Garnetts in return for childcare. In December 1933 she returned to South Wales for Christmas, only to commit suicide on 5 January by throwing herself under a train.

The next two houses are gone. Resident at demolished No.1, until her death in 1952, was Marian Cripps (Lady Parmoor), Quaker philanthropist, political activist and stepmother of the socialist politician Stafford Cripps. At **Nos.1&2** today is the striking white and black façade of former B'nai B'rith Hillel House, built in the 1970s as a social and residential centre for Jewish students – a good modern building, though here arguably out of place, its tiered arcades of round-arched windows nonetheless echoing the shape of its surviving neighbours' doorways. It has now become the Gideon Schreier Wing of the next building along, at the junction with **ENDSLEIGH GARDENS**.

Along its south side to your left, Cubitt's porticoed **Nos.9-11**, now part of John Adams Hall, were the interwar premises of the Caledonian Christian Association. The corner block on the right, at No.8 and named **Bentham House** after the philosopher and jurist Jeremy Bentham (p 86), has been home since 1965 to the UCL Faculty of Laws. Set into the upper floor are carved reliefs by Esmond Burton, depicting industrial workers (and soldiers), the building having been constructed in 1954-58 for the National Union of General & Municipal Workers. Its co-designer, 'H Lidbetter', was presumably Hubert, the architect three decades earlier of Friends' House, almost opposite.

On this site, Bentinck House (No.8 Endsleigh Gardens) served from late-Victorian times as the 'Home for Working Girls in London'. Amy Levy, the feminist poet who in 1889 committed suicide by inhaling carbon monoxide at No.7 next door, was the first Jewish woman in England to be cremated. No.5, as No.56 Euston Square, was home from 1868 to the art critic and literary editor William Michael Rossetti, his wife Lucy (née Madox Brown), his widowed mother and two sisters, including Christina, who in 1876 moved to Torrington Square (p 74). Living in the same house by 1897, and to become a long-term resident, was the Christian ecumenist (Sir) Henry Simpson Lunn; the travel agency he founded here, specialising in Alpine skiing tours, survived into the 21st century as Lunn Poly.

The street's north side is lined by the backs of buildings in Euston Road, together with Leslie Forster House (by Avanti, 1992-94), maisonettes and flats for the elderly with a cylindrical glass-walled entrance.

To their left, and at the east end of Friends' House (p 98), is the recently remodelled Friends' House Garden, a small oasis of open space preserved when the southern half of Euston Square gardens was destroyed. Cross the garden to emerge into Euston Road close to our starting-point at Euston Station across the road.

Sources

Books and pamphlets

Ashton, Rosemary. *Victorian Bloomsbury.* Yale U P, 2012

Bebbington, Gillian. *London street names.* Batsford, 1972

Besant, Sir Walter. *London north of the Thames.* Black, 1911

Blott, Walter. *A chronicle of Blemundsbury.* 1892

Booth, Charles. *Life and labour of the people of London.* Macmillan, 1892-97

Cherry, Bridget & Pevsner, Nikolaus. *London 4: North.* Penguin, 1999 (The buildings of England)

Clark, Catherine M & Mackintosh, James M. *The School and the site: a historical memoir ...* H K Lewis, 1954 (London School of Hygiene & Tropical Medicine memoir, 9)

Clinch, George. *Bloomsbury and St Giles past and present.* Truslove & Shirley, 1890

Clinch, George. *Marylebone and St Pancras.* Truslove & Shirley, 1890

Clunn, Harold. *The face of London.* New ed., rev. by E R Wethersett. Spring Books, 1962

Colvin, H M. *A biographical dictionary of British architects, 1660-1840,* 4th ed. Yale UP, 2008

Cooper, C S. *The outdoor monuments of London: statues, war memorials, tablets and memorial buildings.* Homeland Association, 1928

Crook, J Mordaunt. *The British Museum: a case-study in architectural politics.* Allen Lane, 1972

Davis, Eliza Jeffries. *The University site, Bloomsbury,* reprinted from *London Topographical Record,* vol. 17 (1936)

Dobie, Rowland. *The history of the United Parishes of St Giles in the Fields and St George Bloomsbury.* 1829

Edwards, Percy J. *History of London street improvements 1855-1897.* LCC, 1898

Fairfield, S. *The streets of London: a dictionary ....* Macmillan, 1983

Fletcher, Geoffrey. *London's Pavement Pounders.* Hutchinson, 1967

Girling, Brian. *Bloomsbury and Fitzrovia through time.* Amberley, 2012

Gordon, Edward & Deeson, A F L. *The book of Bloomsbury.* Edward Gordon Arts, 1950

Harte, Negley & North, John. *The world of University College, London 1828.-1978.* UCL, 1978

Hobhouse, Hermione. *Cubitt, master builder.* Macmillan, 1971

Hobhouse, Hermione. *Lost London: a century of demolition and decay.* Macmillan, 1971

Hudson, Roger. *Bloomsbury, Fitzrovia and Soho.* Haggerston Press, 1996 (The London guides)

Kendall, Joshua. *The man who made lists.* J P Putnam Sons, 2008

Lillywhite, Bryant. *London signs: a reference book of London signs from earliest times to about the mid-nineteenth century.* Allen & U, 1972

London County Council. *Survey of London,* vol. 5: *St Giles (Part 2).* LCC, 1914

London County Council. *Survey of London,* vol. 21: *Tottenham Court Road and neighbourhood.* LCC, 1949

Low, Crail. *Rock and pop London.* Handbook Publishing, 1997

McAuliffe, Rona. *The story of the Bloomsbury Dispensary.* [The Trustees], 1973

Meller, Hugh. *St George's Bloomsbury: an illustrated guide to the church.* [The Church], 1975

Miller, E. *That noble cabinet: a history of the British Museum.* Andre Deutsch, 1973.

Murray, Nicholas & Finch, Peter. *Real Bloomsbury.* Seren Books, 2010

Pevsner, Nikolaus. *London, except the Cities of London and Westminster.* 3rd ed., Penguin, 1973 (The buildings of England)

Richardson, John. *A history of Camden.* Historical Publications, 1999

Royal Commission on London Squares. *Report ....* HMSO, 1928 (Cmd. 3195)

Smith, Lyn. *Heroes of the Holocaust.* Random House, 2013

Stow, John. *A survey of the Cities of London and Westminster,* rev. by John Strype. 1720

Summerson, John. *Georgian London.* 4th ed. Penguin, 1988

Tames, Richard. *Bloomsbury past.* Historical Publications, 1993

Tuke, Margaret A. *A history of Bedford College for Women 1836-1937.* Oxford UP, 1939

Walford, E. *Old and new London,* vol. 4. Cassell, 1878

Weinreb, B & Hibbert, C (eds). *The London encyclopaedia,* 3rd ed. Macmillan, 2008

Wilson, Jean Moorcroft. *Virginia Woolf, life and London: a biography of place*. Cecil Woolf, 1987

Also many other biographies and institutional histories, in printed form or digitised

Maps

Ogilby & Morgan 1682;
Strype 1720;
Rocque 1745;
Robert Sawyer 1768;
Faden 1785;
Horwood 1799;
Thompson 1801;
Davies 1834;
Greenwood 1830;
Cassell 1862;
Mair 1866;
Ordnance Survey 1870 & later;
Booth's poverty maps 1889/98;
LCC bomb damage maps

Periodicals and newspapers

Camden History Review (*CHR*)
Camden History Society. *Newsletters*
Camden Journal
Camden New Journal
St Pancras Journal, 1947-1965
West End Extra

Articles

Draper, Marie. 'Bloomsbury gates and bars', *CHR* **12** (1984) 2-4
Gage, John. 'Bloomsbury Market', *CHR* **14** (1986) 20-23
Hamilton Fairley, Sir Neil. 'The Hospital for Tropical Diseases (UCH) London', *Univ Coll Hosp Magazine* **37** (1952) 114-18
Hayes, David A. 'The death of John Dickens …', *CHR* **39** (2015) 30-37
Hayes, David A & Ruth E. 'Bloomsbury blitzed', *CHR* **39** (2015) 2-8
Henderson, John N. 'The Museum Tavern …', *CHR* **16** (1989) 5-9
Morson, A F P. 'An eminent Bloomsbury pharmacist', *CHR*, **15** (1988) 29-31
Romilly, Mimi. 'Sir Samuel Romilly of Russell Square', *CHR* **20** (1996) 5-8
Woodford, F Peter. 'Drs John Radcliffe, Hans Sloane & Richard Mead', *CHR* **32** (2008) 2-7

Other records

Census returns, 1841–1911
Conservation Area Statements (L B Camden)
Crossrail and Transport for London publicity
Goad insurance plans, 1880s & later
Holborn Met. Borough: annual reports; plans of buildings; rate books
Licensed Victuallers Recognizances, 1723 & 1760
London County Council/GLC street lists
Post Office London Directories (Kelly & Co.)
Registers of Electors, Holborn, St Pancras and Camden
St Giles-in-the-Fields & St George Bloomsbury Vestry: Poor Rate
St Giles-in-the-Fields Medical Officer of Health Reports
St Pancras Met. Borough: rate books
St Pancras Vestry: minutes; Poor Rate

Websites

Numerous online resources, including websites of extant local institutions, and also:
Ancestry (ancestry.com)
Bedford Estates, London (bedfordestates.com)
Beginnings: the History of Higher Education in Bloomsbury (beginnings.ioe.ac.uk)
Bloomsbury Conservation Area Advisory Committee (bloomsburylive.co.uk)
Bloomsbury People (bloomsburypeople.blogspot.co.uk)
British History Online (british-history.ac.uk)
L B Camden: Listed Buildings (camden.gov.uk/listedbuildings); Planning (camden.gov.uk/planning)
Charles Booth Online Archive (booth.lse.ac.uk)
Discovery: The National Archives (discovery.nationalarchives.gov.uk/)
Grove Music Online (oxfordmusicoline.com)
Historic England (historicengland.org.uk)
Lost Hospitals of London (ezitis.myzen.co.uk)
Mapping Sculpture (sculpture.gla.ac.uk)
Old Bailey Online (oldbaileyonline.org)
Oxford Dictionary of National Biography (oxforddnb.com)
St Giles-in-the-Fields (stgilesonline.org)
Times Digital Archive 1785-1985 (gale.cengage.co.uk/times.aspx)
UCL: Bloomsbury Project (ucl.ac.uk/bloomsbury-project)
UCL: Legacies of British Slave-Ownership (ucl.ac.uk/lbs)
Wellcome Library (http://archives.wellcome.ac.uk)

Archive centres

British Library
Camden Local Studies & Archives Centre,
Guildhall Library
London Metropolitan Archives
Westminster Archives

Index

Streets included in the survey are indicated in boldface, as are the main entries for these and other selected subjects.
*** = illustration**
***PH* = public house**

S

The British Library (formerly British Museum) Reading Room, 2006 (photo: J Brew)

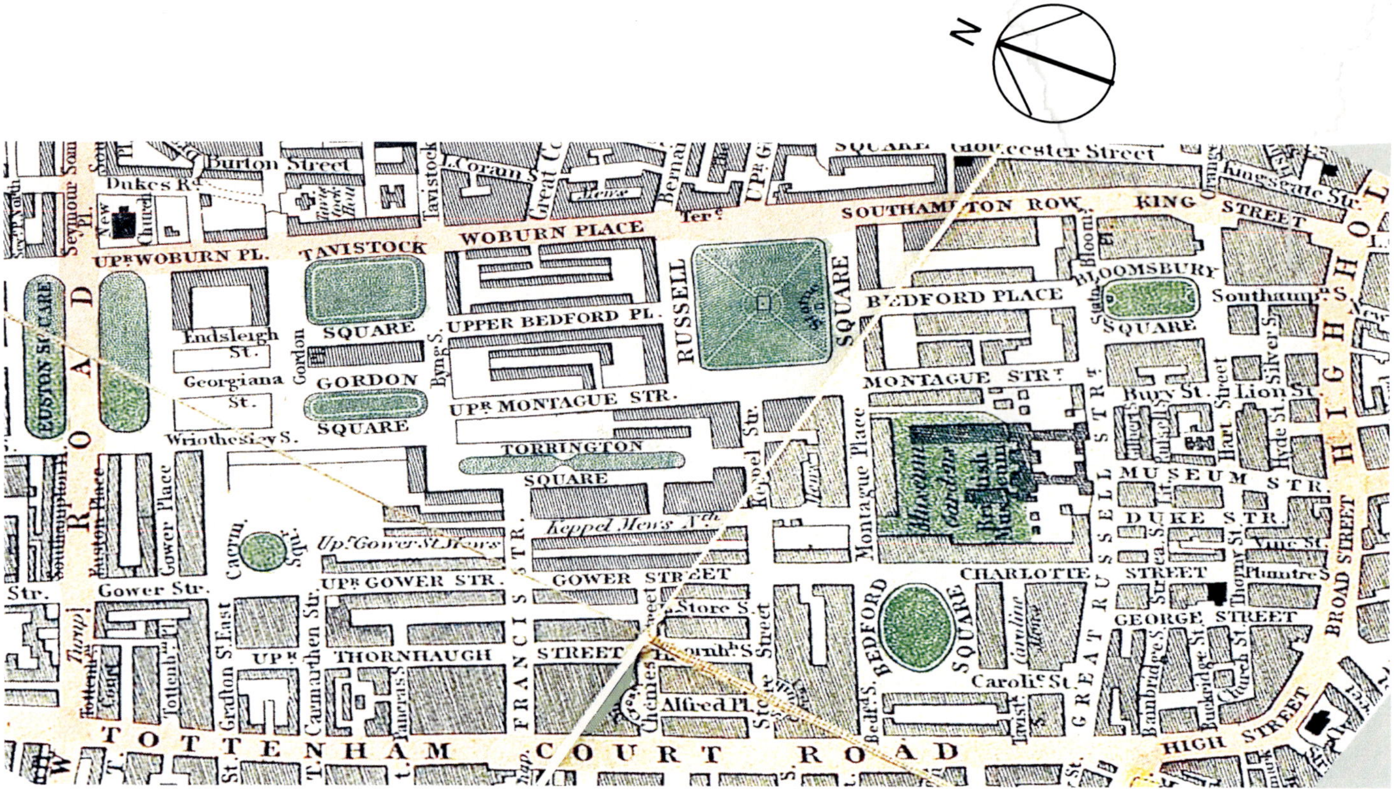

Detail of Cruchley's New Plan of London, 1827. This shows the area just before University College was founded on the site of a projected Carmarthen Square (Caerm. Squr. on the map). Note the names of undeveloped streets nearby, e.g. Wriothesley (now Gordon) and Georgiana (now Taviton); and Upper Montague (now Thornhaugh) Street, continuing across the site of Woburn Square as originally proposed.